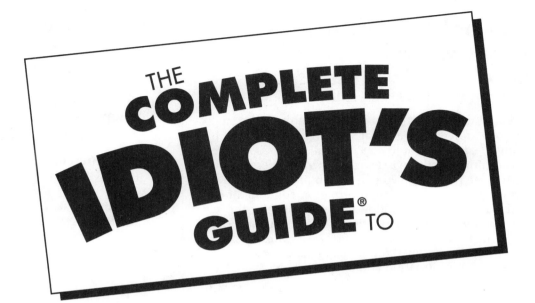

THE COMPLETE IDIOT'S GUIDE® TO

Creating a Web Page, Fourth Edition

Paul McFedries

A Division of Macmillan USA

201 West 103rd Street, Indianapolis, Indiana 46290

The Complete Idiot's Guide to Creating a Web Page, Fourth Edition

International Standard Book Number: 0-7897-2256-9

Library of Congress Catalog Card Number: 99-65790

Printed in the United States of America

First Printing: December 1999

01 00   4 3

Trademarks

Warning and Disclaimer

Associate Publisher
Greg Wiegand

Acquisitions Editor
Stephanie McComb

Development Editor
Gregory Harris

Managing Editor
Thomas F. Hayes

Project Editor
Tricia A. Sterling

Copy Editor
Molly Schaller

Indexer
Sharon Shock

Proofreaders
Maribeth Echard
Linda Morris
Sossity Smith

Technical Editor
Bill Bruns

Illustrator
Judd Winick

Team Coordinator
Sharry Lee Gregory

Media Developer
Jay Payne

Interior Designer
Nathan Clement

Cover Designer
Michael Freeland

Copy Writer
Eric Borgert

Production
Louis Porter, Jr.

Contents at a Glance

Contents

Part 2: A Grab Bag of Web Page Wonders   103

8 Images Can Be Links, Too   105

9 Table Talk: Adding Tables to Your Page   117

10 Making Your Web Pages Dance and Sing   135

About the Author

Paul McFedries has been a computer programmer for more than 20 years and, as a principal in Lone Wolf Software, specializes in database applications. He is the author of many popular computer books, including *The Complete Idiot's Guide to Windows 98*.

Dedication

To Karen, with love and silliness

Tell Us What You Think!

As the reader of this book, *you* are our most important critic and commentator. We value your opinion and want to know what we're doing right, what we could do better, what areas you'd like to see us publish in, and any other words of wisdom you're willing to pass our way.

As an Associate Publisher for Alpha Books, I welcome your comments. You can fax, email, or write me directly to let me know what you did or didn't like about this book—as well as what we can do to make our books stronger.

Please note that I cannot help you with technical problems related to the topic of this book, and that due to the high volume of mail I receive, I might not be able to reply to every message.

When you write, please be sure to include this book's title and author as well as your name and phone or fax number. I will carefully review your comments and share them with the author and editors who worked on the book.

Fax: 317-581-4666

Email: consumer@mcp.com

Mail: Greg Wiegand, Associate Publisher
          Que
          201 West 103rd Street
          Indianapolis, IN 46290 USA

Introduction

A few years ago, after having meandered around the Web's nooks and crannies for quite a while, I got this sudden urge to have my own home page. "Sheesh," I thought to myself, "All these people are doing this wild Web stuff that just seems so, well, *cool*. I want in!" So I scoured the Web and bookstores for information on creating a Web page. What I found were a bunch of highfalutin manuals written in a turgid style that made Web page creation sound like some esoteric business best left to people with advanced engineering degrees.

When I was done, however, one thing was blindingly obvious: *Creating a Web page is actually pretty easy*! So why were there no books out there shouting this from the rooftops? I resolved to take matters into my own hands and write just such a book. The result was the first edition of *The Complete Idiot's Guide to Creating a Web Page*, which saw the light of day back in 1996. I must have struck some kind of chord because, unbelievably, the book has sold over 100,000 copies and you now hold the fourth edition in your would-be Web weaver hands.

Sounds great! But why are you calling me an idiot?

Well, when it comes to producing content for the World Wide Web, a "complete idiot" is someone who, despite having the normal complement of gray matter, wouldn't know HTML from H. G. Wells. This is, of course, perfectly normal and, despite what many so-called Internet gurus may tell you, it does not imply any sort of character defect on your part.

So I might as well get one thing straight right off the bat: the fact that you're reading *The Complete Idiot's Guide to Creating a Web Page, Fourth Edition* (my, that is a mouthful, isn't it?) does *not* make you an idiot. On the contrary, it shows that

➤ You have discriminating taste and you settle for nothing less than the best (and it shows you don't mind immodest authors).

➤ You have a gift for self-deprecation (which is just a fancy-schmancy way of saying that you don't take yourself—or any of this Internet malarkey—too seriously).

➤ You're determined to learn this HTML thing, but you don't want to be bothered with a lot of boring, technical details.

➤ You realize it doesn't make sense to learn absolutely everything about HTML. You just need to know enough to get your Web page up and running.

➤ You're smart enough not to spend your days reading five bazillion pages of arcane (and mostly useless) information. You do, after all, have a life to lead.

In this book, I teach you how to create beautiful Web pages in no time flat. I understand that the very idea of trying to create something that looks as good as what you see on the Web sounds like an intimidating challenge. However, it's my goal in this book to show you that it's really quite simple and that *anyone* can build a page with their bare hands. We even try to have—gasp!—a little irreverent fun as we go along.

You'll also be happy to know that this book doesn't assume you have any previous experience with Web page production. This means that you start from scratch and slowly build your HTML knowledge until, before you know it, you have your very own tract of Web real estate. All the information is presented in short, easy-to-digest chunks that you can easily skim through to find just the information you want.

How This Book Is Set Up

I'm assuming you have a life away from your computer screen, so *The Complete Idiot's Guide to Creating a Web Page, Fourth Edition* is set up so you don't have to read it from cover to cover. If you want to know how to add a picture to your Web page, for example, just turn to the chapter that covers working with images. (Although, having said that, beginners will want to read at least Chapter 2 "Laying the Foundation: The Basic Structure of a Web Page" before moving on to more esoteric topics.) To make things easier to find, I've organized the book into half a dozen more- or less-sensible sections:

Part 1: Creating Your First HTML Web Page

After dipping a toe into the Web publishing waters with some introductory material in Chapter 1, you then dive right into the hurly-burly of HTML. The next five chapters here in Part 1 take you step-by-step, piece-by-piece through the processing of building a spanking new Web page. These chapters build your knowledge of basic HTML slowly and with lots of examples. Then Chapter 7 shows you how to successfully negotiate the big moment: getting your page on the Web for all to admire.

Part 2: A Grab Bag of Web Page Wonders

Part 2 takes you beyond the basics by presenting you with a hodgepodge of HTML topics. You get oh-so-simple instructions on Web page knickknacks such as image links (Chapter 8), tables (Chapter 9), multimedia (Chapter 10), forms (Chapter 11), and frames (Chapter 12).

Part 3: High HTML Style: Working with Style Sheets

Style sheets are the wave of the future in Web page design, so Part 3 devotes no less than three chapters to mastering them. I explain the basics in Chapter 13, and then I show you how to wield styles for fonts, colors, and backgrounds (Chapter 14), as well as dimensions, borders, and margins (Chapter 15).

Part 4: Working with JavaScripts and Java Applets

The three chapters in Part 4 show you how to add tiny little programs to your Web pages to give them that interactive boost. Chapter 16 tells you all about this JavaScript thing that everyone's always blathering on about. It also gives you quite a few examples of scripts that you can plop right inside your pages. Chapter 17 takes the JavaScript ball and runs with it by showing you a whack of other examples that do all kinds of amazingly useful things. Chapter 18 turns your attention to Java and the applets that it creates.

Part 5: Painless Page Production: Easier Ways to Do the HTML Thing

After struggling with all that HTML in Parts 1 through 4, Part 5 shows you a few ways to make this stuff a bit easier. Specifically, I show you how to wield several tools that take some of the drudgery out of putting together a Web page, including Netscape Composer, the Office 2000 HTML tools, FrontPage Express, and even some Web pages that help you create Web pages!

Part 6: Rounding Out Your HTML Education

The main part of the book closes with some chapters that help increase your Webmaster IQ. You get some hints on proper Web page style (Chapter 23), some Internet resources that help you create great pages (Chapter 24), and some proven ways to turn your HTML investment into cash (Chapter 25).

You Want More? You've Got It!

Happily, there's more to this book than 25 chapters of me yammering away. To put a feather in your HTML cap and to make your page publishing adventures a bit easier, I've included a few other goodies:

Tear-out Card: HTML Codes for Cool Characters   This page (it's located on the inside front cover of the book, in case you missed it on the way in) lists all the HTML codes you can use to incorporate characters such as ¢ and © in your Web page. (This is all explained in more detail in Chapter 3, "From Buck-Naked to Beautiful: Dressing Up Your Page.")

Appendix A: Speak Like a Geek Glossary   You can find this section near the back of the book. It's a glossary of Internet, World Wide Web, and HTML terms that should help you out if you come across a word or phrase that furrows your brow.

Appendix B: Frequently Asked Questions About HTML   This section runs through a few dozen of the most common questions asked by beginning Webmasters and, of course, offers simple solutions to each problem.

Appendix C: The CD: Webmaster's Toolkit   The book's major bonus is the CD-ROM that's glued onto the back cover. This little plastic Frisbee contains a complete Webmaster's Toolkit with tons of HTML-related doodads, including all the HTML examples I use in the book, some sample Web pages, HTML programs, lots of graphics you can put in your Web page, and tons more.

The Complete Idiot's HTML Tag Reference   This is also on the CD, and it gives you a complete list of all the HTML tags in the known universe.

The Complete Idiot's Style Sheet Reference   This CD reference runs through all the available style sheet properties, tells you which browsers support them, lists all the possible values, and gives you lots of examples.

Also, as you're trudging through the book, look for the following features that point out important info:

Check This Out

These boxes contain notes, tips, and asides that provide you with interesting and useful (at least theoretically!) nuggets of HTML lore.

Technical Twaddle

This Techno Talk icon points out technical information you can use to impress your friends (and then forget five minutes later).

What's New in This Edition

Sending a book out to market is a little like watching one of your kids leave home. Will they be okay? Will other people accept them? Will they be successful in their chosen field? Will they be displayed prominently at the front of the store? (Well, okay, we probably don't want our kids displayed prominently in the front of stores.) I'm happy to report that *The Complete Idiot's Guide to Creating a Web Page, Fourth Edition* has been a resounding success in its first three ventures into the cold, cruel world. I've received a lot of comments from people saying they liked the book and really enjoyed the approach. Thanks!

The only complaints I heard were from people who wanted more! Well, you got it. This fourth edition includes the same easy-to-digest methods for setting up a Web page, but also includes the following tidbits:

➤ Updated coverage of the basic HTML codes to include the latest and greatest enhancements

➤ Lots of new tips and traps sprinkled throughout the book

➤ Much more extensive coverage of style sheets

➤ Lots more JavaScript examples

➤ A new chapter that runs through proven methods for making money from your Web page know-how

➤ Coverage of the new HTML goodies in Microsoft Office 2000

➤ A complete HTML tag reference

➤ A complete style sheet reference

➤ A complete list of the HTML character codes

➤ An extensive list of Frequently Asked Questions about HTML

➤ Lots of new resources for HTML, Web hosts, JavaScript, and more

➤ Lots of new programs on the CD

Online Resources for Readers

All the stuff that's crammed into this book is only the beginning. I've also set up a few online resources you can use to get more info and continue your HTML education.

This Book's Home Page

For starters, there's the World Wide Web home of *The Complete Idiot's Guide to Creating a Web Page, Fourth Edition*, which is at the following address:

```
http://www.mcfedries.com/books/cightml/
```

Here you get book info, extra material not found in the book, HTML updates, new and changed HTML resources, and much more.

Links to Readers' Web Pages

I was mighty impressed by the pages being cobbled together by the readers of the first edition, so I decided to let other people know about them. To that end, I set up a showcase page that features links to the Web pages created by readers. Here's the address:

```
http://www.mcfedries.com/books/cightml/links.html
```

When you have your own page up and running on the Web, make sure you add it to the list!

The CIGHTML Mailing List

There's nothing like the give-and-take of a mailing list to not only learn more about a topic, but also to foster a sense of community among people who share a common interest. The readers of *The Complete Idiot's Guide to Creating a Web Page, Fourth Edition* share a common interest in stitching together Web pages, so I created a mailing list just for them. To join in our discussions of HTML and Web page design, send an email message to the following address:

```
listmanager@mcfedries.com
```

Include just the following command in the Subject line:

```
join cightml.
```

You'll get back a welcome message that gives you instructions on participating in the list. If you'd like to check out what's happened previously on the list, head for the CIGHTML mailing list archives:

```
http://www.mcfedries.com/books/cightml/list/
```

The Complete Idiot's Guide to Mailing Lists

Not sure what the heck a "mailing list" is? Well, email, as you probably know, is a sort of "virtual conversation." You write to someone, they respond, you rebut their argument, and so on. It's not unlike a telephone conversation, except it takes longer to unfold, and it's in text, and so on.

So if an email exchange is like a phone conversation, a mailing list is like a conference call. That is, there are still messages being sent back and forth, but with a mailing list you have more than two people involved. For example, if the mailing list has 50 subscribers, each message sent to the list goes out to all 50 people. Similarly, if you reply to a list message, the response also goes out to all 50 subscribers.

Let Me Know How You're Doing!

Hey, you paid good money for this book, so it's only reasonable that you should be able to get in touch with its author, right? Sure! So, as long as you have something nice to say (complaints will be acknowledged only grudgingly), why not drop me a line and let me know how your Web page is coming along or, heck, just tell me what you thought of the book. If your page is ready to go, send me its Web address and I'll surf over and take a look. Here's my email address:

```
paul@mcfedries.com
```

If you'd like to drop by my own home page, here's the address:

```
http://www.mcfedries.com/
```

See you in cyberspace!

Acknowledgments (The Giving Credit Where Credit Is Due Department)

Remember the waterfront shack with the sign FRESH FISH SOLD HERE? Of course it's fresh, we're on the ocean. Of course it's for sale, we're not giving it away. Of course it's here, otherwise the sign would be someplace else. The final sign: FISH.

—Peggy Noonan

The wonderful editors at Que have taken my FRESH FISH SOLD HERE manuscript and turned it into a FISH book. That's good news for you because it means you get a book that has no fluff, chaff, or anything else that isn't bookworthy. This takes skillful editing, and the following folks had the necessary skills to get the job done:

Stephanie McComb   Stephanie was the Acquisitions Editor for this edition of the book. She had some great ideas about what to cover (and what to chuck) in this edition, and she did a superb job ensuring that everything went smoothly throughout the project.

Gregory Harris   Otherwise known as "The Proudest Papa on the Planet," Gregory was the book's Development Editor. This means he was the Big Picture guy who made sure that the overall structure of the book and of each chapter made sense. An HTML expert himself, he had many insightful thoughts and ideas on how best to teach HTML.

Tricia Sterling   Tricia's title is Project Editor, which means she was in charge of getting the manuscript ready for the elaborate production process. Tricia's cheerful manner, unmatched competence, and superhuman attention to detail made working with her a delight.

Molly Schaller As the book's Copy Editor, it was Molly's job to make me look good by fixing my spelling slips and correcting my grammatical gaffes. The fact that her eagle editor eyes missed nary a mistake combined with her good humor in the face of a demanding job made her a pleasure to work with (or, should that be a pleasure with which to work; Molly?).

Bill Bruns Bill was the book's Technical Editor, which meant he spent many a long day checking and double-checking my facts, running through my procedures, and verifying all the code. Thanks to Bill's yeoman work, you can rest assured that this book is accurate and won't lead you off the beaten Web page path.

Jay Payne As Media Developer for the book, Jay's job was to put together the top-notch CD that's pasted into the back. Jay negotiated with the software companies, tracked down the samples, cajoled the examples and references out of me, and then put together the entire package. Check out the disc and you'll see what a great job he did.

The members of the editorial team aren't the only people who had their fingers in this publishing pie. Flip back a few pages and you'll find a list of the designers, illustrators, indexers, proofreaders, layout technicians, and other professionals who worked long and hard to produce this book. I tip my authorial hat to all of them. I'd also like to thank the thousands and thousands of readers who have written to me over the years to offer compliments and suggestions. If this is the best edition yet (and I lack just enough humility to think that it is), it's thanks in no small measure to your willingness to offer a couple of cents' worth.

Part 1

Creating Your First HTML Web Page

I know you must be chomping at the bit in anticipation of creating a Web page to call your own. Well, I'm happy to say, your big moment is just around the corner. The seven chapters here in Part 1 will take you through the entire Web page production process, from go to whoa. When the dust settles, you'll have an actual, honest-to-goodness, "Look, ma, I'm in cyberspace!" Web page. You will be, in short, a full-fledged Webmeister and the envy of all your pageless friends.

Chapter 1

A Brief HTML Web Page Primer

In This Chapter

➤ What in the name of blue blazes is HTML?

➤ A look at what kind of havoc you can wreak with HTML

➤ Answers to pressing HTML questions

➤ A veritable cornucopia of Web page examples that show HTML in its best light

---

Before you go off half-cocked and start publishing pages willy-nilly on the World Wide Web, it helps to have a bit of background on HTML. After all, you wouldn't try to set up shop in a new country without first understanding the local geography and customs and learning a few choice phrases, such as "I am sorry I insulted your sister" and "You don't buy beer, you rent it!"

This chapter gives you a handle on the HTML hoo-ha that seems to be such an integral part of Web page construction. What is HTML? Why bother with it? What can you do with it? Why does it sound so darned scary? Will it turn your brain to mush? This chapter answers all these questions and more.

Okay, So Just What Is HTML?

I have some good news, and I have some bad news. The bad news is that HTML stands for—brace yourself—*HyperText Markup Language*. (I'll pause for a sec to let you get the inevitable shudders out of the way.)

The good news, however, is that HTML doesn't stand for Hard To Master Lingo. HTML is, in fact, really a sheep in wolf's clothing: It looks nasty, but it's really quite tame (and, no, it won't turn even a small part of your brain to mush). Basic HTML—which is what 90% of all Web pages use—isn't much tougher than reciting the alphabet. It's way easier than programming your VCR (which is, I'm sure, good news for those of you who sport that scarlet letter of modern technology: The flashing 12:00 on your VCR clock).

That's all well and good, Author Boy, but HyperText Markup Language isn't exactly a phrase that trips lightly off the tongue; it really sounds intimidating.

Well, you're right, it does. So, in the spirit of self-help books everywhere, you need to face your fears and look HTML squarely in the eye. Specifically, you need to examine what each element of "HyperText Markup Language" means in plain English:

HyperText   A hypertext link is a special word or phrase in a Web page that "points" to another Web page. When you click one of these links, your browser transports you immediately to the other Web page, no questions asked. Because these hypertext links are really the distinguishing feature of the World Wide Web, Web pages are often known as *hypertext documents*. So, HTML has the word "HyperText" in it because you use it to create these hypertext documents. (It would be just as accurate to call it WPML—Web Page Markup Language.)

Markup   My dictionary defines "markup" as (among other things) "detailed stylistic instructions written on a manuscript that is to be typeset." For our purposes, I can rephrase this definition as follows: "detailed stylistic instructions typed into a text document that is to be published on the World Wide Web." That's HTML in a nutshell. It has a few simple codes for detailing things like making text bold or italic, creating bulleted lists, inserting graphics, and, of course, defining hypertext links. You just type these codes into the appropriate places in an ordinary text document, and the Web browser software does the dirty work of translating the codes. The result? Your page is displayed the way you want, automatically.

Language   This word might be the most misleading of them all. Many people interpret this to mean that HTML is a programming language, and they wash their hands of the whole thing right off the bat. "You mean I gotta learn programming to get my two cents worth on the Web?" Not a chance, Vance. HTML has nothing, I repeat, *nothing*, whatsoever to do with computer programming. Rather, HTML is a "language" in the sense that it has a small collection of two- and three-letter combinations and words that you use to specify styles such as bold and italic.

What Can You Do with HTML?

All right, so HTML isn't the Hideous, Terrible, Mega-Leviathan that its name might suggest, but rather a Harmless, Tame, and Meek Lapdog. What can you do with such a creature? Well, lots of things, actually. After all, people aren't flocking to the World Wide Web because it's good for their health. Just the opposite, in fact. They're surfing 'til they drop because the Web presents them with an attractive and easily navigated source of information and entertainment (or *infotainment*, as the wags like to call it). It's HTML that adds the attractiveness and ease of navigation. To see what I mean, the next few sections take you through examples of the basic HTML elements.

You Can Format Text

A high Jolts Per Minute (JPM) count is what turns the crank of your average Web-surfing dude and dudette. However, nothing generates fewer jolts (and is harder on the eyes to boot) than plain, unadorned text. To liven things up, you need to use different sizes and styles for your Web page text. Happily, HTML is no slouch when it comes to dressing up text for the prom:

- ➤ You get six different built-in font sizes that you can use for titles, headings, and such.
- ➤ You can display your Web prose as bold.
- ➤ You can emphasize text with italics.
- ➤ You can make text look as though it was produced by a typewriter.
- ➤ You can even use different font sizes for characters.

Figure 1.1 shows examples of each kind of style. (I show you how to use HTML to format Web page text in Chapter 3, "From Buck-Naked to Beautiful: Dressing Up Your Page."

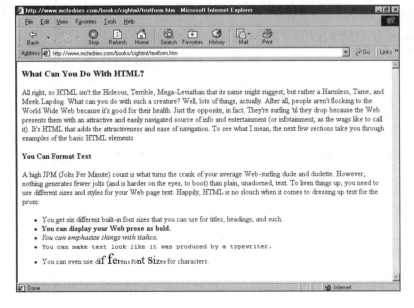

Figure 1.1

Some examples of HTML text styles.

You Can Create Lists of Things

If you're presenting information on your Web page, it helps if you can display your data in a way that makes sense and is easy to read. In some cases, this means arranging the data in lists, such as a numbered list or a bulleted list as shown in Figure 1.1. I fill you in on how to use HTML to create these kinds of lists and more in Chapter 4, "A Fistful of List Grist for Your Web Page Mill."

You Can Set Up Links to Other Pages

Web sessions aren't true surfin' safaris unless you take a flying leap or two. I'm speaking, of course, of selecting hypertext links that take you to the far-flung corners of the Web world.

You can give the readers of your Web pages the same kicks by using HTML to create links anywhere on a page. You can set up three kinds of links:

➤ Links to another of your Web pages.

➤ Links to a different location in the same Web page. (This is useful for pages that contain several sections; you could, for example, put a "table of contents" at the top of the page that consists of links to the various sections in the document.)

➤ Links to any page anywhere on the Web or on your company's intranet.

What's All This Talk About an "Intranet?"

Geez, you just got comfy with the term Internet and now I'm throwing the word "intranet" into your face. What gives? It's no big deal, actually. These days, many companies are rushing to set up their internal networks as mini-Internets. Because these networks exist only within corporate barricades, they're called *intranets* to help distinguish them from the Internet as a whole.

Plenty of sites around the World Wide Web exist only to provide a Web "mouse potato" (like a couch potato, only with a computer) with huge lists of links to pages that are informative, entertaining, or simply "cool." For example, Figure 1.2 shows a page from the Yahoo! Web site, which boasts tens of thousands of links arranged in dozens of categories (Yahoo! is a good place to go if you're looking for Web sites on a particular subject). In this case, the page shows a few links to some "useless" Web pages. ("Beard research"!? "thoughts of cabbage"!?) You find out how to use HTML to sprinkle links all over your Web pages in Chapter 5, "Making the Jump to Hyperspace: Adding Links."

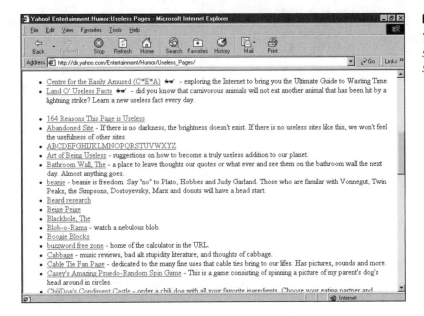

Figure 1.2

This page from Yahoo! shows a few links to some, uh, unusual sites.

You Can Insert Images

Fancy text effects, lists, and lots of links go a long way toward making a Web page a hit. But for a real crowd-pleasing page, you want to throw in an image or two. It could be a picture of yourself, a drawing the kids made, some clip art, or any of the images that are on this book's CD-ROM. As long as you have the image in a graphics file, you can use HTML to position the image appropriately on your page. I give you the details (as well as info on the types of graphics files you can use) in Chapter 6, "A Picture Is Worth a Thousand Clicks: Working with Images."

Figure 1.3 shows an example page with an image. This is a page from my site, and the image is used to illustrate a point from the text.

You Can Format Information in Tables

If your Web page needs to show data formatted in rows and columns, you could try using tabs and spaces to line things up all nice and neat. However, you'll groan in disappointment when you view the page in a browser. Why? Because HTML reduces multiple spaces to a single space, and it ignores tabs completely! This sounds like perverse behavior, but it's just the way HTML was set up.

Figure 1.3

A well-chosen image or two can do wonders for otherwise drab Web pages.

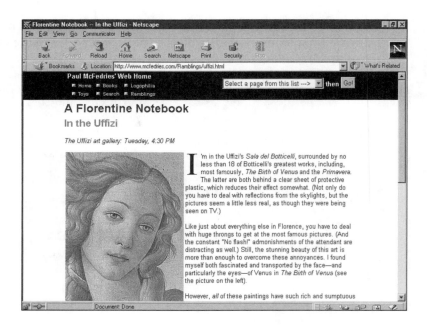

You're not out of luck, though. You can use HTML to create tables to slot your data into slick-looking rows and columns. Figure 1.4 shows an example of a table. I tell you how to use HTML to construct tables in Chapter 9, "Table Talk: Adding Tables to Your Page."

Figure 1.4

Tables: A blessing for neat freaks everywhere.

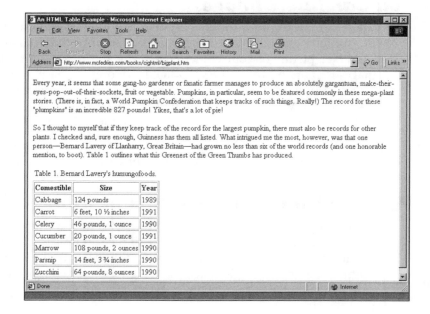

Pages from All Walks of Web Life

Now that you've got some idea of what HTML can do, wouldn't you like to see the rabbits various Web magicians have pulled from their HTML hats? To that end, the next few sections present some real-world examples of Web pages that show you what you can do with a little HTML know-how. In fact, all of the pages featured in these sections were created by a reader of previous editions of *The Complete Idiot's Guide to Creating a Web Page*!

Of course, these examples represent only the smallest subset of the Web world. There are millions of Web pages out there, and each one is like a digital fingerprint—a unique expression of its creator's individuality.

The Personal Touch: Personal Home Pages

The simplest, and probably the most common, type of Web page is the personal home page. This is a page that an individual sets up to tell the Web world a little bit about herself. They're the Web equivalent of those "Hi! My Name is..." stickers that people wear at parties and receptions. They range from warm and fuzzy ("Welcome, friend, to my home page"), to downright vainglorious ("Let me tell you everything there is to know about me"), to frighteningly personal ("Dear diary..."). Figure 1.5 shows the personal home page for a reader known on the Internet as Mulan.

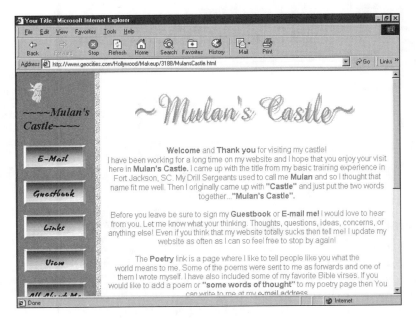

Figure 1.5

The humble home page is perhaps the most common Web page variety.

Hobbyists Do It Themselves with HTML

Sometimes the hardest thing about putting together a Web page is thinking of something to say. (Although there are plenty of garrulous guys and gals out there for whom this is definitely not a problem!) So, what's a body to do about a bad case of Web writer's block? Well, lots of people go with what they know: They talk about their hobbies and interests. Hey, it makes sense. You're more likely to sound enthusiastic and excited about a topic you're keen on, so you're also more likely to hold your reader's interest. You can do lots of things to fill up your page—introduce the hobby to novices, talk about how you got started, show some samples of your work (depending on the hobby, of course), include links to related Web pages, and much more.

As you might imagine, there's no shortage of hobby-related pages on the World Wide Web. You can find info on everything from amateur radio to beekeeping to woodworking. Figure 1.6 shows a bird club page put together by reader Cindy Kime.

Figure 1.6

Hobby pages abound on the Web.

Not for Bathroom Reading: Electronic Magazines

The Web's marriage of text and graphics meant it was only a matter of time before someone decided to "publish" a Web-based magazine. Now it seems that new electronic magazines (they're usually called either Webzines or e-zines) hit the Web's newsstands every few days. The quality, as you might expect, runs the gamut from professional to pathetic, from slick to sick. But the good ones are very good, with well-written articles, handsome graphics, and some unique approaches to the whole magazine thing. There are, literally, hundreds of e-zines out there, so there's no shortage of reading material. John Labovitz maintains a list of e-zines at `http://www.meer.net/johnl/e-zine-list/index.html`.

Figure 1.7 shows the home page for Shock Value, a Webzine published by reader C.J. Cauley.

Figure 1.7

Shock Value: an electronic magazine.

Corporate Culture Hits the Web

One of the biggest engines driving the growth of the World Wide Web is the influx of corporations scrambling to get a "presence" in cyberspace. Companies from mom-and-pop shops to Fortune 500 behemoths are setting up on the Web in anticipation of, well, *something*. Nobody's quite sure why they need a Web site, but they're happy to put one up, just in case something BIG happens one of these days. Hey, who can blame them? With all the Internet hype floating around, no self-respecting CEO is going to be caught with his or her pants down.

Many readers of the previous editions have leveraged their new HTML skills to build pages for their companies. (And a few even managed to get paid to create sites for other companies!) Naturally enough, readers who have their own businesses also become their own site designers. For example, Figure 1.8 shows a nice Web site crafted by reader Verlie Hutchens for her Daughters Too! business.

Figure 1.8

If you run your own business, put up your own business Web page.

Your Tax Dollars at Work—Government Web Pages

If Big Business is rushing to get on the Web, you better believe Big Brother isn't going to be left behind. Yes, governments—local, state, and federal—are putting up Web pages to beat the band. Granted, many of these sites are quite useful. You can use them to contact representatives, read government reports and studies, do research, renew your license, and even file taxes. Some of the pages are even—gasp!—creative.

Reader Bill Eastman put together a fine site for the Texas Commission for the Blind, shown in Figure 1.9.

From Student to Teacher: Webmaster Web Pages

The biggest compliment a teacher can get is to have a student become a teacher. This tells the teacher that a) they taught the student well, and b) they inspired the student to learn more about the subject. Over the years, I've had a number of readers go on to become expert Webmasters. A few of them have decided to share their hard-won knowledge with the rest of the Web community by putting up pages that deal with HTML, site design, JavaScript, and more. One of my favorites is Sitestruct.com by reader Tom Wood, and it's shown in Figure 1.10.

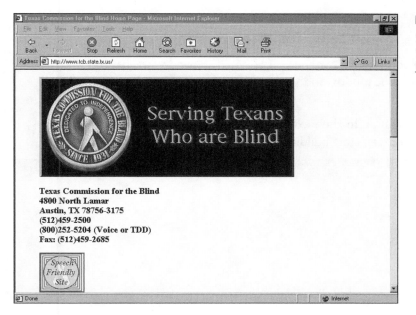

Figure 1.9

The home page for the Texas Commission for the Blind.

Figure 1.10

Sitestruct.com is an excellent Webmaster resource.

The Least You Need to Know

This chapter gave you a quick overview of HTML. I showed you what it is and why it isn't as scary as it sounds, and you saw quite a few examples of what HTML can do.

So much for preliminaries. In the next chapter you get started with the nuts and bolts of HTML so you can start building your first Web page.

WE'RE GONNA KNOCK DOWN THAT NORTH WALL...

Chapter 2

Laying the Foundation: The Basic Structure of a Web Page

In This Chapter

➤ A laundry list of things you need to get started

➤ A quick course on tags, the building blocks of HTML

➤ The basic blueprint for all Web pages

➤ How to add a title, toss in some text, and split your prose into paragraphs

➤ Your field guide to the most fundamental of HTML flora and fauna

---

This book's goal is to help you create your own Web pages and thus lay claim to a little chunk of personal cyberspace real estate: a home page away from home, if you will. Before you can live in this humble abode, however, you have to "pour the concrete" that serves as the foundation for the rest of your digital domicile. In this chapter, I show you a few HTML basics that constitute the underlying structure of all Web pages.

Getting Started

As you saw in Chapter 1, "A Brief HTML Web Page Primer," some Web pages look truly spectacular. To achieve these impressive effects, you might think you need to stretch a fancy word processing or page layout program to its limits. Or you might think you have to rush out and spend beaucoup bucks for some kind of highfalutin' "HTML generator" that's designed specifically for cranking out Web pages. Nah, you're way off. All you really need for creating a basic page is a lowly text editor. Yes,

Starting Notepad

For most versions of Windows, you start the Notepad text editor by selecting **Start**, **Programs**, **Accessories**, **Notepad**.

even a brain-dead program like Windows' Notepad is more than adequate for doing the HTML thing. (Although, having said all that, there are HTML "editors" that can take some of the drudgery out of page production. I'll talk about some of them in Part 5, "Painless Page Production: Easier Ways to Do the HTML Thing.")

Surely a plain old run-of-the-mill text editor won't let me create anything resembling those beautiful pages I see on the Web.

Yes, it will—and stop calling me Shirley. The vast majority of all the Web pages in the world are really just simple text files.

So why in the name of Sam Hill do those pages look so good? Text files I've seen have been ugly with a capital Ugh!

The Web's beauty secret is that it's actually the Web browsers that determine how a page looks. When you surf to a Web page, the browser reads the text, scours the file for HTML markings, and then displays the page accordingly. So, for example, you can mark inside your text file that you want a certain word to appear as bold. When the browser comes to that part of the document, it goes right ahead and formats the word in a bold font. The browser handles all this dirty work behind the scenes, and you never have to give it a second thought (or even a first thought, for that matter).

First, Crank Out a New Text File

So, to get to the point at long last, all you really need to do to get started is fire up your favorite text editor and launch a new document—if the program doesn't do that for you automatically, as most do. (Of course, that isn't to say there aren't other, equally important, accouterments you might need. For me, a good, strong cup of coffee is a must. Other optional HTML accessories include the appropriate mood music—something by The Spinners, perhaps?—a copy of *Feel the Fear and Do It Anyway*, and semi-important things like your creativity and imagination.)

If you prefer, it's okay to use a word processor such as WordPad, the program that comes with Windows 95 and Windows 98, or Microsoft Word. If you take this route, please keep the following caveats in mind:

➤ **Don't try to format the document in any way (such as adding italics or centering paragraphs).** Not only do you run the risk of having a browser choke on these extra formatting codes, but every Web browser on the face of the Earth will completely ignore your efforts. Remember, the only way to make a browser do your bidding and display your Web page properly is to use the appropriate HTML codes.

➤ **Don't save the file in the word processor's native format.** Be sure to save the file as pure text, sometimes referred to as ASCII text. More on this in a sec.

Word Does HTML

Speaking of word processors, Word 97 and Word 2000 both have HTML capabilities built right into the program. To find out more, take a gander at Chapter 20, "Suite Web O' Mine: The Microsoft Office 2000 HTML Tools."

Notes About Saving HTML Files

While slaving away on the text file that will become your Web page, make sure you practice safe computing. That is, make sure you save your work regularly. However, from the thousands of notes that I've received from readers, I can tell you that the number one thing that trips up new Webmeisters is improperly saving their HTML files. To help you easily leap these saving hurdles, here are a few notes to pore over:

➤ **The Save command** You save a file by selecting the program's **File, Save** command. The first time you do this with a new file, the Save As dialog box shows up for work. You use this dialog box to specify three things: the filename, the file type, and the file's location on your hard disk. The next few notes discuss some tidbits about the name and type.

➤ **Use the right file extension** Most Web browsers know how to deal only with files that end with either the .htm or the .html file extension (for example, mypage.html). Therefore, when you name your file, be sure to specify either .htm or .html.

➤ **Use lowercase filenames only** The majority of Web servers (computers that store Web pages) are downright finicky when it comes to uppercase letters versus lowercase letters. For example, the typical server thinks that index.html and INDEX.HTML are two different files. It's dumb, I know. So, to be safe, always enter your filenames using only lowercase letters.

➤ **Don't use spaces** Windows 95, Windows 98, and Windows NT are all happy to deal with filenames that include spaces. Internet Explorer, too, is space-savvy. However, Netscape gets *really* confused if it comes upon any filename that has one or more spaces. So, to be safe, avoid using spaces in your filenames.

Which Extension Should You Use?

Many new HTMLers get confused about whether to use .htm or .html when naming their files. Actually, you're free to use either one because it doesn't make any difference. Note, though, that if you're still using Windows 3.x, then you must use .htm.

➤ **Use the right type**   While in the Save As dialog box, you need to select the correct "file type" for your HTML file. How you do this depends on what program you're using:

> **If you're using Notepad**   Use the **Save as type** list to select **All Files (*.*)**. This ensures that Notepad uses your .htm or .html extension (and not its normal .txt extension).

> **If you're using Windows' WordPad**   Use the **Save as type** list to select **Text Document**. You also need to surround your filename with quotation marks (for example, "index.html") to ensure that WordPad uses your .htm or .html extension.

> **If you're using Microsoft Word**   Use the **Save as type** list to select **Text Only (*.txt)**. Again, you need to surround your filename with quotation marks.

Easier File Extensions

You can see that Windows 95 and Windows 98 are a bit stupid when it comes to file extensions. I'll show you how to overcome this later in this chapter. See the section titled "Help! The Browser Shows My Tags!"

➤ When you've done all that, click **Save** in the Save As dialog box to save the file. (If you're using WordPad, the program might ask if you're sure you want to save the file in "Text-Only format." Say "Duh!" and click **Yes**.)

The Edit-Save-Browse Cycle

By now you've probably figured out the biggest problem associated with fashioning a Web page out of a text file: There's no way to know what the page will look like after it's been foisted onto the Web! Fortunately, all is not lost. Most browsers are more than happy to let you load a text file right from the con-

Opening HTML Files

When you run the **File**, **Open** command, the Open dialog box probably won't show your HTML files. To see them, use the **Files of type** list to select **All Documents** (***.***) (some programs use **All Files** (***.***), instead).

fines of your computer's hard disk. This means you can test drive your page without first having to put it on the Web. So here's the basic cycle you'll use to build your pages:

1. In your text editor or word processor, either start a new file (if one isn't started for you already) or use the **File**, **Open** command to open an existing file.

2. Add some text and HTML stuff (I'll define what this "stuff" is in the next section) to your file.

3. Load the file into your browser of choice to see how things look. As a public service (it's a tough job but, hey, somebody's gotta do it), here are the appropriate instructions for loading a file from your hard disk using the Big Two browsers:

    ➤ In Internet Explorer, select the **File** menu's **Open** command (or press **Ctrl+O**), click the **Browse** button in the Open dialog box that appears, and then pick out the file you need. You can reload the file by selecting the **View** menu's **Refresh** command, or by pressing **F5**.

    ➤ In Netscape Navigator, pull down the **File** menu, select the **Open Page** command (or you can press **Ctrl+O**), click the **Choose File** button, and then find the file by using the Open dialog box that appears. To reload the file, pull down the **View** menu and select **Reload** (or press **Ctrl+R**).

4. Lather. Rinse. Repeat steps 2 and 3. Note that after the file is loaded in the browser, you need only choose the program's **Reload** command to see the effects of your changes.

Tag Daze—Understanding HTML's Tags

As I mentioned earlier, the magic of the Web is wrought by browser programs that read text files and then decipher the HTML nuggets that you've sprinkled hither and thither. These HTML tidbits are markers—called *tags*—that spell out how you want things to look. For example, if you want a word on your page to appear in bold text, you surround that word with the appropriate tags for boldfacing text.

In general, tags use the following format:

```
<TAG>The text to be affected by the tag</TAG>
```

The *TAG* part is a code (usually a one- or two-letter abbreviation, but sometimes an entire word) that specifies the type of effect you want. You always surround these codes with angle brackets <>; the brackets tell the Web browser that it's dealing with a chunk of HTML and not just some random text.

For example, the tag for bold is <B>. So if you want the phrase "BeDazzler Home Page" to appear in bold, you type the following into your document:

```
<B>BeDazzler Home Page</B>
```

The first <B> says to the browser, in effect, "Listen up, Browser Boy! You know the text that comes after this? Be a good fellow and display it in bold." This continues until the browser reaches the </B>. The slash defines this as an *end tag*, which lets the browser know it's supposed to stop what it's doing. So the </B> tells the browser, "Okay, okay. Ixnay on the oldbay!" As you'll see, there are tags for lots of other effects, including italics, paragraphs, headings, page titles, links, and lists. HTML is just the sum total of all these tags.

Don't Forget the Slash!

One of the most common mistakes rookie Web weavers make is to forget the slash (/) that identifies a tag as an end tag. If your page looks wrong when you view it in a browser, a missing slash is the first thing you should look for. The second thing you should look for is another common error: using the backslash (\). Zees ees verboten in zee HTML!

And Now, Some Actual HTML

Okay, you're ready to get down to some brass HTML tacks. (Halle-freakin'-lujah, I hear you saying.) You'll begin by cobbling together a few HTML tags that constitute the underlying skeleton of all Web pages.

Your HTML files will always lead off with the <HTML> tag. This tag doesn't do a whole heckuva lot except tell any Web browser that tries to read the file that it's dealing with a file that contains HTML knickknacks. Similarly, the last line in your document will always be the corresponding end tag: </HTML>. You can think of this end tag as

Check This Out

Tag Case

It makes absolutely no difference if you enter your tag names in upper-case letters or lowercase letters. I always use uppercase letters because it helps me to read the code, so that's the style I use in this book.

the HTML equivalent for "The End." So each of your Web pages will start off with this:

```
<HTML>
```

and end with this:

```
</HTML>
```

The next items serve to divide the document into two sections: the header and the body. The header section is like an introduction to the page. Web browsers use the header to glean various types of information about the page. Although a number of items can appear in the header section, the only one that makes any real sense to us mere mortals is the title of the page, which I talk about in the next section.

To define the header, add a <HEAD> tag and a </HEAD> tag immediately below the <HTML> tag you typed in earlier. So, your Web page should now look like this:

```
<HTML>
<HEAD>
</HEAD>
</HTML>
```

The body section is where you enter the text and other fun stuff that the browser will actually display. To define the body, you place a <BODY> tag and a </BODY> tag after the header section (that is, below the </HEAD> tag), as follows:

```
<HTML>
<HEAD>
</HEAD>
<BODY>
```

Use 'Em Once Only!

For best results, make sure you use each of these six basic structural tags only once in each page.

A Not-So-Necessary Evil?

To relieve some of the inevitable boredom of these early stages of Web page creation, you'll find some help on the CD-ROM that comes with this book. I've included a file named **skeleton.htm** that contains all the tags that make up the bare bones of a Web page. You can use this file as a template each time you start a new Web page.

```
</BODY>
</HTML>
```

Hmm. It's not exactly a work of art, is it? On the excitement scale, these opening moves rank right up there with watching the grass grow and tuning in to C-SPAN on a slow news day. Well, just file it under "Necessary Evils" and move on.

A Page by Any Other Name: Adding a Title

If you try loading your Web page into a browser, you'll just get a whole lot of nothingness because you haven't given the browser anything meaty that it can sink its teeth into. The first snack you can offer a hungry browser program is the title of the Web page. The page's title is just what you might think it is: the overall name of the page (not to be confused with the name of the file you're creating). If someone views the page in a graphical browser (such as Netscape Navigator or Internet Explorer), the title appears in the title bar of the browser's window.

The <TITLE> Tag

To define a title, you surround the text with the <TITLE> and </TITLE> tags. For example, if you want the title of your page to be "My Home Sweet Home Page," you enter it as follows:

```
<TITLE>My Home Sweet Home Page</TITLE>
```

Note that you always place the title inside the head section, so your basic HTML document now looks like so:

```
<HTML>
<HEAD>
<TITLE>My Home Sweet Home Page</TITLE>
</HEAD>
<BODY>
</BODY>
</HTML>
```

Figure 2.1 shows this document loaded into the Windows version of Netscape Navigator. Notice how the title appears in the window's title bar.

The page title

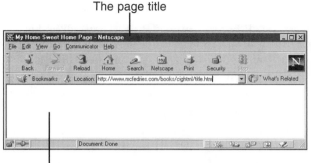

Figure 2.1

Most Windows Web browsers display the title in the title bar (duh).

The body text will appear here.

Title Do's and Don'ts

Here are a few things to keep in mind when thinking of a title for your page:

➤ Do make sure your title describes what the page is all about.

➤ Don't make your title too long. If you do, the browser might chop it off because there's not enough room to display it in the title bar. Fifty or sixty characters are usually the max.

➤ Do use titles that make sense when someone views them out of context. For example, if someone really likes your page, she might add it to her list of bookmarks (hey, it could happen). The browser displays the page title in the bookmark list, so it's important that the title makes sense when she looks at her bookmarks later on.

➤ Don't use titles that are cryptic or vague. Titling a page "Link #42" or "A Page" might make sense to you, but your readers might not appreciate it.

Fleshing Out Your Page with Text

With your page title firmly in place, you can now think about putting some flesh on your Web page's bones by entering the text you want to appear in the body of the page. For the most part, you can simply type the text between the <BODY> and </BODY> tags, like so:

```
<HTML>
<HEAD>
<TITLE>My Home Sweet Home Page</TITLE>
</HEAD>
<BODY>
This text appears in the body of the Web page.
</BODY>
</HTML>
```

Before you start typing willy-nilly, however, there are a few things you should know:

➤ You might think you can line things up and create some interesting effects by stringing together two or more spaces. Ha! Web browsers chew up all those extra spaces and spit them out into the nether regions of cyberspace. Why? Well, the philosophy of the Web is that you can use only HTML tags to lay out a document. So, a run of multiple spaces (or whitespace, as it's called) is ignored. (There are a couple of tricks you can use to get around this, however. I tell you about them in the next chapter.)

➤ Tabs also fall under the rubric of white space. You can enter tabs all day long, but the browser ignores them completely.

➤ Another thing that browsers like to ignore is the carriage return. It might sound reasonable to the likes of you and me that pressing **Enter** starts a new paragraph, but that's not so in the HTML world. I talk more about this in the next section.

➤ If HTML documents are just plain text, does that mean you're out of luck if you need to use characters such as ©, ™, and ¶? Luckily, no, you're not. HTML has special codes for these kinds of characters, and I talk about them in the next chapter.

More Character Assassinations

Note, too, that the angle bracket characters < and > can't be displayed in HTML pages because you use them to identify tags. Again, if you need to use them, I show you some special codes in the next chapter that get the job done.

➤ Word processor users, it bears repeating here that it's not worth your bother to format your text. The browser cheerfully ignores even the most elaborate formatting jobs because, as usual, browsers only understand HTML-based formatting. (And besides, a document with formatting is, by definition, not a pure text file, so a browser might bite the dust trying to load it.)

How to Do Paragraphs

As I mentioned earlier, carriage returns aren't worth a hill of beans in the World Wide Web. If you type one line, press **Enter**, and then type a second line, the browser simply runs the two lines together, side by side.

If a new paragraph is what you need, you have to stick the browser's nose in it, so to speak, by using the <P> tag. For example, consider the following text:

```
<HTML>
<HEAD>
<TITLE>My Home Sweet Home Page</TITLE>
</HEAD>
<BODY>
This text appears in the body of the Web page.
This is the second line (not!).
<P>
This is the third line.
</P>
</BODY>
</HTML>
```

Figure 2.2 shows how this text looks in the browser. As you can see, the first two lines appear beside each other, despite the fact that they're on separate lines in the original text. However, the third line sits nicely in its own paragraph thanks to the <P> tag that precedes it. Note, too, that I used the </P> end tag to finish the paragraph. This isn't strictly necessary (because the end of one paragraph automatically implies the beginning of the next one), but it's a good idea to get into the habit of using both <P> and </P> to define your paragraphs.

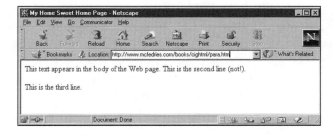

Figure 2.2

You need to use the <P> tag to create paragraphs in HTML.

"Help! The Browser Shows My Tags!"

When you view your HTML file in the browser, you might be dismayed to see that it shows not only your page text, but all the HTML tags, as well (see Figure 2.3).

Figure 2.3

The browser might show your tags along with your text.

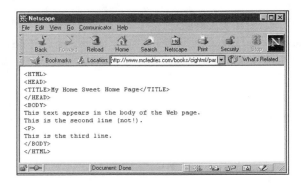

This kind of problem is almost always caused by one of the following:

➤ The file isn't a pure text file but is, rather, in a word processor format. As I mentioned earlier, if you're using a word processor to create your HTML files, make sure that when you save the file, you save it as a text file.

➤ The file doesn't have a .htm or .html extension. If you're using Windows 95 or 98 and saving a file as text, Windows has a perverse tendency to always want to add the .txt extension onto the end of the filename. Even if you specify the .htm or .html extension when you save the file, Windows just adds the .txt extension anyway (so you end up with something like index.htm.txt).

Assuming the latter is the problem, you saw earlier how you can overcome it by surrounding your filename with quotes in the Save As dialog box. To avoid that hassle, tell Windows to display file extensions. That way, the system always honors the extensions you enter by hand and won't force documents saved as text to always use the .txt extension. Here's how you do it:

1. Select **Start**, **Programs**, **Windows Explorer**.
2. Pull down the **View** menu and select the **Options** command (or the **Folder Options** command, depending on which version of Windows you're using).
3. In the Options dialog box (you might need to select the **View** tab, again depending on which flavor of Windows you have), deactivate the **Hide MS-DOS extensions for the file types that are registered** check box.
4. Click **OK**.

After that's done, you're able to add the .htm or .html extension to the end of your filenames without having to use quotation marks.

Note, too, that you should check your existing HTML files to see if they have .txt extensions. For example, you might have files named index.htm.txt, or whatever. If so, edit the filename to remove the .txt at the end.

The Least You Need to Know

This chapter got you started on your way to earning your Webmaster merit badge by showing you the basic HTML structure of a Web page. In the next chapter, I show you how to make the rather plain text you've got so far look more attractive.

Chapter 3

BEFORE   AFTER

From Buck-Naked to Beautiful: Dressing Up Your Page

In This Chapter

➤ HTML tags for formatting characters

➤ How to create impressive-looking headings

➤ Miscellaneous text tags

➤ How to insert special characters in your page

➤ A complete makeover for your Web page text

In the early, pre-text stages of the Web-page production process, your page is essentially naked. It passes its days exposed to the elements, shivering and teeth-chatteringly cold. Brrr! To put some color in your page's cheeks and prevent it from catching its death, you need to clothe it with the text you want everyone to read, as described in Chapter 2, "Laying the Foundation: The Basic Structure of a Web Page."

These new text garments might be warm, but they aren't much to look at. I mean, face it, a plain-text Web page just doesn't present your prose in the best light. I'm definitely talking Worst Dressed List here.

However, this really doesn't matter for those times when you're just kicking around the Web house. At this stage, you're the only one who sees your Web page, so you usually don't care how it looks. But what about when it's time to go out on the town? What do you do when you want the rest of the Web world to see your creation? Heck, you can't send your Web page out into cyberspace looking like *that*!

Before your page has its coming-out party, you need to dress it up in clothes appropriate for the occasion. In short, you need to format your text so it looks its best. This chapter is your Web page fashion consultant as it examines the various ways you can use HTML to beautify your words.

Sprucing Up Your Text

The first of our Web page makeover chores is to examine some tags that alter the look of individual words and phrases. The next few sections fill you in on the details.

Yer Basic Text Formatting Styles

The good news about text formatting is that most browsers support only four basic kinds: **bold**, *italic*, underline, and monospace. The bad news is that HTML has about a billion different tags that produce these styles. However, I'll take mercy on you and only let you in on the easiest tags to use. Table 3.1 shows the tags that produce each of these formats.

Table 3.1   Basic Text Formatting Tags

Text Style	Begin Tag	End Tag
Bold	\<B\>	\</B\>
Italic	\<I\>	\</I\>
Underline	\<U\>	\</U\>
Monospace	\<TT\>	\</TT\>

Here's a sample HTML document that shows each of these styles in action. Figure 3.1 shows how the styles look when viewed with Internet Explorer.

```
<HTML>
<HEAD>
<TITLE>Yer Basic Text Formatting Styles</TITLE>
</HEAD>
<BODY>
<U>My Excellent Bookstore Adventure</U>
<P>
The other day, I went to a unique bookstore called
<TT>Mary, Mary, Quite Contrary</TT>. There were
<I>tons</I> of unexpected delights, including, believe
it or not, a <B>Self-Helpless</B> section! For real.
I saw titles like <I>Got a 50-Cent Head? Here's How To
Get a Ten Dollar Haircut!</I> and <I>A Few Geese Shy of
a Gaggle—And Proud Of It!</I>
</BODY>
</HTML>
```

Alternative Text Tags

Just in case you're a glutton for punishment, here's a rundown of some alternative tags you can use for these text styles:

Text Style	Alternative Tags
Bold	\<STRONG\>
Italic	\<EM\> or \<CITE\> or \<ADDRESS\>
Monospace	\<CODE\> or \<KBD\>

Unfortunately, there's no way to predict how a given browser will display these styles, so I don't recommend using them. Other folks swear by them, however, so I wanted to let you know about these tags in case you trip over them when viewing other Web pages.

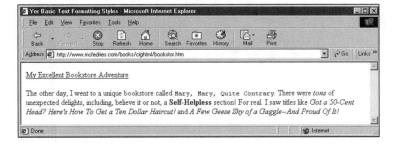

Figure 3.1

A Web page showing the four basic text formatting styles.

Keep in mind that this book's disc includes all the HTML examples you read about in the book. (For instructions on installing the disc—if you haven't already done so—see Appendix C, "The CD: The Webmaster's Toolkit.") This helps make your Web-building chores easier because you can use the examples to get started with your own pages. To get your mitts on the example I used previously, look for the file named bookstor.htm on the CD-ROM. If you don't have a CD-ROM drive on your computer, or if the CD is damaged, you can get the examples from my Web site at the following URL:

```
http://www.mcfedries.com/books/cightml/examples.html
```

Combining Text Formats

You should note, as well, that all modern browsers are perfectly happy to let you combine these text styles. So, for example, if you need bold italic text, you can get it by throwing the <B> and <I> tags together, like so:

```
<B><I>This'll give you, like, bold italic
➥text</I></B>
```

Accessorizing: Displaying Special Characters

You might think that because HTML is composed in text-only documents (documents that include only the characters and symbols you can peck out from your keyboard), non-standard characters such as ¢ and ¥ would be taboo. It's true that there's no way to add these characters to your page directly, but the Web wizards who created HTML thought up a way around this limitation. Specifically, they came up with special codes (called—a name only a true geek would love—*character entities*) that represent these and other oddball symbols.

These codes come in two flavors: a *character reference* and an *entity name*. Character references are basically just numbers, and the entity names are friendlier symbols that describe the character you're trying to display. For example, you can display the cents sign by using either the ¢ character reference or the ¢ entity name, as shown here:

```
    Got a 50&#162; Head? Here's How To Get a $10 Haircut!
```

or

```
    Got a 50&cent; Head? Here's How To Get a $10 Haircut!
```

Note that both character references and entity names begin with an ampersand (&) and end with a semi-colon (;) . Don't forget either symbol when using special characters in your own pages.

Table 3.2 lists a few other popular characters and their corresponding codes. You'll find a more complete list in the tearout card in the front of the book.

Table 3.2   A Few Common Characters

Symbol	Character Reference	Entity Name
Non-breaking space		
<	&#060;	&lt;

Symbol	Character Reference	Entity Name
>	>	>
¢	¢	¢
£	£	£
¥	¥	¥
©	©	©
®	®	®
°	°	°
1/4	¼	¼
1/2	½	½
3/4	¾	¾
×	×	×

What's a Non-Breaking Space?

The table contains a bizarre entry called a "non-breaking space." What's up with that? Remember back in Chapter 2 when I told you that HTML simply scoffs at whitespace (multiple spaces and tabs)? Well, you use the non-breaking space thingamajig when you want to force the browser to display white space. For example, if you want to indent the first line of a paragraph by three spaces, you'd start it like so:

```
   This line appears indented by three spaces.
```

You can also use the non-breaking space to position images, line up text, and much more.

A Few Formatting Features You'll Use All the Time

This section takes you through five more formatting tags that should stand you in good stead throughout your career as a Web engineer. You use these tags for adding headings, aligning paragraphs, displaying "preformatted" text, inserting line breaks, and displaying horizontal lines. The next few sections give you the details.

Techno Talk

Displaying < and >

Notice that I forced the browser to display a less-than sign (<) by using the character code &lt, and to display a greater-than sign (>) by using the code >.

Sectioning Your Page with Headings

Like chapters in a book, many Web page creators divide their contents into several sections. To help separate these sections and thus make life easier for the reader, you can use headings. Ideally, headings act as mini-titles that convey some idea of what each section is all about. To make these titles stand out, HTML has a series of heading tags that display text in larger, bold fonts. There are six heading tags in all, ranging from <H1>, which uses the largest font, down to <H6>, which uses the smallest font.

What's with all the different headings? Well, the idea is that you use them to outline your document. As an example, consider the headings I've used in this chapter and see how I'd format them in HTML.

The overall heading, of course, is the chapter title, so I'd display it using, say, the <H1> tag. The first main section is the one titled "Sprucing Up Your Text," so I'd give its title an <H2> heading. That section contains three subsections, "Yer Basic Text Formatting Styles," "Combining Text Formats," and "Accessorizing: Displaying Special Characters." I'd give each of these titles the <H3> heading. Then I come to the section called "A Few Formatting Features You'll Use All the Time." This is another main section of the chapter, so I'd go back to the <H2> tag for its title, and so on.

The following HTML document (look for headings.htm on the CD) shows how I'd format all the section titles for this chapter, and Figure 3.2 shows how they appear in Internet Explorer. (Notice that I don't need to use a <P> tag to display headings on separate lines; that's handled automatically by the heading tags.)

```
<HTML>
<HEAD><TITLE>Some Example Headings</TITLE>
</HEAD>
<BODY>
<H1>From Buck-Naked to Beautiful: Dressing Up Your Page</H1>
<H2>Sprucing Up Your Text</H2>
<H3>Yer Basic Text Formatting Styles</H3>
<H3>Combining Text Formats</H3>
<H3>Accessorizing: Displaying Special Characters</H3>
<H2>A Few Formatting Features You'll Use All the Time</H2>
<H3>Sectioning Your Page With Headings</H3>
<H3>Aligning Paragraphs</H3>
<H3>Handling Preformatted Text</H3>
<H3>Them's the Breaks: Using &lt;BR&gt; for Line Breaks</H3>
<H3>Inserting Horizontal Lines</H3>
<H2>Textras: Fancier Text Formatting</H2>
```

```
<H3>The &lt;FONT&gt; Tag I: Changing the Size of Text</H3>
<H3>The &lt;BASEFONT&gt; Tag</H3>
<H3>The &lt;FONT&gt; Tag II: Changing the Typeface</H3>
<H3>Changing the Color of Your Page Text</H3>
<H3>The &lt;FONT&gt; Tag III: Changing the Color</H3>
<H3>The Dreaded &lt;BLINK&gt; Tag</H3>
</BODY>
</HTML>
```

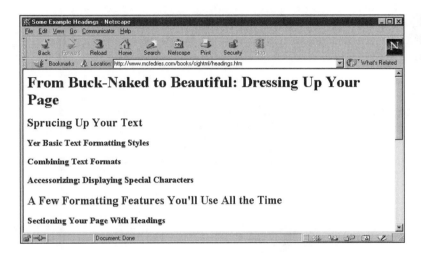

Figure 3.2

Examples of HTML's heading tags.

Aligning Paragraphs

Centering text and graphics is a time-honored way to give reports and brochures a professional look and feel. To provide the same advantage to your Web pages, the <CENTER> tag gives you centering capabilities for your page headings, paragraphs, lists, and even graphics. Here's how <CENTER> works:

```
<CENTER>
[Headings, text, and graphics that you want centered go here.]
</CENTER>
```

The <CENTER> tag is a nice, simple way to shift things to the middle of a page. However, you can also use the ALIGN attribute for the <P> tag and the heading tags. For example, to center the next paragraph, you use the following variation on the <P> tag theme:

```
<P ALIGN=CENTER>
```

Similarly, you can center, say, an <H1> heading like so:

```
<H1 ALIGN=CENTER>
```

35

The advantage to this approach is that you can also use either LEFT or RIGHT with the ALIGN attribute to further adjust your paragraph alignment.

Handling Preformatted Text

In the previous chapter, I told you that Web browsers ignore whitespace (multiple spaces and tabs) as well as carriage returns. Well, I lied. Sort of. You see, all browsers normally *do* spit out these elements, but you can talk a browser into swallowing them whole by using the <PRE> tag. The "PRE" part is short for "preformatted," and you normally use this tag to display preformatted text exactly as it's laid out. Here, "preformatted" means text in which you use spaces, tabs, and carriage returns to line things up.

Let's look at an example. The following bit of code is an HTML document (look for pre_tag.htm on the CD) in which I set up two chunks of text in a pattern that uses spaces and carriage returns. The first bit of doggerel doesn't make use of the <PRE> tag, but I've surrounded the second poem with <PRE> and </PRE>. Figure 3.3 shows the results. Notice that the lines from the first poem are strung together, but that when the browser encounters <PRE>, it displays the whitespace and carriage returns faithfully.

<PRE> Text Is Ugly!

You'll notice one other thing about how the browser displays text that's ensconced within the <PRE> and </PRE> tags: It formats the text in an ugly monospaced font. The only way to get around this is to use something called a "style sheet" to specify the font you want the browser to use with the <PRE> tag. I show you how this works in Part 3, "High HTML Style: Working with Style Sheets."

```
<HTML>
<HEAD>
<TITLE>The &lt;PRE&gt; Tag</TITLE>
</HEAD>
<BODY>
<H3>Without the &lt;PRE&gt; Tag:</H3>
          Here's
        some ditty,
```

```
          specially done,
       to lay it out all
     formatted and pretty.
Unfortunately, that is all
  this junk really means,
        because I admit I
         couldn't scrawl
           poetry for
             beans.
<H3>With the &lt;PRE&gt; Tag:</H3>
<PRE>
             Here's
          some ditty,
        specially done,
       to lay it out all
     formatted and pretty.
Unfortunately, that is all
  this junk really means,
        because I admit I
         couldn't scrawl
           poetry for
             beans.
</PRE>
</BODY>
</HTML>
```

Figure 3.3

How preformatted text appears in Explorer.

Them's the Breaks: Using <BR> for Line Breaks

As you saw in the previous chapter, you use the <P> tag when you need to separate your text into paragraphs. When a browser trips over a <P> tag, it starts a new paragraph on a separate line and inserts an extra, blank line after the previous paragraph. However, what if you don't want that extra line? For example, you might want to display a list of items with each item on a separate line and without any space between the items. (Actually, there are better ways to display lists than the method I show you here; see Chapter 4, "A Fistful of List Grist for Your Web Page Mill.")

Well, you could use the <PRE> tag, but your text would appear in that ugly, monospaced font. A better solution is to separate your lines with <BR>, the line break tag. A browser starts a new line when it encounters <BR>, but it doesn't toss in an extra blank line. Here's an example (it's the file named linebrks.htm on the CD):

```
<HTML>
<HEAD>
<TITLE>Line Breaks</TITLE>
</HEAD>
<BODY>
<H2>My Excellent Bookstore Adventure</H2>
<HR>
The other day, I went to a unique bookstore called
<TT>Mary, Mary, Quite Contrary</TT>. There were
<I>tons</I> of unexpected delights, including, believe
it or not, a <B>Self-Helpless</B> section! For real.
Here's a list of just some of the great titles I saw:
<P>
Got a 50&#162; Head? Here's How To Get a $10 Haircut!<BR>
A Few Geese Shy of a Gaggle—And Proud Of It!<BR>
The Seven Habits of Highly Ineffective Couch Potatoes<BR>
Dieting? No, Sorry, You're <I>Way</I> Too Late For That!<BR>
"Dumb and Dumber": A Yahoo Way of Knowledge
</BODY>
</HTML>
```

In the list of books, I added the <BR> tag to the end of each line (except the last one; I don't need it there). As you can see in Figure 3.4, Netscape dutifully displays each line separately, with no space in between.

Inserting Horizontal Lines

The eagle-eyed among you might have noticed a horizontal line extending across the browser screen shown in Figure 3.4. What gives? Well, while you weren't looking, I surreptitiously inserted an <HR> tag into the HTML text. <HR>, which stands for "horizontal rule," produces a line across the page, which is a handy way to separate sections of your document.

If you use <HR> by itself, you get a standard line that goes right across the page. However, Internet Explorer and Netscape support various enhancements to the <HR> tag that enable you to change the line's size, width, alignment, and more. Table 3.3 shows a rundown.

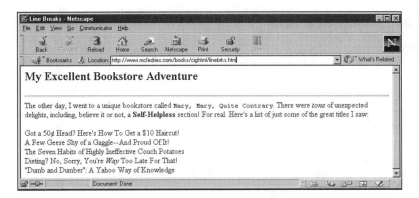

Figure 3.4
Use the <BR> tag to force a line break in your text.

Table 3.3　Extra Attributes for the <HR> Tag

<HR> Extension	What It Does
<HR WIDTH=x>	Sets the width of the line to *x* pixels
<HR WIDTH=x%>	Sets the width of the line to *x* percent of the screen
<HR SIZE=n>	Sets the thickness of the line to *n* pixels (where the default thickness is 1 pixel)
<HR ALIGN=LEFT>	Aligns the line with the left margin
<HR ALIGN=CENTER>	Centers the line
<HR ALIGN=RIGHT>	Aligns the line with the right margin
<HR NOSHADE>	Displays the line as a solid line (instead of appearing etched into the screen)

Fancier Lines

The <HR> tag draws a plain horizontal line. You might notice some Web pages have fancier lines that use color and other neat texture effects. Those lines are actually graphic images; I show you how to add those in Chapter 6, "A Picture Is Worth a Thousand Clicks: Working with Images."

Textras: Fancier Text Formatting

As you saw a bit earlier in this chapter, you can display your text in a different font size by using one of the heading tags (such as <H1>). Unfortunately, you can't use heading tags to adjust the size of individual characters because headings always appear on a line by themselves. To fix this, you use two tags: <FONT> and <BASE-FONT>, which I discuss in the next couple of sections. I'll also show you how to change the color of your text.

The <FONT> Tag I: Changing the Size of Text

The <FONT> tag adjusts (among other things) the size of any text placed between <FONT> and its corresponding end tag, </FONT>. Here's how it works:

```
<FONT SIZE=size>Affected text goes here</FONT>
```

The *size* part is a number that pinpoints how big you want the text to appear. You can use any number between 1 (tiny) and 7 (gargantuan); 3 is the size of standard-issue text. Here's an example (see fontsize.htm on the CD-ROM):

```
<HTML>
<HEAD>
<TITLE>Text Size Extensions</TITLE>
</HEAD>
<BODY>
<H1>Changing Font Size with the &lt;FONT&gt; Tag</H1>
<HR>
<FONT SIZE=7>This text uses a font size of 7.</FONT><BR>
<FONT SIZE=6>This text uses a font size of 6.</FONT><BR>
<FONT SIZE=5>This text uses a font size of 5.</FONT><BR>
<FONT SIZE=4>This text uses a font size of 4.</FONT><BR>
<FONT SIZE=3>This text uses a font size of 3 (normal).</FONT><BR>
<FONT SIZE=2>This text uses a font size of 2.</FONT><BR>
<FONT SIZE=1>This text uses a font size of 1.</FONT><BR>
<HR>
<FONT SIZE=7>Y</FONT>ou can mix and match sizes:
<BR>
Here at Shyster & Son Brokerage, you'll see your investments
<FONT SIZE=7>s<FONT SIZE=6>h<FONT SIZE=5>r<FONT SIZE=4>i
<FONT SIZE=3>n<FONT SIZE=2>k</FONT> while our commissions
<FONT SIZE=4>g<FONT SIZE=5>r<FONT SIZE=6>o<FONT SIZE=7>w!</FONT>
</BODY>
</HTML>
```

Figure 3.5 shows the results as they appear with Internet Explorer.

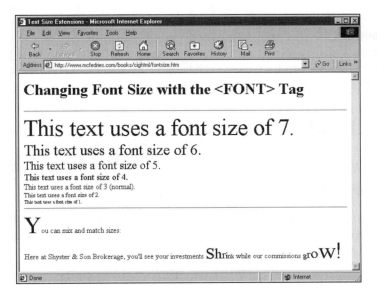

Figure 3.5
Use the <FONT> tag to adjust the size of your Web page text.

The <BASEFONT> Tag

I mentioned earlier that the standard font size in a Web page is 3. This is called the *base font*, and you'll be interested to know that it's not set in stone. To change it, use the <BASEFONT> tag:

```
<BASEFONT SIZE=size>
```

Once again, *size* is a number between 1 and 7 that specifies the base font size you want. For example, if you enter **<BASEFONT=7>** at the top of your document (the top of the body section, that is), then all the text will appear with font size 7.

You might be wondering what the heck's the big deal with <BASEFONT>. After all, couldn't you just insert a <FONT SIZE=7> tag at the top of the document? Good point. (Gee, you *are* paying attention, aren't you?) The beauty (if beauty is the right term) of base fonts is that they enable you to set up relative font sizes. A relative font size is one that's so many sizes larger or smaller than the base font. Here's an example:

```
<BASEFONT=6>
This text is displayed in the base font size. However
<FONT SIZE=-2>these three words</FONT> were displayed in
a font size that was two sizes smaller than the base font.
```

The <FONT SIZE=-2> tag tells the browser to display the text in a font size that's two sizes smaller than the base font (to get larger fonts, you'd use a plus sign , instead). Because I specified a base font of 6, the text between the <FONT> and </FONT> tags appears with a font size of 4.

Why not simply use <FONT SIZE=4>, instead? Well, suppose you plaster your document with dozens of font changes and then, when you display it in the browser, the fonts appear too small. If you're using explicit font sizes, you have to painstakingly adjust each <FONT> tag. However, if you're using relative font sizes, you only have to change the <BASEFONT> tag.

The <FONT> Tag II: Changing the Typeface

By default, the browser uses a plain typeface to render your pages. However, you can change that by shoehorning the FACE attribute into the <FONT> tag, like so:

```
<FONT FACE="typeface">
```

Here, *typeface* is the name of the typeface you want to use. The following page (it's typeface.htm on the disc) shows a few FACE-enhanced <FONT> tags in action, and Figure 3.6 shows what Netscape thinks of the whole thing.

```
<HTML>
<HEAD>
<TITLE>Font Typeface Extensions</TITLE>
</HEAD>
<BODY>
<H1>The &lt;FONT&gt; Tag Can Also Do Different Typefaces</H1>
<HR>
<FONT SIZE=6>
This is the default browser typeface (Times New Roman).<BR>
<FONT FACE="Arial">This is the Arial typeface.</FONT><BR>
<FONT FACE="Courier New">This is the Courier New typeface.</FONT><BR>
<FONT FACE="Comic Sans MS">This is the Comic Sans MS
typeface.</FONT><BR>
<FONT FACE="Not My Typeface">Doh! This is NOT the Not My Typeface
typeface!</FONT><BR>
<BODY>
<HTML>
```

Sounds easy, right? Not so fast, bucko. The problem with the FACE attribute is that it only works if the typeface you specify is installed on the user's computer. If it's not, you're out of luck because the browser will just use its default typeface. In the previous example, notice that the browser doesn't render anything for the Not My Typeface typeface because it's not installed. (It doesn't even exist because I just made up the name!)

To increase your chances, however, you're allowed to add multiple typeface names to the FACE attribute:

```
<FONT FACE="Arial, Verdana, Helvetica">
```

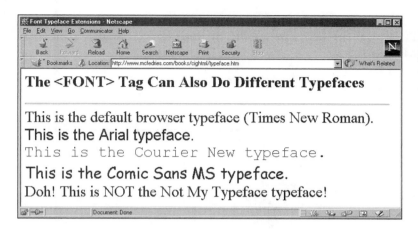

Figure 3.6

Use the <FONT> tag's FACE attribute to try different typefaces on for size.

Some Notes About Working with Colors

The next couple of sections show you how to change text colors. You'll find that you often have to work with colors when constructing Web pages, so it's probably a good idea to take a minute or two now and get the HTML color techniques down pat.

Most of the time, you specify a color by entering a six-digit code that takes the following form:

    #rrggbb

This sure looks weird, but there's method in its mathematical madness. Here, *rr* is the red part of the color, *gg* is the green part, and *bb* is the blue part. In other words, each code represents a combination of the three primary colors, and it's this combination that produces the final color. These are called *RGB values*.

The truly nerdish aspect of all this is that each two-digit primary color code uses *hexadecimal* numbers. These are base 16 (instead of the usual base 10 in decimal numbers), so they run from 0 through 9, then A through F. Yeah, my head hurts, too.

Table 3.4 lists the appropriate values for some common colors.

Table 3.4   RGB Codes for Common Colors

If You Use This Value...	You Get This Color...
#000000	Black
#FFFFFF	White
#FF0000	Red
#00FF00	Green
#0000FF	Blue

continues

43

Table 3.4   Continued

If You Use This Value...	You Get This Color...
#FF00FF	Magenta
#00FFFF	Cyan
#FFFF00	Yellow

Using "Safe" Colors

There are millions of these RGB codes. However, a mere 216 of them have been deemed "safe" for use on the Web. This just means that these 216 colors will look good on any monitor, no matter what settings the surfer is using. I have a complete list of all these safe colors in the CD's reference section.

Rather than working with these bizarre RGB values, you might prefer to use the standard HTML color names, which are supported by Internet Explorer 3.0 and later, as well as Netscape Navigator 3.0 and later. These color names use nice English words such as "Blue" and "Tan" (as well as plenty of bizarre words such as "Bisque" and "Orchid"). A complete list of the color names, their corresponding RGB values, and a swatch that shows the color are available in the file x11color.htm on the CD (see Figure 3.7 for a black-and-white version of that document).

Changing the Color of Your Page Text

Browsers display your text in basic black, which is readable but not all that exciting. To put some color in your text's cheeks, let's look at a few extra goodies.

For starters, the <BODY> tag has a TEXT attribute:

```
<BODY TEXT="color">
```

Here, *color* is either a color name or an RGB value that specifies the color you want to use.

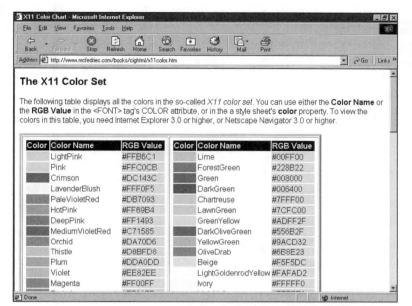

Figure 3.7

The colors, color names, and their RGB equivalents.

Compare and Contrast

Because you can change the color of your page's background, links, and text, it's very important that you choose a color combination that makes for easy reading. Light yellow text on white, or bright green text on red, can be a little hard on the eyes.

Changing the Color of Your Links

There are also ways to specify colors for the links you include in your page. Here's how they work:

```
<BODY LINK="color" VLINK="color" ALINK="color">
```

Use LINK to specify the color of new links (links the reader has never clicked before); use VLINK to set up a color for visited links; use ALINK to set up a color for active links. (An *active link* is a link you've clicked and are waiting for the page to display.)

The <FONT> Tag III: Another Way to Change Text Color

The problem with these <BODY> tag attributes is that they affect the entire page. What if you only want to change the color of a heading, a word, a link, or even a single letter? For that you need to return to our old friend the <FONT> tag, which also supports a COLOR attribute:

```
<FONT COLOR="color">
```

Here's an example:

```
<FONT COLOR="#FF0000">This text is red.</FONT>
```

Web Page Fashion Tips

The HTML elements I discussed in this chapter (and many of the ones I talk about in subsequent chapters) can make a Web page actually look worse if you misuse or overuse them. If you're interested in making your pages look their best, be sure to read Chapter 23, "The Elements of Web Page Style," where I discuss the dos and don'ts of Web page design.

The Least You Need to Know

This chapter showed you a few ways to dress up your Web page for a night on the town. Next on the agenda is how to display lists in your pages, and I get to that in the following chapter.

Chapter 4

A Fistful of List Grist for Your Web Page Mill

In This Chapter

➤ Creating numbered lists on your Web page

➤ How to set up bulleted lists

➤ Cobbling together a definition list

➤ More list examples than you can shake a stick at

Are you making a list and checking it twice? Gonna find out who's naughty and...oops, drifted off to the North Pole for a second! But if you do want to include a list in your Web page, what's the best way to go about it? You saw in the previous chapter how you can use the
 (line break) tag to display items on separate lines. That works well enough, I guess, but hold your list horses—there's a better way. HTML has a few tags that are specially designed to give you much more control over your list-building chores. In fact, HTML offers no less than three different list styles: numbered lists, bulleted lists, and definition lists. This chapter takes you through the basics of each list type and provides you with plenty of examples.

Putting Your Affairs in Order with Numbered Lists

If you want to include a numbered list of items—it could be a top 10 list, bowling league standings, or any kind of ranking—don't bother adding in the numbers yourself. Instead, you can use HTML ordered lists to make the Web browser generate the numbers for you.

Ordered lists use two types of tags:

➤ The entire list is surrounded by the <OL> (ordered list) and </OL> tags.

➤ Each item in the list is preceded by the <LI> (list item) tag.

The general setup looks like this:

```
<OL>
<LI>First item.
<LI>Second item.
<LI>Third item.
<LI>You get the idea.
</OL>
```

Here's an example (see numlist1.htm on the CD):

```
<HTML>
<HEAD>
<TITLE>Numbered Lists - Example #1</TITLE>
</HEAD>
<BODY>
<H3>My Ten Favorite U.S. City Names</H3>
<OL>
<LI>Toad Suck, Arkansas
<LI>Panic, Pennsylvania
<LI>Dismal, Tennessee
<LI>Boring, Maryland
<LI>Hell, Michigan
<LI>Two Egg, Florida
<LI>Muck City, Alabama
<LI>Rambo Riviera, Arkansas
<LI>King Arthur's Court, Michigan
<LI>Buddha, Indiana
</OL>
</BODY>
</HTML>
```

Notice that I didn't include any numbers before each list item. However, when I display this document in a browser (see Figure 4.1), the numbers get inserted automatically. Pretty slick, huh?

The items you toss into your numbered lists don't have to be short words and phrases, however. For example, if you're explaining how to perform a certain task, a numbered list is the perfect way to take your readers through each step. Here's a more involved example (it's numlist2.htm on the CD) that uses a numbered list to explain how to juggle:

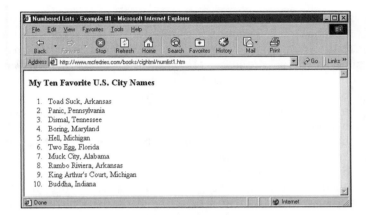

Figure 4.1

How the numbered list appears in Internet Explorer (it will look pretty much the same in any browser).

Spice Up Your List Items

Your list items don't have to be just plain text, so you're free to go crazy and insert other HTML tags. For example, you could use <B> and </B> to boldface a word or two in the item, you could use a heading tag to increase the font size of the item, or you could make an item a hypertext link to another Web page. Just make sure to start each line with the <LI> tag. (I discuss this linking stuff in the next chapter.)

```
<HTML>
<HEAD>
<TITLE>Numbered Lists - Example #2</TITLE>
</HEAD>
<BODY>
<H3>The Complete Idiot's Guide to Juggling</H3>
<HR>
Here are the basic steps for the most fundamental of juggling
moves&#151;the three-ball cascade:
<OL>
<LI>Place two balls in your dominant hand, one in front of the other,
and hold the third ball in your other hand. Let your arms dangle
naturally and bring your forearms parallel to the ground (as though
you were holding a tray).
<LI>Of the two balls in your dominant hand, toss the front one towards
your left hand in a smooth arc. Make sure the ball doesn't spin too
```

```
much and that it goes no higher than about eye level.
<LI>Once the first ball has reached the top of its arc, you need to
release the ball in your other hand. Throw it towards your dominant
hand, making sure it flies <I>under</I> the first ball. Again, watch
that the ball doesn't spin or go higher than eye level.
<LI>Now things get a little tricky . Soon after you release the
second ball, the first ball will approach your other hand (gravity
never fails). Go ahead and catch the first ball.
<LI>When the second ball reaches its apex, throw the third ball (the
remaining ball in your dominant hand) under it.
<LI>At this point, it just becomes a game of catch-and-throw-under,
catch-and-throw-under. Keep repeating steps 1-5 and, before you know
it, you'll be a juggling fool. (However, I'd recommend holding off on
the flaming clubs until you've practiced a little.)
</OL>
</BODY>
</HTML>
```

As you can see, most of the items are quite long; and it's kind of hard to tell where each <LI> item begins and ends. However, as shown in the Figure 4.2, the list looks pretty good when viewed in a Web browser.

Figure 4.2

Numbered lists are perfect for outlining the steps in a procedure.

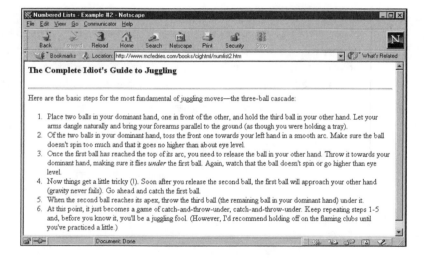

Using a Different Numbering Scheme in Numbered Lists

That <OL> tag's TYPE attribute enables you to define a different numbering scheme. Here's how it works:

```
<OL TYPE=type>
```

Here, *type* is one of the characters shown in Table 4.1.

Table 4.1   TYPE Attribute Values

Type	Numbering Scheme	Example
1	Standard numbers	1, 2, 3
a	Lowercase letters	a, b, c
A	Uppercase letters	A, B, C
i	Small Roman numerals	i, ii, iii
I	Large Roman numerals	I, II, III

Here's an example (see oltype.htm on the CD):

```
<HTML>
<HEAD>
<TITLE>Numbered List Extensions</TITLE>
</HEAD>
<BODY>
<H3>Using the &lt;OL TYPE=<I>type</I>&gt; Tag</H3>
<B>TYPE=a:</B><BR>
<OL TYPE=a>
<LI>Win.
<LI>Place.
<LI>Show.
</OL>
<B>TYPE=A:</B><BR>
<OL TYPE=A>
<LI>Gold.
<LI>Silver.
<LI>Bronze.
</OL>
<B>TYPE=i:</B><BR>
<OL TYPE=i>
<LI>Miss America.
<LI>First runner-up.
<LI>Second runner-up.
</OL>
<B>TYPE=I:</B><BR>
<OL TYPE=I>
<LI>Picard.
<LI>Riker.
<LI>Data.
</OL></BODY>
</HTML>
```

Figure 4.3 shows how Internet Explorer handles the various types of lists.

Figure 4.3

The <OL> tag extensions in action.

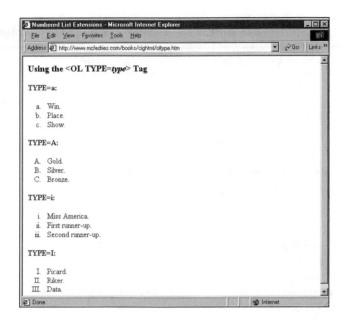

Scoring Points with Bulleted Lists

Numbered lists, of course, aren't the only kinds of lists. If you just want to enumerate a few points, a bulleted list might be more your style. They're called "bulleted" lists because a Web browser displays a cute little dot or square (depending on the browser) called a *bullet* to the left of each item.

The HTML tags for a bulleted list are pretty close to the ones you saw for a numbered list. As before, you precede each list item with the same <LI> tag, but you enclose the entire list with the <UL> and </UL> tags. Why "UL"? Well, what the rest of the world calls a bulleted list, the HTML powers-that-be call an *unordered list*. Yeah, that's real intuitive. Ah well, here's how they work:

```
<UL>
<LI>First bullet point.
<LI>Fifty-seventh bullet point.
<LI>Sixteenth bullet point.
<LI>Hey, whaddya want-it's an unordered list!
</UL>
```

Here's an HTML document (look for bulleted.htm on the disc) that demonstrates how to use the bulleted list tags:

```
<HTML>
<HEAD>
```

```
<TITLE>Bulleted List Example</TITLE>
</HEAD>
<BODY>
<H3>Products I'd Like To See</H3>
<UL>
<LI>Water-resistant sponge
<LI>Self-soiling oven
<LI>Tineless fork
<LI>Silent alarm clock
<LI>Inflatable dartboard
<LI>Teflon bath mat
<LI>Helium-filled paperweight
<LI>Flame-retardant firewood
<LI>Sandpaper bathroom tissue
<LI>Water-soluble dishcloth
</UL>
</BODY>
</HTML>
```

Figure 4.4 shows how the Netscape browser renders this file—little bullets and all.

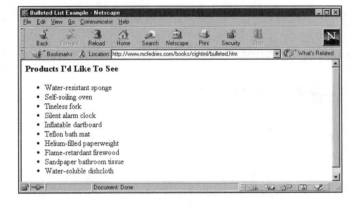

Figure 4.4

A typical bulleted list.

Changing the Bullet Type in Bulleted Lists

The basic bulleted-list bullet is a small circle. However, Netscape and Internet Explorer also support an extra TYPE attribute that modifies the bullet:

```
<UL TYPE=type>
```

In this case, *type* can be either disc (the standard bullet), circle, or square. Here's a for-instance (look for ultype.htm on the disc):

```
<HTML>
<HEAD>
<TITLE>Bulleted List Extensions</TITLE>
```

53

```
</HEAD>
<BODY>
<H3>Using the &lt;UL TYPE=<I>type</I>&gt; Tag</H3>
<HR>
<UL TYPE=disc>
<LI>Compact disc.
<LI>Disc jockey.
<LI>Disc brake.
</UL>
<HR>
<UL TYPE=circle>
<LI>Circle the wagons!
<LI>Circle all that apply.
<LI>Chalk Circle.
</UL>
<HR>
<UL TYPE=square>
<LI>Square root.
<LI>Three square meals.
<LI>Times square.
</UL>
</BODY>
</HTML>
```

And Figure 4.5 shows how it looks from Internet Explorer's point of view.

Figure 4.5

The TYPE extension to the <UL> tag enables you to choose from any of three different bullet styles.

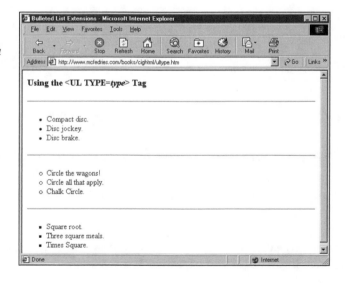

Defining Definition Lists

The final type of list is called a *definition list*. Originally, people used it for dictionary-like lists where each entry had two parts: a term and the definition of the term. As you'll see, though, definition lists are useful for more than just definitions.

To mark the two different parts of each entry in these lists, you need two different tags. The term is preceded by the <DT> tag, and the definition is preceded by the <DD> tag, like so:

```
<DT>Term<DD>Definition
```

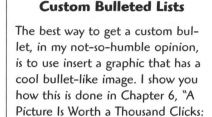

Custom Bulleted Lists

The best way to get a custom bullet, in my not-so-humble opinion, is to use insert a graphic that has a cool bullet-like image. I show you how this is done in Chapter 6, "A Picture Is Worth a Thousand Clicks: Working with Images."

You can, if you like, put the <DT> part and the <DD> part on separate lines, but I prefer this style (and either way, they end up looking the same in the browser). You then surround the whole list with the <DL> and </DL> tags to complete your definition list. Here's how the whole thing looks:

```
<DL>
<DT>A Term<DD>Its Definition
<DT>Another Term<DD>Another Definition
<DT>Yet Another Term<DD>Yet Another Definition
<DT>Etc.<DD>Abbreviation of a Latin phrase that means "and so forth."
</DL>
```

Let's look at an example. The HTML document shown next (it's on the CD in the file named defnlist.htm) uses a definition list to outline a few words and phrases and their definitions. (Notice that I've applied bold face to all the terms; this helps them stand out more when the browser displays them.)

```
<HTML>
<HEAD>
<TITLE>Definition List Example</TITLE>
</HEAD>
<BODY>
<H3>Some Techno-Terms You Should Know</H3>
<DL>
<DT><B>Barney Page</B><DD>A Web page that tries to capitalize on a
current craze.
<DT><B>Bit-Spit</B><DD>Any form of digital correspondence.
<DT><B>Byte-Bonding</B><DD>When computer users discuss things that
nearby noncomputer users don't understand. See also <I>geeking
out</I>.
<DT><B>Clickstreams</B><DD>The paths a person takes as she negotiates
```

```
various Web pages.
<DT><B>Cobweb Page</B><DD>A Web page that hasn't been updated in a
while.
<DT><B>Geek</B><DD>Someone who knows a lot about computers and very
little about anything else.
<DT><B>Geeking Out</B><DD>When <I>geeks</I> who are <I>byte-
bonding</I>
start playing with a computer during a non-computer-related social
event.
<DT><B>Luser</B><DD>A "loser user." Someone who doesn't have the
faintest
idea what they're doing and, more importantly, refuses to do anything
about it.
<DT><B>Nerd</B><DD>A <I>geek</I> totally lacking in personal hygiene
and
social skills.
</DL>
</BODY>
</HTML>
```

Figure 4.6 shows how the definition list appears in the Netscape scheme of things.

Figure 4.6

A few definitions arrayed, appropriately enough, in a definition list.

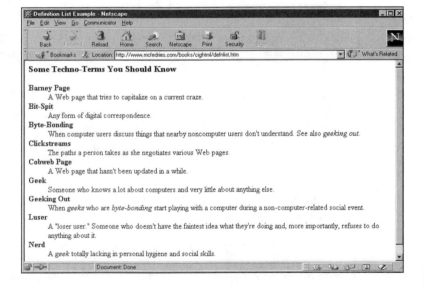

More Than Just Definitions

People often use definition lists for things other than definitions. Some Web welders like to use the term (the <DT> part) as a section heading and the definition (the <DD> part) as the section text. You can also leave out the term and just use the <DD> tag by itself. This is handy for those times when you need indented text (say, if you're quoting someone at length).

Combining Lists Inside Lists

These three types of HTML lists should serve you well for most of your Web page productions. However, you're free to mix and match various list types to suit the occasion. Specifically, it's perfectly legal to plop one type of list inside another (this is called *nesting lists*). For example, suppose you have a numbered list that outlines the steps involved in some procedure. If you need to augment one of the steps with a few bullet points, you can simply insert a bulleted list after the appropriate numbered list item.

As an example, I'll take the definition list from the last section and toss in both a numbered list and a bulleted list. Here's the result (I've lopped off some of the lines to make it easier to read; you can find the full document on the CD in the file named combo.htm):

```
<DL>
<DT><B>Barney Page</B><DD>A Web page that tries to capitalize on a
current craze. Here are some recent Barney page subjects:

<UL>
<LI>Pokemon
<LI>The Y2K problem
<LI>Ricky Martin
</UL>

<DT><B>Bit-Spit</B><DD>Any form of digital correspondence.
<DT><B>Byte-Bonding</B><DD>When computer users discuss things that
nearby noncomputer users don't understand. Here are the three stages
of byte-bonding that inevitably lead to <I>geeking out</I>:

<OL>
```

```
<LI>"Say, did you see that IBM ad where the nuns are talking about
surfing the Net?"
<LI>"Do you surf the Net?"
<LI>"Let's go surf the Net!"
</OL>

<DT><B>Clickstreams</B><DD>The paths a person takes as she negotiates
various Web pages.
...
</DL>
```

After the first definition list entry—the one for Barney Page—I've inserted a bulleted list that gives a few examples. (I've added blank lines above and below the bulleted list to make it stand out better. Note that I added these lines for cosmetic purposes only; they don't affect within listss how the page appears in the browser.) Then, after the third definition list entry—Byte-Bonding—I've put in a numbered list. Figure 4.7 shows how all this looks when a browser gets hold of it.

Figure 4.7

HTML is more than happy to let you insert lists inside each other.

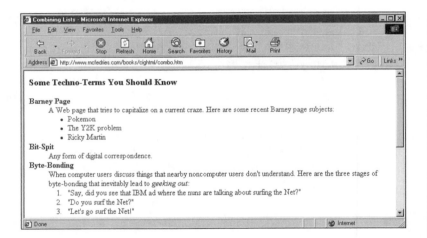

The Least You Need to Know

This chapter took you through the wacky world of HTML lists. You might not need to use them all that often, but they can really come in handy.

Next up: the monent you've been waiting for, I'm sure. (Insert drum roll here.) Chapter 5 shows you how to add those all-important links to your Web pages.

Making the Jump to Hyperspace: Adding Links

As a would-be Web page publisher, you've gotta give the people what they want, right? And what today's modern surfer wants more than anything else is to *interact* with a Web page. Unfortunately, truly interactive pages are still on the bleeding edge of Web technology. (I'll talk about some of this stuff in Chapter 10, "Making Your Web Pages Dance and Sing.") And you usually can't create the semi-interactive Web pages that are quite common (they're called *forms*) without recourse to some heavy-duty programming (although be sure to read Chapter 11, "Need Feedback? Create a Form!" for some ways around this).

However, there is a way to throw at least a small interactive bone to the readers of your Web creations: Give 'em a few hypertext links that they can follow to the four corners of the Web world (or even just to another part of your own cyberspace plot). It's an easy way to give your pages a dynamic feel that'll have people coming back for more. This chapter explains links and shows you how to put the "hypertext" into HTML.

The URL of Net: A Cyberspace Address Primer

Before the hypertext festivities commence, there's a bit of background info I need to slog through for you. As I mentioned in Chapter 1, "A Brief HTML Web Page Primer," a *hypertext link* is a special word or phrase in a Web page that, when the user clicks it, takes her to a different Web document (or to an FTP site, or whatever). Each Web page (and, indeed, any Internet resource) has its own address, which is called a *Uniform Resource Locator* (or URL, for short).

When you combine these two factoids, you realize that for a hypertext link to work properly, you need to know the correct address of the resource to which you're linking. To do that, you need to understand the anatomy of these URL things. Unfortunately, the whole URL concept seems to have been invented by some insane Geek of Geeks who never believed normal human beings would actually use the darn things. They're long, they're confusing, they're messy, and they're almost impossible to type correctly the first time. Not to worry, though. I've gone *mano-a-mano* with this URL foofaraw, and I've come up with a plan that's designed to knock some sense into the whole mess.

The idea is that, like journalists and their 5 Ws (who, what, where, when, and why), you can reduce any URL to 3 Ws (who, what, and where) and an H (how). So, the basic form of any URL ends up looking like this:

> *How://Who/Where/What*

Hmm. I'm definitely talking serious weirdness here, so let's see what the heck I mean by all that:

How   The first part of the URL specifies how the data is going to be transferred across Net lines. This is called the *protocol* and, luckily, mere mortals like you and I don't need to concern ourselves with the guts of this stuff. All you need to know is which protocol each resource uses, which is easy. For example, the World Wide Web uses something called HTTP (I tell you which protocols other resources use later in this chapter). So, the "how" part of the URL is the protocol, followed by a colon and two slashes (//). (I told you this stuff was arcane; it makes alchemy look like "The Cat In the Hat.") So, a Web page URL always starts like this (lowercase letters are the norm, but they're not necessary):

```
http://
```

Who   Calling the next part the "who" of the URL is, I admit, a bit of a misnomer because there's no person involved. Instead, it's the name of the computer where the resource is located—in geek circles, this is called the *hostname*. (This is the part of an Internet address that has all those dots you're always hearing, such as ncsa.uiuc.edu or www.yahoo.com.) For example, this book's home page is located on a computer named www.mcfedries.com. You just tack this "who" part onto the end of the "how" part, as shown here:

```
http://www.mcfedries.com
```

Where   The next part of the address specifies where the resource is located on the computer. This generally means the directory in which the resource is stored; the directory might be something like /pages or /pub/junk/software. This book's home page is in its own directory, which is /books/cightml. (To get your own directory, you need to sign up with a company that puts pages on the Web; see Chapter 7, "Publishing Your Page on the Web," for details.) So now you just staple the directory onto the URL and then add another slash on the end, for good measure:

```
http://www.mcfedries.com/books/cightml/
```

What   Almost there. The "what" part is just the name of the file you want to use. For a Web page, you use the name of the document that contains the HTML codes and text. The file containing this book's home page is called index.html, so here's the full URL:

```
http://www.mcfedries.com/books/cightml/index.html
```

Make Sure You're on the Case

I mentioned earlier that you can use uppercase or lowercase letters (the latter are normally used) for the "how" part of the URL. The same is true for the "who" part, but case is crucial when entering the directory and filename. If you enter even a single letter of a directory or filename in the wrong case, you won't get to where you want to go. That's why I always tell people to use nothing but lowercase letters for directory and filenames; it just keeps things simpler (and saves wear-and-tear on your typing fingers by not having to stretch over to the Shift key).

Okay, so lemme ask you another thing. I visit your Web site all the time, but to get there, I only have to enter http://www.mcfedries.com/books/cightml/. *How come I can get away without entering a filename?*

Ah, that's because most Web servers have something they call a *default filename*. This means that if the user doesn't specify a filename, the server just assumes they want the default file. On most servers, the default file is named index.html, so if you enter this:

```
http://www.mcfedries.com/books/cightml/
```

what you really get is this:

```
http://www.mcfedries.com/books/cightml/index.html
```

When you sign up with a Web host, you need to find out what the default filename is and then be sure to use that name for your main page. (Otherwise, your site visitors will just see an ugly list of all the files in your directory.)

Got all that? Yeah, I know—it's as clear as mud. Well, have no fear. If you can keep the "how, who, where, and what" idea in your head, it'll all sink in eventually.

Getting Hyper: Creating Links in HTML

Okay, with that drivel out of the way, it's time to put your newfound know-how to work (assuming, that is, I haven't scarred you for life!). To wit, this section shows you how to use HTML to add hypertext links to your Web page.

The HTML tags that do the link thing are <A> and </A>. (Why "A"? Well, as you'll find out later on—see the section "Anchors Aweigh: Internal Links"—you can create special links called *anchors* that send your readers to other parts of the same document instead of to a different document.) The <A> tag is a little different from the other tags you've seen (you just knew it would be). Specifically, you don't use it by itself but, instead, you shoehorn the URL of your link into it. Here's how it works:

```
<A HREF="URL">
```

Here, HREF stands for *Hypertext REFerence*. Just replace *URL* with the actual URL of the Web page you want to use for the link (and, yes, you have to enclose the address in quotation marks). Here's an example:

```
<A HREF="http://www.mcfedries.com/books/cightml/index.html">
```

Now you can see why I made you suffer through all that URL poppycock earlier: It's crucial for getting the <A> tag to work properly.

You're not done yet, though, not by a long shot (insert groan of disappointment here). What are you missing? Right, you have to give the reader some descriptive link text to click. Happily, that's easier done than said because all you do is insert the text between the <A> and </A> tags, like so:

```
<A HREF="URL">Link text goes here</A>
```

Need an example? You got it (see the file link.htm on the CD):

```
Why not head to this book's
<A HREF="http://www.mcfedries.com/books/cightml/index.html">home page
</A>?
```

Figure 5.1 shows how it looks in a Web browser. Notice how the browser highlights and underlines the link text and when I point my mouse at the link, the URL I specified appears in the status bar.

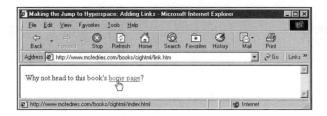

Figure 5.1

How the hypertext link appears in Internet Explorer.

Hypertext links are generally divided into two categories: external and internal. An *external link* sends the person who clicks it to a different document. You have two choices here:

➤ You can link to a Web page in a different directory, to a location on your company's internal Web (that intranet thing I mentioned back in Chapter 1), or to a different Web site altogether. I call this a "faraway" link.

➤ You can link to a Web page in the same directory as the current page. I call this a "nearby" link.

An *internal link* (an anchor) sends the reader to a different part of the same document. The next few sections describe both types of link.

External Links to Faraway Pages

The most common type of link is one that whisks the reader off to a page at some other Web site. Many Webmeisters use these kinds of external links to provide their readers with a quick method of surfing to related sites. For example, if you're putting together a page extolling the virtues of, say, the Helsinki Formula, you might want to include some links to pages about Helsinki or Finland or even *The Man From U.N.C.L.E.* For these types of links, make sure your <A> tag includes the full address of the new location, as described in the preceding section.

Lots of pages also include links that point to the author's fave rave Web sites and to those sites that the author deems "cool." These so-called "hot lists" are a popular item on home pages, and they can be fun for surfers (providing, of course, they share the Web page creator's taste in what's cool).

External Links to Nearby Pages

When putting Web pages together, the operating principle is "Bet you can't create just one!" That is, people usually get so juiced by getting a page on the Web that they're inspired to do it once more from the top. It's not at all unusual for a prolific Websmith to have 5, 10, or even 20 different pages!

Chances are that if you create more than one Web page, at least a few of your pages are related, so you'll probably want to include links that take your readers to other examples of your Web handiwork. You'll probably store all your Web pages in the same directory, so the how, who, and where parts of the URL are the same as the current document. For example, compare the URL of this book's home page with the URL of the HTML file (called links.html) that contains the links to Web pages created by the book's readers:

```
http://www.mcfedries.com/books/cightml/index.html

http://www.mcfedries.com/books/cightml/links.html
```

As you can see, the two addresses are identical right up to (but not including) the filenames. This is good because if I want to include a link to links.html in the book's home page, I only have to include the filename in the <A> tag. That's right: If you're creating a link to a document in the same directory, you can simply lop off the how, who, and where parts of the URL. Here's how such a link looks:

```
Check out the <A HREF="links.html">links to readers' Web pages</A>
```

Organizing Your Site

Even at this early stage in your Webmaster career, it's worthwhile to start thinking about how you want to organize your site. If you just plan to create a page or two, no organization is necessary because it's easiest to plop everything into a single directory. However, prolific Web authors should consider dividing their material into separate directories. I discuss this in greater detail in Chapter 7, "Publishing Your Page on the Web."

Anchors Aweigh: Internal Links

Most of your HTML pages will probably be short and sweet, and the Web surfers who drop by will have no trouble navigating their way around. But if, like me, you suffer from a bad case of terminal verbosity combined with bouts of extreme long-windedness, you'll end up with Web pages that are lengthy, to say the least. Rather than force your readers to scroll through your tome-like creations, you can set up links to various sections of the document. You can then assemble these links at the top of the page to form a sort of "hypertable of contents."

Unlike the links you've looked at so far, internal links don't connect to a different document. Instead, they link to a special version of the <A> tag—called an *anchor*—that you've inserted somewhere in the same document. To understand how anchors work, think of how you might mark a spot in a book you're reading. You might dog-ear the page, attach a note, or place something between the pages, such as a book-mark or your cat's tail.

An anchor performs the same function: It "marks" a particular spot in a Web page, and you can then use a regular <A> tag to link to that spot.

I think an example is in order. Suppose I want to create a hypertext version of this chapter. (As a matter of fact, I did! Look for the file named chapter5.htm on the CD.) To make it easy to navigate, I want to include a table of contents at the top of the page that includes links to all the section headings. My first chore is to add anchor tags to each heading. Here's the general format for an anchor:

```
<A NAME="Name">Anchor text goes here</A>
```

As you can see, an anchor tag looks a lot like a regular hypertext link tag. The only difference is that the HREF part is replaced by NAME="*Name*"; *Name* is the name you want to give the anchor. You can use whatever you like for the name, but most people choose relatively short names to save typing. For example, this chapter's first section is titled "The URL of Net: A Cyberspace Address Primer." If I want to give this section the uninspired name Section1, I use the following anchor:

```
<A NAME="Section1">The URL of Net: A Cyberspace Address Primer</A>
```

Now, when I set up my table of contents, I can create a link to this section by using a regular <A> tag (with the HREF thing) that points to the section's name. And, just so a Web browser doesn't confuse the anchor name with the name of another document, I preface the anchor name with a number sign . Here's how it looks:

```
<A HREF="#Section1">The URL of Net: A Cyberspace Address Primer</A>
```

Just so you get the big picture, here's an excerpt from the HTML file for this chapter (Figure 5.2 shows how it looks in a browser):

```
<H3>Hypertable of Contents:</H3>
<DL>
<DD><A HREF="#Section1">The URL of Net: A Cyberspace Address
Primer</A>
<DD><A HREF="#Section2">Getting Hyper: Creating Links in HTML</A>
<DL>
<DD><A HREF="#Section2a">External Links to Faraway Pages</A>
<DD><A HREF="#Section2b">External Links to Nearby Pages</A>
<DD><A HREF="#Section2c">Anchors Aweigh: Internal Links</A>
</DL>
<DD><A HREF="#Section3">Creating an Email Link</A>
```

```
<DD><A HREF="#Section4">The Least You Need to Know</A>
</DL>
<HR>
 [Rambling introduction goes here]
<A NAME="Section1"><H2>The URL of Net: A Cyberspace Address
Primer</H2>
</A>
```

Sneakily Hiding Text in a Web Page

This chapter's introduction doesn't appear in the figure above, but the text is there if you look at the chapter5.htm file. Is this some kind of HTML hocus-pocus? Not at all. You can hide any chunk of text from a browser by surrounding it with the <!-- tag at the beginning and the --> tag at the end, like so:

```
<!--The browser won't show this-->
```

This technique is useful for adding comments to a Web page without having those comments displayed for all to see.

Figure 5.2

The hypertext version of this chapter.

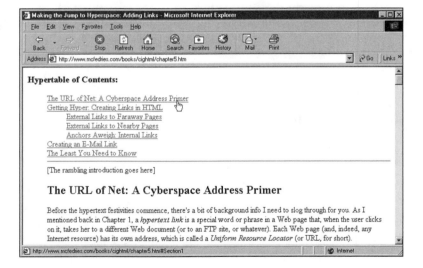

Although you'll mostly use anchors to link to sections of the same Web page, there's no law against using them to link to specific sections of other pages. All you do is add the appropriate anchor to the other page and then link to it by adding the anchor's name (preceded, as usual, by #) to the end of the page's filename. For example, here's a tag that sets up a link to a section named Grumpy in an HTML file named dwarves.html:

Web Email Doesn't Work

Setting up an email link doesn't work if the user has a Web-based email service such as Hotmail.

```
<A HREF="dwarves.html#Grumpy">Info
on Grumpy</A>
```

Creating an Email Link

As I mentioned earlier, there's no reason a link has to lead to a Web page. In fact, all you have to do is alter the "how" part of the URL, and you can connect to most other Internet services, including FTP and Usenet.

In this section, however, I'll concentrate on the most common type of non-Web link: email. In this case, someone clicking an email link is presented with a window (assuming their browser supports this kind of link, which most recent browsers do) they can use to send a message to your email address. Now that's interactive!

This type of link is called a *mailto link* because you include the word *mailto* in the <A> tag. Here's the general form:

```
<A HREF="mailto:YourEmailAddress">The link text goes here</A>
```

Here, *YourEmailAddress* is your Internet email address. For example, suppose I want to include an email link in one of my Web pages. My email address is paul@mcfedries.com, so I'd set up the link as follows:

```
You can write to me at my
<A HREF="mailto:paul@mcfedries.com">email address.</A>
```

Figure 5.3 shows how it looks in Internet Explorer.

Figure 5.3

A Web page with an email link.

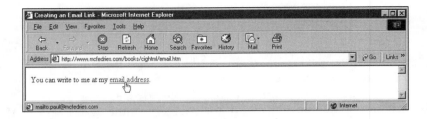

How to Link to Other Net Resources

If you want to try your hand at linking to other Net resources, here's a run-down of the types of URLs to use:

Resource	URL
FTP (directory)	`ftp://Who/Where/`
FTP (file)	`ftp://Who/Where/What`
Gopher	`gopher://Who/`
Usenet	`news:newsgroup.name`
Telnet	`telnet://Who`

Note that *who, where,* and *what* are the same as I defined them earlier in this chapter. Also, *newsgroup.name* is just the name of the newsgroup that has articles you want to see. Note that not all browsers support all of these resources.

The Least You Need to Know

This chapter gave you the lowdown on using HTML to include hypertext links in your Web pages. The next piece of the Web page puzzle involves adding spiffy images to your pages. I'll show you how it's done in the next chapter.

Chapter 6

A Picture Is Worth a Thousand Clicks: Working with Images

In This Chapter

➤ A quick look at some image basics

➤ Using the <IMG> tag to insert an image on your Web page

➤ How to make text and images get along

➤ Using an image as the page background

➤ Using a "pixel shim" for precise positioning

➤ Adding the finishing touches to your Web page with icons, bullets, buttons, and other graphical glad rags

You've probably seen those TV ads proclaiming in no uncertain terms (true hipsters are never uncertain about their hipness) that "image is everything." You know they couldn't put it on TV if it wasn't true , so you need to think about what kind of image your Web page presents to the outside world.

You've seen how tossing a few text tags, a list or two, and a liberal dose of links can do wonders for drab, lifeless pages. But face it: Anybody can do that kind of stuff. If you're looking to make your Web abode really stand out from the crowd, you need to go graphical with a few well-chosen images. To that end, this chapter gives you the ins and outs of images, including some background info on the various graphics formats, tags for inserting images, and lots more. (You can even use images as links. I'll show you how it's done in Chapter 8, "Images Can Be Links, Too.")

Images: Some Semi-Important Background Info

Before you get down to brass tacks and start trudging through the HTML tags that plop pictures onto your pages, there are a few things I need to discuss. Not to worry, though; it's nothing that's overly technical. (That, of course, would be contrary to *The Complete Idiot's Guide* bylaw 4.17c: "Thou shalt not cause the eyes of thy readers to glaze over with interminable technical clap trap.") Instead, I just look at a few things that help you choose and work with images, and that should help make all this stuff a bit clearer.

No, Images Aren't Text, But That's Okay

First off, let me answer the main question that's probably running through your mind even now about all this graphics rumpus:

If the innards of a Web page are really just text and HTML tags, then how in the name of h-e-double-hockey-sticks am I supposed to get an image in there?

Hey, that's a darn good question. Here's the easy answer: you don't.

Huh?

Yeah. As you see later on (in the section "The Nitty-Gritty, at Last: the <IMG> Tag"), all you're really doing is, for each image you want to use, adding a tag to the document that says, in effect, "Yo! Mr. Browser! Insert image here." That tag specifies the name of the graphics file, so the browser just opens the file and displays the image. In other words, you have two files: your HTML file and a separate graphics file. It's the browser's job to combine them into your beautiful Web page.

Graphics Formats: Can't We All Just Get Along?

Some computer wag once said that the nice thing about standards is that there are so many of them! Graphics files are no exception. It seems that every geek who ever gawked at a graphic has invented his own format for storing them on disk. And talk about alphabet soup! Why, there are images in GIF, JPEG, BMP, PCX, TIFF, DIB, EPS, and TGA formats, and those are just off the top of my head. How's a budding Web page architect supposed to make sense of all this acronymic anarchy?

Well, my would-be Web welders, I bring tidings of great joy. You can toss most of that graphic traffic into the digital scrap heap because the Web has standardized on just two formats—GIF and JPEG—that account for 99% of all Web imagery. Oh happy day! Here's a quick look at them:

➤ **GIF**   This was the original Web graphics format. It's limited to 256 colors, so it's best for simple images: line art, clip art, text, and so on. GIFs are also useful for setting up images with transparent backgrounds (see "Giving a GIF a Transparent Background," later in this chapter) and for creating simple animations (see Chapter 10, "Making Your Web Pages Dance and Sing").

➤ **JPEG** This format (which gets its name from the Joint Photographic Experts Group that invented it; gee, don't *they* sound like a fun bunch of guys to hang out with?) supports complex images that have many millions of colors. The main advantage of JPEG files is that, given the same image, they're smaller than GIFs, so they take less time to download. This doesn't matter much with simple images, but digitized photographs and other high-quality images tend to be huge, but the JPEG format *compresses* these images so they're easier to manage.

Graphics Extensions

When you work with graphics files, bear in mind that GIF files use the .gif extension, while JPEG files use the .jpg extension.

"Can I Use BMP Images?"

If you use Windows, then you're probably familiar with the BMP images that you can create with the Paint program. Although Internet Explorer is willing to work with these types of images, Netscape isn't. Therefore, I suggest that you avoid them and use only GIFs and JPEGs.

How Do I Get Graphics?

The text part of a Web page is, at least from a production standpoint, a piece of cake for most folks. After all, even the most pathetic typist can peck out at least a few words a minute. Graphics, on the other hand, are another kettle of digital fish entirely. Creating a snazzy logo or eye-catching illustration requires a modicum of artistic talent, which is a bit harder to come by than basic typing skills.

However, if you have such talent, you're laughing: Just create the image in your favorite graphics program and save it in GIF or JPEG format. (If your program gives you several GIF options, use GIF87 or, even better, GIF89, if possible. If your software doesn't know GIF from a hole in the ground, see the next section, where I show you how to convert the file.)

The non-artists in the crowd have to obtain their graphics goodies from some other source. Fortunately, there's no shortage of images floating around. Here are some ideas:

➤ Many software packages (including Microsoft Office and most paint and illustration programs) come with clip art libraries. *Clip art* is professional-quality artwork that you can freely incorporate in your own designs. If you don't have a program that comes with its own clip art, most software stores have CD-ROMs for sale that are chock-full of clip art images.

➤ Grab an image from a Web page. When your browser displays a Web page with an image, the corresponding graphics file is stored temporarily on your computer's hard disk. Most browsers have a command that lets you save that file permanently. Here are some examples:

Internet Explorer   Right-click the graphic and then select **Save Picture As** from the shortcut menu.

Netscape   Right-click the graphic and choose **Save Image As** from the menu that appears.

➤ Take advantage of the many graphics archives on the Internet. There are sites all over the Net that store dozens, even hundreds, of images. I give you some specifics in Chapter 24, "Some HTML Resources on the Web."

➤ If you have access to a scanner, you can use it to digitize photos, illustrations, doodles, or whatever.

➤ Use the images that come with this book. I've included hundreds of GIF and JPEG images on this book's CD-ROM that I hope will come in handy.

The Copyright Conundrum

Don't forget that many images are the property of the individuals who created them in the first place. Unless you're sure the picture is in the public domain, you need to get permission from the artist before using it. This is particularly true if your Web page has a commercial slant. Note, however, that all the graphics that come on the CD-ROM are public domain, so you can use them at will.

Converting Graphics to GIF or JPEG

What do you do if you've got the perfect image for your Web page, but it's not in GIF or JPEG format? You need to get your hands on a graphics program that's capable of converting images into different formats. Here are three that are commonly used by Web graphics gurus:

➤ **Paint Shop Pro**   An excellent all-around graphics program that's great not only for converting graphics, but also for manipulating existing images and for creating new images. Best of all, there's no download required because this program is available on the book's CD.

See `http://www.jasc.com/`

➤ **GraphX**   This is a neat little program that's happy to convert a whack of graphics formats into GIF or JPEG. This one's also available on the CD.

See `http://www.group42.com/`

➤ **ACDSee32**   This is a simple program that works best as a graphics viewer. However, it can also convert many different graphics formats into JPEG (but not GIF, unfortunately). This program is available on the CD, as well.

See `http://www.acdsystems.com/`

➤ **LView Pro**   Can perform some image manipulation, but it's best as a graphics converter.

See `http://www.lview.com/`

➤ **PolyView**   A good converter with some interesting graphics features (such as the ability to create a Web page from a set of images).

See `http://www.polybytes.com/`

➤ **Graphic Workshop**   This program has a bit of a clunky interface, but it does a good job of converting graphics.

See `http://www.mindworkshop.com/alchemy/gwspro.html`

For most of these programs, you use the same steps to convert an image from one format to another:

1. In the program, select the **File**, **Open** command and use the Open dialog box to open the image file you want to convert.
2. Select the **File**, **Save As** command. The Save As dialog box drops by.
3. In the **Save as type** list, choose either JPEG or GIF. (In some programs, the latter is called CompuServe Graphics Interchange format.)
4. Click **Save**.

MacGraphics

Mac users have several graphics conversion programs to play with, including GraphicConverter (see `http://www.lemkesoft.de/index.html`) and GIFConverter (see `http://www.kamit.com/gifconverter/`).

The Nitty-Gritty at Last: The <IMG> Tag

Okay, enough of all that. Let's get the lead out and start squeezing some images onto our Web pages. As I mentioned earlier, there's an HTML code that tells a browser to display an image: the <IMG> tag. Here's how it works:

```
<IMG SRC="filename">
```

Here, SRC is short for "source" and *filename* is the name of the graphics file you want to display. For example, suppose you have an image named logo.gif. To add it to your page, you use the following line:

```
<IMG SRC="logo.gif">
```

For this to work, bear in mind that your HTML file and your graphics file need to be sitting in the same directory on your computer (if you're just testing things at home) or on your Web host (if you're trying things out online).

Let's check out an example. Most folks are constantly tinkering with their Web site—modifying existing pages, pruning dead wood (I know I do a lot of that!), and adding new stuff. Until the new pages are ready, however, you don't want to subject your visitors to them. Instead, you can just display a generic page (I call it a "Procrastination Page") that tells people the new module isn't quite ready for prime time just yet.

If you'd like something similar for your Web pages, here's some HTML code that does the job (look for the file named undercon.htm on the CD):

```
<HTML>
<HEAD>
<TITLE>Detour!</TITLE>
</HEAD>
<BODY>
<IMG SRC="constru1.gif">
<H2>Web Work In Progress!</H2>
```

```
<HR>
Sorry for all the mess, but I haven't quite got around to
implementing this section yet. Hopefully I'll have everything
up and running real soon.
<P>
<A HREF="index.html">Click here to go back to my home page.</A>
</BODY>
</HTML>
```

To emphasize the work-in-progress feel, this page includes a small graphic (constru1.gif) that says "Contents Under Construction" and shows a construction worker in action (see Figure 6.1). Note, too, that the page includes a link that gives the reader an easy way to get back to your home page. (In the <A> tag, make sure you change "index.html" to the appropriate name of your home page. Refer to Chapter 5, "Making the Jump to Hyperspace: Adding Links," if you need a refresher course on this link stuff.)

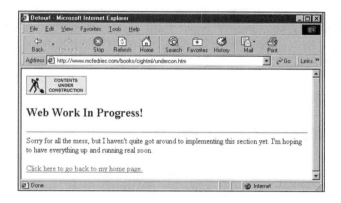

Figure 6.1

A Web page to use as a substitute for pages you're still slaving away at.

"Help! The #%@*&! Browser Won't Display My Images!"

After adding your <IMG> tag, you might be dismayed to find that the browser refuses to display the image. Instead, it just shows a little "X" icon where the image should be. Grrrr. Here are some possible solutions to the all-too common problem:

➤ If you're viewing your page on your home machine, the HTML file and the image files might be sitting in separate directories on your computer. Try moving your image file into the directory that holds your HTML file.

➤ If you're viewing your page on the Web, perhaps you didn't send the image file to your server.

➤ Make sure you have the correct match for uppercase and lowercase letters. If an image is on your server and it's named "image.gif", and your IMG tag refers to "IMAGE.GIF", your image won't show up. In this case, you'd have to edit your IMG tag so that it refers to "image.gif".

➤ If you're using Netscape to view the page, make sure there are no spaces in the image's filename. Remember, too, that Netscape doesn't understand BMP graphics.

➤ Make sure you're not missing a quotation mark in the SRC attribute.

Consider a Graphics Subdirectory

If you only have a few images for your pages, it's easiest to store everything—your HTML files and your graphics files—in the same directory. However, Webmeisters who deal with tons of images like to store their graphics files in a separate directory to keep things organized. In this case, you also need to specify the name of the directory as part of the SRC value. For example, it's common to set up a subdirectory named graphics, which then requires an <IMG> tag like this:

```
<IMG SRC="graphics/image.jpg">
```

Specifying Image Height and Width

When surfing Web sites that contain graphics, have you ever wondered why it sometimes takes quite a while before anything appears on the screen? Well, one of the biggest delays is that most browsers won't display the entire page until they've calculated the height and width of all the images. The ever-intrepid browser programmers realized this, of course, and decided to do something about it. "What if," they asked themselves, "there was some way to tell the browser the size of each image in advance? That way, the browser wouldn't have to worry about it, and things would show up onscreen much faster."

Thus was born two extensions to the <IMG> tag: the HEIGHT and WIDTH attributes:

```
<IMG SRC="filename" WIDTH=x HEIGHT=y>
```

Here, *filename* is, as usual, the name of the graphics file. For the new attributes, use *x* for the width of the graphic, and *y* for the height. Both dimensions are measured in *pixels* (short for *picture elements*), which are the tiny dots that make up any computer screen image. Any good graphics program tells you the dimensions of an image.

Alternatively, you can express the width and height as percentages of the browser window. For example, the following line displays the image bluebar.gif so its width always takes up 90% of the screen:

```
<IMG SRC="bluebar.gif" WIDTH=90%>
```

The advantage here is that, no matter what size screen someone is using, the graphic always takes up the same amount of room across the screen. As proof, check out the next two figures showing the bluebar.gif image with WIDTH set to 90%. As you can see in Figures 6.2 and 6.3, the image always usurps 90% of the available width, no matter how big the Internet Explorer window. (Note, too, that because I didn't specify the HEIGHT, Internet Explorer adjusts the height in proportion to the increase or decrease of the width.)

Figure 6.2

The bluebar.gif image in a relatively narrow window.

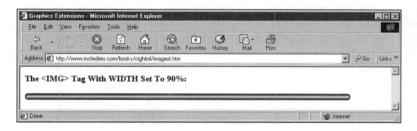

Figure 6.3

The same image in a wider window.

Aligning Text and Images

In the Work-In-Progress example you saw earlier, the image appears on a line by itself. However, that only happened because I used a heading tag—<H2>—immediately after the <IMG> tag, and heading tags always start on a fresh line. However, if you insert an image inside regular page text, the browser will display the image and the text on the same line.

This is all very reasonable, but you might run into problems with tall images, because the bottom of the image is aligned with the bottom of the line of text. If you prefer your text to appear at the top or the middle of the image, or if you want text to wrap around the image, the <IMG> tag has an extra ALIGN attribute that you can use. Here's how it works:

```
<IMG SRC="filename" ALIGN=VALUE>
```

Here, the *VALUE* can be any one of the following:

TOP   Text is aligned with the top of the image.

MIDDLE   Text is aligned with the middle of the image.

BOTTOM   Text is aligned with the bottom of the image.

LEFT   The image appears on the left side of the browser window, and text wraps around the image on the right.

RIGHT   The image appears on the right side of the browser window, and text wraps around the image on the left.

The following HTML listing (align.htm) gives you a demo (Figure 6.4 shows the results):

```
<HTML>
<HEAD>
<TITLE>Aligning Text and Images</TITLE>
</HEAD>
<BODY>
<IMG SRC="constru1.gif" ALIGN=TOP> This text appears at the top of the
image.
<P>
<IMG SRC="constru1.gif" ALIGN=MIDDLE> This text appears in the middle
of the image.
<P>
<IMG SRC="constru1.gif" ALIGN=BOTTOM> This text appears at the bottom
of the image.
<P>
<IMG SRC="constru1.gif" ALIGN=LEFT>
In the "Work In Progress" example you saw earlier, the image appears
on a line by itself. However, that only happened because I used a
heading tag&#151;&lt;H2&gt;&#151;immediately after the &lt;IMG&gt;
tag, and heading tags always start on a fresh line. However, if you
insert an image inside regular page text, the browser will display the
image and the text on the same line.
<IMG SRC="constru1.gif" ALIGN=RIGHT>
This is all very reasonable, but you might run into problems with tall
images, because the bottom of the image is aligned with the bottom of
the line. If you prefer your text to appear at the top or the middle
of the image, or if you want text to wrap around the image, the
&lt;IMG&gt;
tag has an extra ALIGN attribute that you can use.
</BODY>
</HTML>
```

78

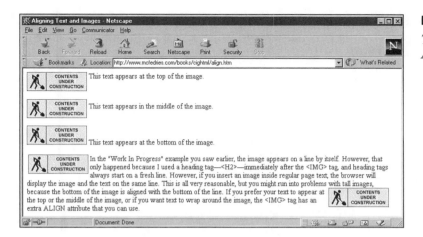

Figure 6.4
The <IMG> tag's ALIGN options.

Techno Talk

Breaking Free of an Image

What happens if you're using ALIGN=LEFT or ALIGN=RIGHT to wrap text around an image, but then you want to start a new line or a new paragraph *after* the image? The solution here is to toss in a
 (line break) tag that uses the CLEAR attribute:

```
<BR CLEAR=LEFT¦RIGHT¦ALL>
```

Use CLEAR=LEFT to start the next line when the left margin is clear; use CLEAR=RIGHT to start the next line when the right margin is clear; use CLEAR=ALL to start the next line when both margins are clear.

Handling Graphically Challenged Text Browsers

Some browsers are text-only and wouldn't know how to display a graphics file if it bit them in the face. Instead, they usually just display [IMAGE] in the spot where your <IMG> tag appears, and then they wash their hands of this whole graphics rigmarole.

That looks pretty ugly (and not particularly descriptive, either), so you should have mercy on the image-deprived users of such browsers. How? Well, the <IMG> tag has an extra ALT attribute you can throw in to provide alternative text that appears in place of the image. Here's the general format:

```
<IMG SRC="filename" ALT="alternative text">
```

Here, *alternative text* is whatever text you want to use instead of the graphic. For example, if you have a picture of your hometown in your page, you can display the words *A lovely pic of my hometown* with the following line:

```
<IMG SRC="hometown.gif" ALT="A lovely pic of my hometown">
```

Two Other Reasons to Use ALT

If you think the number of Internauts using text-only browsers is too small for you to bother with the ALT attribute, here's another reason: Most graphical browsers allow you to turn off the display of images. This feature is a favorite among people with slow Internet connections; so there might be more people in "text mode" than you think.

And even if a surfer does have graphics turned on, using ALT is still a good idea because most modern browsers display the ALT text in a banner when users hover their mouse pointers over the image.

Separating Text and Images

If you surround your images with text, you'll find that the text often bumps up against the image borders. To create a margin between the image and the surrounding text, add the HSPACE and VSPACE attributes to the <IMG> tag:

```
<IMG SRC="filename" HSPACE=h VSPACE=v>
```

HSPACE creates a margin between the image and the text above and below (where *h* is the size of the margin, in pixels). VSPACE creates a margin between the image and the text to its left and right (where *v* is the size of the margin, in pixels).

Good Uses for Images on Your Web Page

Images are endlessly useful, and they're an easy way to give your page a professional look and feel. Although I'm sure you can think of all kinds of ways to put pictures to work, here are a few suggestions:

➤ A company logo on a business-related page

➤ Graphics from an ad

➤ Drawings done by the kids in a paint program

➤ Charts and graphs

➤ Fancy-schmancy fonts

➤ Your signature

➤ Using a graphic line in place of the <HR> tag

➤ Using graphic bullets to create a better bulleted list

You might be wondering how to do that last item. Well, there are a number of ways to go about it, but the one I use for short lists is to create a definition list (see Chapter 4, "A Fistful of List Grist for Your Web Page Mill") and precede each item in the list with a graphic bullet. For example, the following code uses a file called redball.gif:

```
<DL>
<DD><IMG SRC="redball.gif">First item
<DD><IMG SRC="redball.gif">Second item
<DD><IMG SRC="redball.gif">Third item
</DL>
```

If the text in one or more of the bullets is quite long, a better approach is to create a table. I show you how to do this in Chapter 9, "Table Talk: Adding Tables to Your Page."

Graphics Are Slooooooowwwww

Although graphics have a thousand-and-one uses, that doesn't mean you should include a thousand-and-one images in each page. Bear in mind that many of your readers are accessing your site from a slow modem link, so graphics take forever to load. If you have too many images, most folks give up and head somewhere else.

Using an Image As the Page Background

Depending on the browser you use, Web page text and graphics often float in a sea of dull, drab gray, or plain white. It's about as exciting as a yawning festival. To give things a little pep, you can change the background color your page appears on to whatever suits your style. You can also specify an image to appear as the background.

Modifying the <BODY> Tag

The guts of your page appears within the body, so it makes sense that you do this by tweaking the <BODY> tag. The simplest method is specifying a new background color:

```
<BODY BGCOLOR="#rrggbb">
```

Yes, you're right: The *rrggbb* part is the same color code that I talked about back in Chapter 3, "From Buck-Naked to Beautiful: Dressing Up Your Page." Figure 6.5 shows an example page that uses a black background (see blakback.htm on the CD). Note, too, that I had to use white for the page text so the surfer can read the page (which is kind of important).

Figure 6.5

A page that uses a black background and white text.

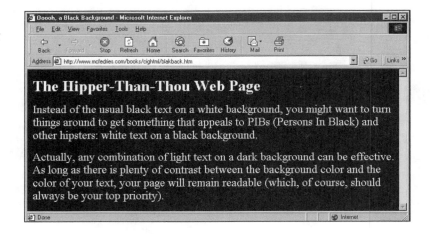

Instead of a color, you can specify an image to use as the background (similar to the way Windows lets you cover the desktop with wallpaper). This doesn't have to be (nor should it be) a large image. The browser takes smaller graphics and *tiles* them so they fill up the entire window. The secret to background images is the <BODY> tag's BACKGROUND attribute:

```
<BODY BACKGROUND="filename">
```

Here, *filename* is the name of the graphics file you want to use.

In general, I recommend sticking with just a different background color. Tiled background images take longer to load, and they can make text devilishly difficult to read. On the other hand, many new browsers understand the BACKGROUND attribute, but not the BGCOLOR attribute. So, a compromise solution is to create a small graphics file that displays only the background color you want to use and then to reference that file by using BACKGROUND.

Margined Backgrounds

One of the most popular styles of Web page backgrounds these days is the margined background which features a colored strip down the left (and sometimes also the right) side of the page. I show you how to create this attractive background style in Chapter 9, "Table Talk: Adding Tables to Your Page."

Giving a GIF a Transparent Background

One of the features you get with a GIF image is the ability to set the background color to be "transparent." This just means that the browser doesn't show the background when it displays the file. This can make an image look much neater. For example, compare the two images shown in Figure 6.6. See how the one on the right doesn't show the black background?

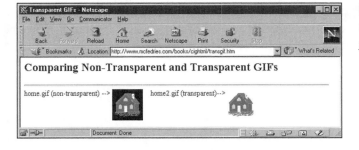

Figure 6.6

GIF files can have transparent backgrounds.

Here's how you give a GIF file a transparent background in Paint Shop Pro:

1. Load your image into the program.
2. Select the **Colors, Set Palette Transparency** command.
3. If Paint Shop Pro mumbles something about reducing the number of layers and colors, click **Yes** and then click **OK** in the Decrease Color Depth dialog box.
4. In the Set Palette Transparency dialog box, activate the **Set the transparency value to palette entry** option.
5. Move the mouse pointer into the image and then click the color that you want to be transparent.
6. Click **OK**.

7. Select **File**, **Save As** to open the Save As dialog box.
8. In the **Save as type** list, choose **CompuServe Graphics Interchange (*.gif)**.
9. Click **Options**, activate the **Version 89a** option, and click **OK**.
10. Click **Save**.

Note that this doesn't change the appearance of the image in Paint Shop Pro. That is, if your image has a black background, you'll still see the background. The transparency effect only comes into play when you view the image in a browser.

It's also possible to make a "truly transparent" background in Paint Shop Pro when you start an image from scratch. In the New Image dialog box, select **Transparent** in the **Background color** list box. Then select **Colors, Set Palette Transparency**. In the dialog box, activate **Set the transparency value to the current background color** and then click **OK**.

A Special Image: The Pixel Shim (spacer.gif)

One of the biggest problems faced by Web designers is positioning text and images with precision. Regular HTML just doesn't have any way of manipulating the position of any object.

You can get around this limitation by using something called a *pixel shim*. A pixel shim is a transparent GIF that's 1 pixel wide and 1 pixel tall. Because it's transparent, it doesn't show up on the page. However, by manipulating the <IMG> tag's HEIGHT and WIDTH attributes, you can create any amount of blank space that you need, which is great for precise positioning of text and images (I'll show you an example in Chapter 9).

I've put a pixel shim on this book's CD. Look for the file named spacer.gif.

The Least You Need to Know

This chapter showed you how to turn your Web pages into veritable works of art by adding an image or two. Now the Big Moment is at hand because in the next chapter I'll show you how to get your newly minted page onto the Web.

Chapter 7

Publishing Your Page on the Web

In This Chapter

➤ A rundown of the various choices for publishing your page

➤ A review of some companies that will put your pages on the Web (hosting providers)

➤ How to get your Web pages to the provider

➤ Advertising your page

➤ A blow-by-blow description of the whole Web page publishing thing

---

I've covered a lot of ground in the past few chapters, and no doubt you've worked your fingers to the bone applying the electronic equivalent of spit and polish to buff your Web page to an impressive sheen. However, there's still one task you need to perform before you can cross "Make Web Page" off your to-do list. I'm talking, of course, about getting your page published on the Web so surfers the world over can eyeball your creation.

This chapter shows you how to help your Web pages emigrate from their native land (your hard disk) to the New World (the Web). I show you how to best prepare them for the journey, how to select a mode of transportation and an ultimate destination, and how to settle your pages when they've arrived.

A Plethora of Web Publishing Possibilities

The third most common question posed by Web page publishing neophytes is "Where the heck do I put my page when I'm done?" (The most common question, in case you're wondering, is "How do I get started?" The second most common question is "Why is Jerry Lewis so popular in France?") If you've asked that question yourself, then you're doing okay, because it means you're clued into something crucial: Just because you've created a Web page and you have an Internet connection doesn't mean your page is automatically a part of the Web.

The reasons for this are mind-numbingly technical, but the basic idea is that people on the Net have no way of "getting to" your computer and, even if they did, your computer isn't set up to hand out documents (such as Web pages) to visitors who ask for them.

Computers that can do this are called *servers* (because they "serve" stuff out to the Net), and computers that specialize in distributing Web pages are called *Web servers*. So, to get to the point at long last, your Web page isn't on the Web until you store it on a Web server. (Because this computer is, in effect, playing "host" to your pages, such machines are also called *Web hosts*. Companies that run these Web hosts are called *hosting providers*.)

Okay, that's all more or less reasonable. Now, just how does one go about finding one of these Web server thingamajigs? Well, the answer to that depends on a bunch of factors, including the type of page you have, how you got connected to the Internet in the first place, and how much money you're willing to shell out for the privilege. In the end, you have three choices:

➤ Use your existing Internet provider

➤ Try to find a free hosting provider

➤ Sign up with a commercial hosting provider

Use Your Existing Internet Provider

If you access the Internet via a corporate or educational network, your institution might have its own Web server that you can use. If you get your Net jollies through an access provider, ask them if they have a Web server available. Many providers put up personal pages free of charge. (This is particularly true of the big online service providers such as CompuServe and America Online.)

Try to Find a Free Hosting Provider

If you qualify, there are a few hosting providers that will bring your Web pages in from the cold out of the goodness of their hearts. What do I mean by "qualify?" Well, in most cases, these services are open only to specific groups, such as students, artists, non-profit organizations, less fortunate members of the Partridge Family, and so on.

However, there are plenty of providers that put up personal home pages free of charge. What's the catch? Well, there are almost always restrictions both on how much data you can store and on the type of data you can store (no ads, no dirty pictures, and so on). You'll probably also be required to display on your pages some kind of "banner" advertisement for the hosting provider.

A couple of years ago, you could count all the free Web hosting services on one hand. These days, however, there are dozens of them, with more coming online every week. The proverbial space limitations prevent me from listing all of these sites. However, a few intrepid Net souls have put together lists of free Web hosting providers. To help you out on your search, I've put together a list-of-lists that points you to these pages.

One-Click Host Shopping

For your shopping convenience, I've gathered the links shown here and in the next section and dropped them into a Web page. It's called hostlist.htm, and you'll find it on the CD. To check out a list, open the page in your favorite browser, click the link, and you're there!

Free Webpage Provider Review

`http://fwpreview.ngworld.net/`

Max Lee maintains this excellent resource. Not only do you get links to sites that offer free Web hosting, but Max also tells you how much disk space you get, whether or not the service provides an HTML editor, and more (see Figure 7.1).

FreeIndex

`http://www.freeindex.com/`

This site contains not only a decent list of free Web hosts, but also info on free email, counters, CGI hosting, graphics, guest books, chat rooms, and more.

Free Homepage Center

`http://www.freehomepage.com/`

This page divides free Web hosting providers into three categories: Personal, Business, and Special Interest. The site also includes short descriptions for each provider.

Figure 7.1

The Free Webpage Provider Review gives you lots of good info on Web freebies.

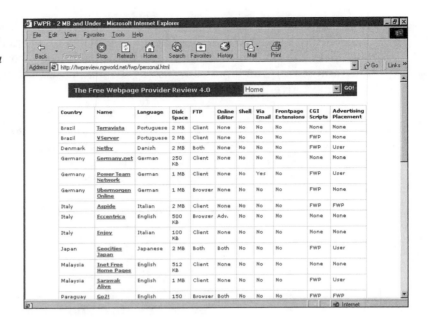

FreeWebspace.net

`http://www.freewebspace.net/`

One of the nice features about this site is that it includes a large number of user reviews for various free Web hosts. There are also discussion areas, news stories about hosts, and much more.

Yahoo!'s Index of Free Web Presence Providers

`http://www.yahoo.com/Business_and_Economy/Companies/`
`Internet_Services/Web_Services/Free_Web_Pages/`

As usual, Yahoo! is one of the best places to go for information. In this case, they offer an extensive index of free Web hosting providers (which they call Web *presence* providers). And, as usual, the URL is finger-numbingly long.

Sign Up with a Commercial Hosting Provider

For personal and business-related Web pages, most Web artisans end up renting a chunk of a Web server from a commercial hosting provider. You normally fork over a setup fee to get your account going, and then you're looking at a monthly fee that gets you two things:

➤ **A specified amount of storage on the Web server for your files** The amount of acreage you get determines the amount of info you can store. For example, if you get a 1MB (megabyte) limit, you can't store more than 1MB worth of files on the server. HTML files don't take up much real estate, but large graphics sure do, so you need to watch your limit.

➤ **A specified amount of bandwidth** *Bandwidth* is a measure of how much data the server serves. For example, suppose the HTML file for your page is 1KB (kilobyte) and the graphics associated with the page consume 9KB. If someone accesses your page, the server ships out a total of 10KB; if ten people access the page (either at the same time or over a period of time), the total bandwidth is 100KB. *Caveat emptor*: Most providers charge you an extra fee for exceeding your bandwidth limitation, so check this out before signing up.

The world's capitalists—efficient free-market types that they are—smelled plenty of money to be had after the explosive growth of the Web became apparent. This means there's certainly no shortage of Web hosting providers available. In fact, there are hundreds of the darn things. Once again, here are some sites that can supply you with lists of commercial providers.

FindAHost.com

http://www.findahost.com/

This site lets you search for a Web host by selecting the features you need.

Host Finders

http://www.hostfinders.com/

As the name implies, this site also offers a search feature for finding a Web host that has what you want.

HostIndex.com

http://www.hostindex.com/

This site offers a large index of Web hosts. However, its best feature is a monthly ranking of Web hosts based on user feedback, features, pricing, and more (see Figure 7.2).

The List

http://thelist.internet.com/

This is *the* site for listings of Internet service providers. For our purposes, it also tells you whether or not the providers host Web pages.

Figure 7.2

HostIndex.com's monthly ranking is a great tool when you're trying to decide which host to go with.

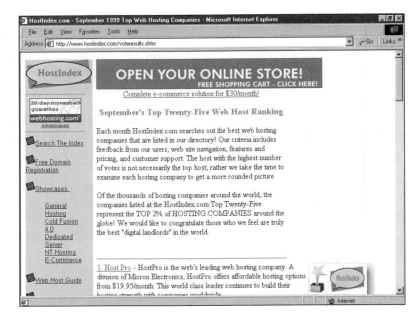

The Ultimate Web Host List

`http://webhostlist.internetlist.com/`

This excellent site lives up to its name! It divides hosts into various categories, including alphabetical, region, "specialty hosting" (e-commerce, Windows NT, and so on), and it also offers various "Top Hosts" lists so you can see who's the best.

Yahoo!'s Index of Commercial Web Presence Providers

`http://www.yahoo.com/Business_and_Economy/Companies/`
`➥Internet_Services/Web_Services/Hosting/Complete_Listing/`

Yahoo! maintains a list of hundreds of commercial Web hosting providers at this site.

What Does Your Web Home Look Like?

What happens when you sign up with one of these providers? Well, after you establish your account, the Web administrator creates two things for you: a directory on the server computer that you can use to store your Web page files, and your very own URL. (This is also true if you're using a Web server associated with your corporate or school network.)

The directory usually takes one of the following forms:

```
/usr/login/
/users/login/
/usr/login/www-docs/
```

In each case, *login* is the login name or user name that the provider assigns to you. Your URL will normally take the following shape:

```
http://provider/~login/default.html
```

Here, *provider* is the host name of your provider (for example, `www.angelfire.com`), *login* is your login name (note the tilde in front, which on most keyboards is beside the 1), and *default* is the recommended name for your home page (which is usually either index.html or default.html).

Why the Default Name for a Home Page?

Why does the hosting provider often insist that your home page have a certain name? Well, they need to allow for someone trying to access your URL without specifying an HTML document (if they don't know the name of your home page, for example). Let's suppose your provider's host name is `www.host.com` and your login name is biff. Now suppose someone uses the following URL to access your site:

```
http://www.host.com/~biff/
```

The server has to display something, so it will usually look for a default HTML file (such as index.html). If your home page is named something else, the reader might get an ugly listing of the files in your directory, or even an error.

If you're only putting together a few pages, the directory supplied by the provider should be more than adequate. If you're constructing a larger site, however, you should give some thought to how you organize your files. Why? Well, think of your own computer. It's unlikely that you have everything crammed into a single directory. Instead, you probably have separate directories for the different programs you use and other directories for your data files.

There's no reason why you can't cook up a similar scheme in your Web home. On my site, to give you an example, I have a separate directory called books, and that directory is divided further into various subdirectories. For example, the directory that stores all the files related to this book is called books/cightml. I also have a directory called ramblings that stores miscellaneous writings, another called toys that has a few online applications, a graphics subdirectory to store all my image files, and so on.

If you go this route, it's crucial that you set up your home computer to have the same directory structure as the one you use at your Web site. That way, when you transfer your HTML files to their new Web home, you won't have to make any changes to account for a different directory configuration. You can go about this in a number of ways, but here's the simplest:

➤ Create a directory on your computer that acts as the "home base" for all your HTML files. This is the equivalent of your home directory at your Web hosting provider. Note that you can name this directory whatever you like (for example, HTML or Home).

➤ Create your subdirectories under this home base directory. In this case, the subdirectories you create must have the same names as the ones you create on your Web site (I show you how to do the latter later in this chapter).

However, even with this simple setup, how you reference files in other directories can be a bit tricky. As an example, consider a Web site that has four directories:

```
/ (this is the main directory)
graphics/
writings/
stuff/
```

Here, graphics, writings, and stuff are all subdirectories of the main directory. There are three scenarios to watch out for:

➤ **Referencing a file in the same directory** This is the easiest because you don't have to include any directory information. Suppose that the HTML file you're working on is in the writing directory and that you want to reference a page named tirade.html that's also in that directory. In this case, you just use the name of the file, like so:

```
<A HREF="tirade.html">
```

➤ **Referencing a file in a subdirectory from the main directory** This is a common scenario because your home page (which is almost certainly in the main directory) is likely to have links to files in subdirectories. For example, suppose in your home page you want to use an image named bullet.gif from the graphics subdirectory. Then your <IMG> tag looks like this:

```
<IMG SRC="graphics/bullet.gif">
```

Similarly, suppose you want to link to a page named doggerel.html in the writings subdirectory from your home page. Then your <A HREF> tag takes the following form:

```
<A HREF="writings/doggerel.html">
```

➤ **Referencing a file in a subdirectory from a different subdirectory** This is the trickiest scenario. For example, suppose you have a page in the writing subdirectory and you want to use an image named home.gif from the graphics subdirectory. Here's what your <IMG> tag is

```
<IMG SRC="../graphics/home.gif">
```

Weird, eh? The ".." thing represents the main directory. It essentially says, "From here, go up the main directory, and then go down in the graphics subdirectory." Let's see a similar example. Suppose you're working on a page in the writings subdirectory and you want to link to a page named duh.html in the stuff subdirectory. Here's the <A HREF> tag:

```
<A HREF="../stuff/duh.html">
```

Figure 7.3 shows a simplified version of the directory structure that I use. My home directory is called HTML Stuff, I have a subdirectory called graphics for my image files, and I have four subdirectories that store related HTML files: books (which has its own subdirectories), daily-word, ramblings, and toys.

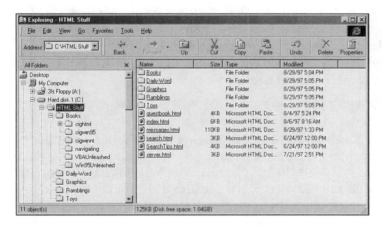

Figure 7.3

The directory structure I use for my HTML files.

A Pre-Trip Checklist

After you decide on a hosting provider and a directory structure, you're just about ready to transfer your files to your directory on your hosting provider's server. Before you do that, however, you need to do the look-before-you-leap thing. That is, you need to give your files the once-over to make sure everything's on the up-and-up. Here's a short checklist to run through:

➤ HTML isn't hard, but it's fussy, persnickety stuff. If you miss even the smallest part of a single tag, your entire page could look like a real dog's breakfast. To avoid this, recheck your tags to make sure they look right. In particular, make sure that each tag's opening angle bracket has a corresponding closing angle bracket . Also, make sure that links and <IMG> tags have both opening and closing quotation marks , and that tags—such as <B>, <I>, <U>, <H1>, <OL>, <DL>, and <A>—have their appropriate closing tags (</B>, </I>, and so on).

➤ URLs are easy to mistype, so double-check all your links. The best way to do this is to load the page into a browser and then try clicking the links.

➤ Different browsers have different ways of interpreting your HTML codes. To make sure your Web page looks good to a large percentage of your readers, load the page into as many different browsers as you can. Note that Netscape Navigator and Internet Explorer together control about 98% of the browser market, so you should always run your page through these two programs.

Versions of the Big Two

The Big Two browsers—Internet Explorer and Netscape Navigator—have come out with various versions over the years, and they render HTML in subtly different ways. So, if possible, you should check your page with as many different versions as you can. At the very least, you should try out Internet Explorer 4.0 and later, as well as Netscape Navigator 4.0 and later.

➤ Pages can also look radically different depending on the screen resolution. If your video card supports them, make sure you view your page using the following resolutions: 640×480, 800×600, and 1,024×768. (To change the resolution in Windows 95 and 98, select **Start**, **Settings**, **Control Panel**, open the **Display** icon, and then select the **Settings** tab.)

➤ One of the advantages of using a word processor to create HTML files is that you usually have access to a spell checker. If so, make sure you use it to look for spelling gaffes in your page. You might want to add all the HTML tags to your custom dictionary so they don't constantly trip up the spell checker. In any case, you should always reread your text to make sure things make sense and are at least semi-grammatical.

➤ Create a list of all the files you need. This includes not only the HTML documents, but also any graphics files referenced in your pages. This way, you can make sure you don't miss any files during the transfer.

➤ Make backup copies of all your files before beginning the transfer. If anything untoward should happen while you're sending your files, you'll be able to recover gracefully.

Putting Your Page into Analysis

If you want to give your page a thorough HTML check, there are resources on the Web that do the dirty work for you. These so-called HTML "analyzers" check your page for improper tags, mismatched brackets, missing quotation marks, and more. One of the best is called Weblint (because it picks the lint off your Web pages). To try it out, point your browser to the following site:

```
http://www.unipress.com/cgi-bin/WWWeblint/
```

Copy your entire HTML code and then paste it in the DATA box near the bottom of the Weblint screen. Click **Check it**, and Weblint goes to work. After a few seconds, a new page appears with a complete analysis of your page. It's the easy way to good HTML mental health!

Okay, Ship It!

Now, at long last, you're ready to get your page on the Web. If the Web server is on your company's or school's network, you send the files over the network to the directory set up by your system administrator. Otherwise, you send the files to the directory created for you on the hosting provider's Web server.

In the latter case, you probably need to use the Internet's FTP (File Transfer Protocol) service. (Note, however, that AOL and some Web hosts offer their own file upload services.) For this portion of the show, you have a number of ways to proceed:

➤ Use the CuteFTP software that comes on the CD-ROM with this book. This is a Windows FTP program that makes it easy to send files from your computer to the Web server. The next couple of sections show how to configure and use CuteFTP to get the job done. (See Appendix C, "The CD: The Webmaster's Toolkit," for information on installing CuteFTP.)

➤ If you use Office 97, you can FTP files to and fro using Microsoft Word (or even Excel or PowerPoint).

Automatic Initial Directory

If you didn't get a specific directory assigned to you, it's probably because the Web host will automatically plop you into your directory when you connect to them.

➤ If you're an America Online user, you can use AOL's FTP service to ship your files to your "My Place" home directory.

➤ Mac users can try a couple of FTP programs to see which one suits their styles. These programs are called Fetch and Anarchie, and you can get them via TUCOWS (`http://www.tucows.com/`). Click the `Macintosh` link.

Adding Your Web Provider's Site

Before you can send anything to the Web server, you have to tell CuteFTP how to find it and which directory to use. Thankfully, you only have to do this once, and you're set for life (or at least until you move to another Web host). Here's how it's done:

1. Start CuteFTP. The FTP Site Manager dialog box appears.

2. In the box on the left, make sure Personal FTP Sites is highlighted, and then select the **Add site** button. The FTP Site Edit dialog box appears.

3. In the **Site Label** text box, enter a name for this site (something like "My Web Home" is just fine).

4. In the **Host Address** text box, enter the hostname of your provider (for example, **www.*myhost*.com**). If your provider has a separate host address for FTP stuff, enter that address, instead.

5. Enter your login name in the **User ID** box and your password in the **Password** box. (Note that, for security reasons, the password appears as asterisks.)

6. In the **Initial Remote Directory** text box, enter the Web server directory that was assigned to you (such as **/usr/*login*/**).

7. In the **Initial Local Directory** box, enter the drive and directory on your computer that contains your Web page files.

8. Click **OK** to store your settings. Figure 7.4 shows an example of a completed dialog box.

Sending the Files Via FTP

With CuteFTP ready for action, you can get down to it. Here are the basic steps to follow to send your files to the Web server via FTP:

1. If you haven't done so already, establish a connection with your regular Internet access provider.

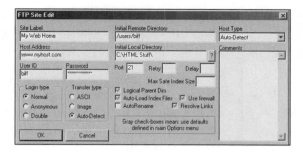

Figure 7.4

An example of a completed FTP Site Edit dialog box.

2. In CuteFTP's FTP Site Manager dialog box, make sure the site you just added is highlighted and then click the **Connect** button. After you're logged in to the server, CuteFTP might display a Login Messages dialog box.

3. If so, click **OK**. You're now at the main CuteFTP window. As you can see in Figure 7.5, this window shows your computer's files on the left and your Web server files on the right. (Note, as well, that the example shown has the same directory structure on both sides. You can establish this "synchronized structure" with CuteFTP—see the section, "Creating a New Directory.")

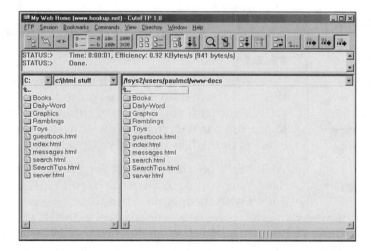

Figure 7.5

CuteFTP shows your computer's files on the left and your Web server files on the right.

4. If you've set up subdirectories, make sure you open the appropriate directory on both sides.

5. Select all the files on your computer that you want to send. The easiest way to do this is to hold down the **Ctrl** key, move your mouse into the left box, and then click each file that you're sending. When you finish selecting the files, release the **Ctrl** key.

6. Pull down the **Commands** menu and select **Upload**. CuteFTP sends the files one by one to the Web server.

Directory Directions

In CuteFTP, you open a subdirectory by double-clicking it. If you want to back up the main directory, double-click the upward pointing arrow that appears just above the directory list.

Upload Tip

A quick way to send files to the server is to use your mouse to drag the highlighted files from the left pane and drop them on the right pane. When CuteFTP asks you to confirm, click **Yes**.

7. After the files have arrived safely, pull down the **FTP** menu and select **Exit** to shut down the connection.

To make sure everything's working okay, plug your URL into your browser and give your page a test surf. If all goes well, then congratulations are in order, because you've officially earned your Webmeister stripes!

Creating a New Directory

If you need to create separate subdirectories for your graphics or HTML files, CuteFTP makes it easy. Just open the server directory you want to work with and then select the **Commands** menu's **Make new dir** command. In the dialog box that appears, enter the name of the new subdirectory and then click **OK**.

Making Changes to Your Web Files

What happens if you send an HTML file to your Web provider and then realize you've made a typing gaffe? Or what if you have more information to add to one of your Web pages? How do you make changes to the files that you've already sent?

Well, here's the short answer: You don't. That's right, after you've sent your files, you never have to bother with them again. That doesn't mean you can never update your site, however. Instead, you make your changes to the HTML files that reside on your computer and then send these revised files to your Web provider. These files replace the old files, and your site is updated with no questions asked.

Getting the Word Out: Advertising Your Page

Okay, your page is floating out there in Webspace. Now what? How are people supposed to know that your new cyberhome is up and running and ready for visitors? Well, people won't beat a path to your door unless you tell them how to get there. For starters, you can spread the news via word of mouth, email notes to friends and colleagues, and by handing out your shiny, new business cards that have your home page URL plastered all over them. Also, it's worth checking to see if your hosting provider has a section devoted solely to announcing new customer pages. And don't forget that I've set up a page that contains nothing but links to reader Web pages. Here's the address:

```
http://www.mcfedries.com/books/cightml/links.html
```

Watch Your Case!

I mentioned back in Chapter 5 that the UNIX computers that play host to the vast majority of Web servers are downright finicky when it comes to the uppercase and lowercase letters used in file and directory names.

Therefore, it's crucial that you check your <A> tags and <IMG> tags to make sure that the file and directory names you use match the combination of uppercase and lowercase letters used on your server. For example, suppose you have a graphics file on your server that's named vacation.gif. If your <IMG> tag points to, say, vacation.gif, the image won't appear.

For the Internet at large, however, you need to engage in a bit of shameless self-promotion. Although there's no central database of Web pages, there are a few spots you can use to get some free publicity for your new page. These include Usenet newsgroups, "What's New" pages, Web directories, Web search engines, mailing lists, and more. The best place to get a complete rundown of all these sources is the article titled "FAQ: How to Announce Your New Web Site." You can eyeball this article in either of the following locales:

➤ In the `comp.infosystems.www.announce` newsgroup.
➤ Via FTP at `ftp://rtfm.mit.edu/pub/usenet-by-group/comp.infosystems.` `www.announce/`.

Using the <META> Tag to Make Search Engines Notice Your Site

The big search engines such as AltaVista and Excite scour the Web for new and updated sites. Chances are they'll stumble upon your humble home one of these days and add your pages to their massive databases. That's fine, but is there any way to

Avoid Spamdexing!

You might think you could conjure yourself up a better search result placement by repeating some of your keywords a few times. Don't do it! Search engines call this *spamdexing* and they'll usually disqualify your site if they think you're trying to pull the Web wool over their eyes.

ensure that your pages will come out near the top if someone runs a search for topics related to your site? Well, no, there's no way to guarantee a good placement. However, you can help things along tremendously by adding a couple of special <META> tags that you insert between the <HEAD> and </HEAD> tags.

The first of these tags defines a description of your site:

```
<META NAME="Description" CONTENT="Your
description goes here">
```

Most search engines use this description when they display your page in the results of a Web search.

The second <META> tag defines one or more keywords that correspond to the key topics in the page. The search engines use these keywords to match your page with keywords entered by users when they perform a Web search. Here's the syntax:

```
<META NAME="Keywords" CONTENT="keyword1, keyword2, etc.">
```

Here's an example:

```
<HTML>
<HEAD>
<TITLE>Tickle Me Elmomentum</TITLE>
<META NAME="Description"
CONTENT="This page examines the Tickle Me Elmo
phenomenon and attempts to understand its social ramifications.">
<META NAME="Keywords" CONTENT="tickle me elmo, toy, doll, giggle,
frenzy, fad, parental pressure">
</HEAD>
<BODY>
etc.
```

To ensure compatibility with most search engines, you should put all of your keywords in lowercase.

Good luck!

The Least You Need to Know

This chapter completed your course on creating your first Web page by showing you how to get your page out onto the Net. In Part 2, you take your Web page publishing efforts to a new level by examining a huge array of tag tricks and techniques.

Part 2
A Grab Bag of Web Page Wonders

The HTML hoops I made you jump through in Part 1 will stand you in good stead for the majority of your Web page projects. In fact, you now have enough HTML trivia crammed into your brain to keep you going strong for the rest of your career as a Web author. But that doesn't mean you should rip out the rest of this book and turn it into confetti. Heck no. You still have quite a few nuggets of HTML gold to mine, and that's just what you do here in Part 2. Think of the next few chapters as page-bound piñatas, stuffed full of various HTML candies and toys. You only have to whack each one with a stick (metaphorically speaking, of course) to spill out things like using images as links (Chapter 8), creating tables (Chapter 9), adding sounds (Chapter 10), forms (Chapter 11), and frames (Chapter 12), and lots more.

Images Can Be Links, Too

In This Chapter

➤ How to set up an image as a hypertext link

➤ Some handy ideas for using image links

➤ A few image pitfalls to watch out for

➤ How to create your own image maps—without programming!

➤ Lots of nifty techniques for turning image *lead* into link *gold*

You might think that Web page images are all show and no go, but I assure you they can "go" with the best of them. Specifically, I mean you can use them as hypertext links, just like regular text. The reader just clicks the image, and he goes off to whatever corner of the Web you specify. This chapter shows you not only how to set up an image as a link but also how to create *image maps*—graphics that contain multiple links.

Turning an Image into a Link

Recall from Chapter 5, "Making the Jump to Hyperspace: Adding Links," that you use the <A> tag to build a hypertext link into a Web page:

```
<A HREF="URL">The link text goes here</A>
```

The *URL* part is the Internet address of the Web page (or whatever) to which you want to link.

Designating an image as a hypertext link is not a whole lot different than using text. You use the same <A> tag, but you insert an <IMG> tag between the <A> and </A> tags, like this:

```
<A HREF="URL"><IMG SRC="filename"></A>
```

Again, *URL* is the address of the linked page, and *filename* is the name of the graphics file that you want the surfer to click.

For example, it's often a good idea to include a link from all your other Web pages back to your home page. This makes it easy for your readers to start over again. Here's a document (backhome.htm on the CD) that sets up an image of a house as the link back to the home page:

```
<HTML>
<HEAD>
<TITLE>Images Can Be Links, Too</TITLE>
</HEAD>
<BODY>
Click this house <A HREF="index.htm"><IMG SRC="house.gif"></A>
to return to my home page.
</BODY>
</HTML>
```

Figure 8.1 shows how it looks. Notice how the browser displays a border around the image to identify it as a link.

Figure 8.1

An image masquerading as a hypertext link.

"Why Should I Use an Image As a Link?"

That's a good question, and I can answer it with two simple words: eye candy. You already know that adding images is a great way to liven up a dull-as-dishwater Web page. So if it's your goal to encourage people to surf your site and see what you have to offer, it's just more tempting for would-be surfers to click interesting-looking images.

That's not to say you have to turn every last one of your links into an image. As always, prudence is the order of the day, and a page with just a few image links is more effective than a page that's covered in them. So, for example, you might want to add links to get people back to your home page, to enable visitors to send you an email message, or for important areas of your site. The next two sections also take you through two common uses for image links: toolbars and navigation buttons.

Example 1: A Web Page "Toolbar"

Most modern programs have toolbars with various buttons that give you one-click access to the program's most-used commands and features. You can use image links to provide similar convenience to the folks who trudge through your site.

The basic process for setting this up involves three steps:

1. Use your favorite graphics program to create button-like images that represent important sections of your Web site (your home page, your guest book, your list of links to *Animaniacs* sites, and so on).

2. Create <IMG> tags to set up these buttons as image links that point to the appropriate pages.

3. Insert these <IMG> tags consecutively (that is, on a *single* line) at the top or bottom of each page. The consecutive <IMG> tags cause the images to appear side-by-side. Presto: instant Web toolbar!

Borderless Image Links

The link border that appears around an image link isn't usually very flattering to the image. To keep your images looking good, get rid of the border by adding BORDER=0 to your <IMG> tag:

```
<IMG SRC="house.gif"
➥BORDER=0>
```

Adding Text to Graphics

Every good graphics program has some kind of "Text" tool that enables you to add text to an image.

The design of your buttons is entirely up to you, but most Web toolbars use some combination of image and text. Personally, I don't have an artistic bone in my body, so I prefer to use "text-only" images, as shown in Figure 8.2. This toolbar is just six linked images displayed on a single line. Here's the HTML code that I used to create this toolbar:

```
<HTML>
<HEAD>
<TITLE>A Web Page Toolbar</TITLE>
</HEAD>
<BODY>
<A HREF="/Books/index.html">
```

107

```
➥<IMG SRC="books.gif" BORDER=0></A>
➥<A HREF="/Ramblings/index.html">
➥<IMG SRC="ramblings.gif" BORDER=0></A>
➥<A HREF="/Toys/index.html">
➥<IMG SRC="toys.gif" BORDER=0></A>
➥<A HREF="/guestbook.html">
➥<IMG SRC="guestbk.gif" BORDER=0></A>
➥<A HREF="/search.html">
➥<IMG SRC="search.gif" BORDER=0></A>
➥<A HREF="/index.html">
➥<IMG SRC="homepage.gif" BORDER=0></A>
</BODY>
</HTML>
```

Remember: the key here is that all these <A> tags and <IMG> tags must by typed out on a single line.

Figure 8.2

Cram consecutive image links together for a handy Web page toolbar.

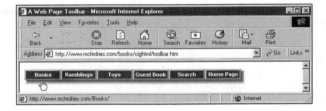

Example 2: VCR-Style Navigation Buttons

Some Web sites contain material that could (or should) be read serially. That is, you read one page and then the next page, and so on. In these situations, it's convenient to give the reader an easy method for navigating back and forth through these pages. The solution that many sites use is to set up VCR-style buttons on the page. These are usually arrows that point forward or backward, as well as a "rewind" button that takes the reader to the first page in the series.

For example, Figure 8.3 shows a Web page from the CIGHTML mailing list archives. These archived messages are arranged by threads, and the buttons at the top of each page enable you to navigate to the next message (the Next Msg button), the previous message (the Prev Msg button), the next thread (the Next Thread button), and so on.

The Ins and Outs of Image Links

If you plan on using images and links on your Web pages, here are a few tidbits to bear in mind when designing these links:

Figure 8.3

An example of a Web page that uses image links as VCR-style navigation buttons.

➤ **Don't use massive images for your links.** It's frustrating enough waiting for a humongous image to load if you have a slow Internet connection. However, it's doubly frustrating if that image is an important part of the site's navigation system. In this case, most folks simply take their surfing business elsewhere. As a general rule, it shouldn't take more than a few seconds for surfers with slow connections to download your image.

➤ **Try to use images that have at least some connection to the link.** For example, suppose you want to set up a link back to your home page. You might have some kind of personal logo or symbol that might seem appropriate, but how many of your surfers will know what this means? A simple icon of a house would probably be more effective.

➤ **Unless your image is ridiculously obvious, you should always accompany the graphic with explanatory text.** A simple line such as "Click the mailbox icon to send me a message" does wonders for making your site easier to figure out.

Check This Out

Take Advantage of ALT Text

Remember that most modern browsers display the <IMG> tag's ALT text has a banner when the user hovers the mouse over an image. With an image link, you can use the ALT text to tell the surfer where the link takes her.

➤ **Consider turning the explanatory text itself into a link that points to the same page as the image.** That way, if the surfer is using a text-only browser or a graphical browser with images turned off, she can still navigate your site. Figure 8.4 shows an example. Here, I've augmented the toolbar with the equivalent text links.

Figure 8.4

It's often useful to supplement your image links with the equivalent text links.

Images Can Be Maps, Too

An *image map* is a Web page graphic with several defined "clickable" areas. (These areas are also called *hot spots*.) Click one area and a particular Web page loads; click a different area and a different page loads. In other words, each of these areas is just a special kind of hypertext link. Image maps give you much more flexibility than simple image links because you have more freedom to arrange the links and you can use more elaborate graphics (but not *too* elaborate; remember those poor surfers with slow modem connections).

Originally, setting up an image map was a complicated affair in which you actually had to write a program that would decipher clicks on the image and tell the Web server which page to load. Although gluttons for punishment can still take that road, the rest of us now have an easier method. The tall-forehead types call this method *client-side image maps*, but a better name would probably be *browser-based image maps*. In other words, in contrast to the old method that required the intervention of a program and a Web server, this new method has everything built right into the browser. You also get the following extra benefits:

➤ Browser-based image maps are faster because the Web server doesn't have to process any image map info.

➤ The browser shows the actual URL of each image map link. With server-based image maps, all you get are the coordinates of the map.

➤ You can test out your map on your own computer before you load everything onto the Web.

For your image map to work correctly, you have to perform three steps:

1. Decide which distinct image regions you want to use and then determine the coordinates of each region.

2. Use the <MAP> and <AREA> tags to assign a link to each of these regions.

3. Add a special version of the <IMG> tag to your Web page.

The next few sections take you through each of these steps to show you how to create your own browser-based image maps.

Step 1: Determine the Map Coordinates

All the information that you see on your computer screen is divided into tiny little points of light called *pixels*. Suppose you went insane one day and decided you wanted to invent a way to specify any particular pixel on the screen. Well, because a typical screen arranges these pixels in 640 columns by 480 rows, you might do this:

➤ Number the columns from left to right starting with 0 as the first column (remember, you're insane) and 639 as the last column.

➤ Number the rows from top to bottom starting with 0 as the first row and 479 as the last row.

So far, so good(!). Now you can pinpoint any pixel just by giving its column number followed by its row number. For example, pixel 10,15 is the teensy bit of light in the 11th column and 16th row. And, because your insanity has math-geek overtones, you call the column value "X" and the row value "Y."

This "coordinate system" that you've so cleverly developed is exactly what you use to divide an image map, where the top-left corner of the image is 0,0. For example, check out the image displayed in Figure 8.5. This image is 600 pixels wide and 100 pixels high, and it's divided into three areas, each of which is 200 pixels wide and 100 pixels high:

Area A   This area is defined by coordinate 0,0 in the upper-left corner and coordinate 199,99 in the lower-right corner.

Area B   This area is defined by coordinate 199,0 in the upper-left corner and coordinate 399,99 in the lower-right corner.

Area C   This area is defined by coordinate 399,0 in the upper-left corner and coordinate 599,99 in the lower-right corner.

Why bother with all this coordinate malarkey? Well, it's how you let the browser know what to do when the user clicks the image. For example, suppose you want to load a page named a.htm when the surfer clicks inside area A in the preceding image. Then you'd tell the browser (this is explained in the next section) that if the mouse pointer is within the rectangle bounded by the coordinates 0,0 and 199,99, load a.htm.

Figure 8.5

Use a coordinate system to divide your image.

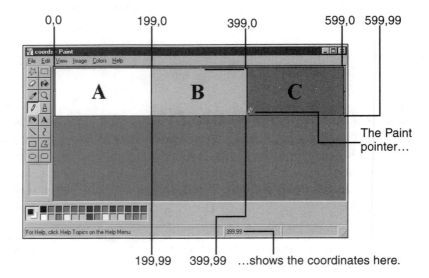

That's all well and good, but how the heck are you supposed to figure out these coordinates? One way would be to load the image into a graphics program. Paint, for example, shows the current coordinates in the status bar when you slide the mouse around inside the image (as shown in the previous figure).

If you don't have a graphics program that does this, there's a method you can use to display the coordinates within the browser. What you have to do is set up an HTML file with a link that uses the following format:

```
<A HREF="whatever"><IMG SRC="YourImageMap" ISMAP></A>
```

Here, replace *YourImageMap* with the name of the image file you want to use for your map. The ISMAP attribute fools the browser into thinking this is a server-based image map. So what? So this: Now load this HTML file into a browser, move your mouse pointer over the image and—voilà!—the image coordinates of the current mouse position appear in the status bar! As shown in Figure 8.6, you just point at the corners that define the image areas and record the coordinates that appear.

Step 2: Use <MAP> to Define the Image Map

With your image coordinates now scribbled on a piece of paper, you can set about defining the image map. To do this, you start with the <MAP> tag, which uses the following general form:

```
<MAP NAME="MapName">
</MAP>
```

The *MapName* part is a name that you assign to this map definition. Next, you have to specify the clickable areas on the image. You do this by using the <AREA> tag:

```
<AREA SHAPE="Shape" COORDS="Coords" HREF="URL">
```

112

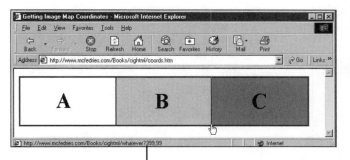

Figure 8.6
To determine coordinates, set up your image as a link with the ISMAP attribute, and Netscape does all the hard work for you.

Jot down the coordinates for each image area.

ISMAP and Internet Explorer

The ISMAP trick works with all flavors of Netscape, and it also works with Internet Explorer 4.0 and higher. If you're using an earlier version of Internet Explorer, there's a way to get the coordinates via VBScript. To see how it works, visit the following page on my Web site:

```
http://www.mcfedries.com/toys/vb-coords.html
```

Looks pretty ugly, doesn't it? Well, it's not too bad. The SHAPE attribute determines the shape of the area, the COORDS attribute defines the area's coordinates, and the HREF attribute specifies the Web page that loads when the user clicks this area.

The COORDS attribute depends on what value you use for the SHAPE attribute. Most image map areas are rectangles, so you specify RECT as the SHAPE and set the COORDS attribute equal to the coordinates of the area's upper-left corner and lower-right corner. For example, here's an <AREA> tag for area A in the example we've been using:

```
<AREA SHAPE="RECT" COORDS="0, 0, 199, 99" HREF="a.htm">
```

You then stuff all your <AREA> tags between the <MAP> and </MAP> tags, like so:

```
<MAP NAME="TestMap">
<AREA SHAPE="RECT" COORDS="0, 0, 199, 99" HREF="a.htm">
<AREA SHAPE="RECT" COORDS="199, 0, 399, 99" HREF="b.htm">
<AREA SHAPE="RECT" COORDS="399, 0, 599, 99" HREF="c.htm">
</MAP>
```

Other Image Map Shapes

The <AREA> tag's SHAPE attribute also accepts the values CIRCLE (for, duh, a circle) and POLY (for a polygon).

For a circle, the COORDS attribute takes three values: the x coordinate of the circle's center point, the y coordinate of the center point, and the radius of the circle.

For a polygon, the COORDS attribute takes three or more sets of coordinates. The browser determines the area by joining a line from one coordinate to the other.

Step 3: Add the Image Map to Your Web Page

Okay, it's all over but the shouting, as they say. To put all that coordinate stuff to good use, you just toss a special version of the <IMG> tag into your Web page:

```
<IMG SRC="YourImageMap" USEMAP="#MapName">
```

As before, you replace *YourImageMap* with the name of the image map file. The key, though, is the USEMAP attribute. By setting this attribute equal to the name of the map you just created (with an extra # tacked on the front), the browser treats the graphic as an image map. For example, here's an <IMG> tag that sets up an image map for the example we've been using:

```
<IMG SRC="coords.gif" USEMAP="#TestMap">
```

Figure 8.7 shows you that this stuff actually works. Notice that when I point to area A, the name of the linked page (a.htm, in this case) appears in the status bar.

Figure 8.7

The image map is now ready for prime time.

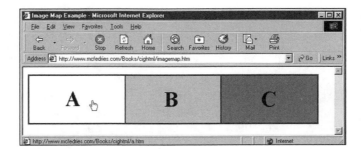

The Least You Need to Know

This chapter expanded your link knowledge by showing you how to set up image links and image maps. You saw, in particular, that client-side image maps are a bit persnickety to set up, but at least it's easier than programming! The next chapter delves even deeper into the Web page goodies bag to pull out a new and very useful HTML structure: the table.

Chapter 9

Table Talk: Adding Tables to Your Page

In This Chapter

➤ What are tables, and why are they useful?

➤ Creating simple tables

➤ Ever-so-slightly advanced tables

➤ Tons of table tips and techniques

In this chapter, you learn a bit of computer carpentry as I show you how to build and work with *tables*. Don't worry if you can't tell a hammer from a hacksaw; the tables we're dealing with are purely electronic. An HTML table is a rectangular grid of rows and columns on a Web page, into which you can enter all kinds of info, including text, numbers, links, and even images. This chapter tells you everything you need to know to build your own table specimens.

What Is a Table?

Despite the name, HTML tables aren't really analogous to the big wooden thing you eat on every night. Instead, as I've said, a table is a rectangular arrangement of rows and columns on your screen. Figure 9.1 shows an example table.

To make sure you understand what's going on (that *is* my job, after all), let's check out a bit of table lingo:

Figure 9.1

An HTML table in a Web document.

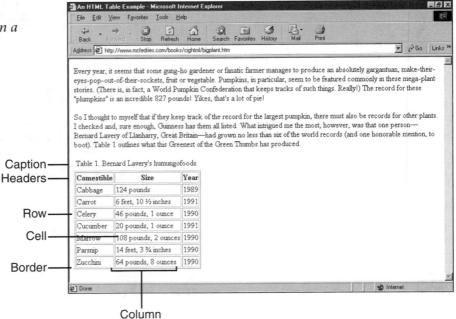

Row   A single "line" of data that runs across the table. In the example shown in the previous figure, there are eight rows in all.

Column   A single vertical section of data. The previous example has three columns.

Cell   The intersection of a row and column. The cells are where you enter the data that appears in the table.

Caption   This is text that appears (usually) above the table and is used to describe the contents of the table.

Headers   The first row of the table. The headers are optional, but many people use them to label each column.

Borders   These are the lines that surround the table and each cell.

Nothing too rocket science-y there.

Wait a minute. Way back in Chapter 3, "From Buck-Naked to Beautiful: Dressing Up Your Page," you showed me how to use the <PRE> tag to make text line up all nice and neat. So why use a table when <PRE> can do a similar job?

Good question. Here are just a few advantages that tables bring to the, uh, table:

➤ Getting text to line up using <PRE> is frustrating at best, and a hair-pulling, head-pounding, curse-the-very-existence-of-the-@#$%&!-World-Wide-Web chore at worst. With tables, though, you can get your text to line up like boot camp recruits with very little effort (and without having to yell orders at the top of your lungs).

➤ Each table cell is self-contained. You can edit and format the contents of a cell without disturbing the arrangement of the other table elements.

➤ The text "wraps" inside each cell, making it a snap to create multiple-line entries.

➤ Tables can include not only text, but images and links as well (even other tables!).

➤ Most text tags (such as <B>, <I>, <H1>, and so on) are fair game inside a table, so you can format the table to suit your needs. Recall that text stuck between <PRE> and </PRE> is displayed in an ugly, typewriter-like font.

Web Woodworking: How to Build a Table

Okay, it's time to put the table pedal to the HTML metal and start cranking out some of these table things. The next few sections take you through the basic steps. As an example, I show you how I created the table in Figure 9.1.

The Simplest Case: A One-Row Table

Tables always use the following basic container:

```
<TABLE>
</TABLE>
```

All the other table tags fit between these two tags. There are two things you need to know about the <TABLE> tag:

➤ If you want your table to show a border, use the <TABLE BORDER> tag instead of <TABLE> (you still close the table with the </TABLE> tag, though).

➤ If you don't want a border, just use <TABLE>.

Use a Border to Start

I can't tell you how many table troubles I've solved just by turning on the border to get a good look at the table structure. Therefore, I highly recommend that you use a border while constructing your table. You can always get rid of it after you're done.

After you do that, most of your remaining table chores involve the following four-step process:

1. Add a row.
2. Divide the row into the number of columns you want.
3. Insert data into each cell.
4. Repeat steps 1–3 until done.

To add a row, you toss a <TR> (table row) tag and a </TR> tag (its corresponding end tag) between <TABLE> and </TABLE>:

```
<TABLE BORDER>
<TR>
</TR>
</TABLE>
```

Now you divide that row into columns by placing the <TD> (table data) and </TD> tags between <TR> and </TR>. Each <TD></TD> combination represents one column (or, more specifically, an individual cell in the row), so if you want a three-column table (with a border), you do this:

```
<TABLE BORDER>
<TR>
<TD></TD>
<TD></TD>
<TD></TD>
</TR>
</TABLE>
```

Now you enter the row's cell data by typing text between each <TD> tag and its </TD> end tag:

```
<TABLE BORDER>
<TR>
<TD>Cabbage</TD>
<TD>124 pounds</TD>
<TD>1989</TD>
</TR>
</TABLE>
```

Remember that you can put any of the following within the <TD> and </TD> tags:

➤ Text
➤ HTML text-formatting tags (such as <B> and <I>)
➤ Links
➤ Lists
➤ Images

Adding More Rows

When your first row is firmly in place, you simply repeat the procedure for the other rows in the table. For our example table, here's the HTML that includes the data for all the rows:

```
<TABLE BORDER>
<TR>
<TD>Cabbage</TD><TD>124 pounds</TD><TD>1989</TD>
</TR>
<TR>
<TD>Carrot</TD><TD>6 feet, 10 &#189; inches</TD><TD>1991</TD>
</TR>
<TR>
<TD>Celery</TD><TD>46 pounds, 1 ounce</TD><TD>1990</TD>
</TR>
<TR>
<TD>Cucumber</TD><TD>20 pounds, 1 ounce</TD><TD>1991</TD>
</TR>
<TR>
<TD>Marrow</TD><TD>108 pounds, 2 ounces</TD><TD>1990</TD>
</TR>
<TR>
<TD>Parsnip</TD><TD>14 feet, 3 &#190; inches</TD><TD>1990</TD>
</TR>
<TR>
<TD>Zucchini</TD><TD>64 pounds, 8 ounces</TD><TD>1990</TD>
</TR>
</TABLE>
```

Creating a Row of Headers

If your table displays stats, data, or other info, you can make your readers' lives easier by including labels at the top of each column that define what's in the column. (You don't need a long-winded explanation; in most cases, a word or two should do the job.) To define a header, use the <TH> and </TH> tags within a row, like so:

```
<TR>
<TH>First Column Header</TH>
<TH>Second Column Header</TH>
<TH>And So On, Ad Nauseum</TH>
</TR>
```

As you can see, the <TH> tag is a lot like the <TD> tag. The difference is that the browser displays text that appears between the <TH> and </TH> tags as bold and centered within the cell. This helps the reader differentiate the header from the rest of the table data. Remember, though, that headers are optional; you can bypass them if your table doesn't need them.

Here's how I added the headers for the example you saw at the beginning of the chapter:

```
<TABLE BORDER>
<TR>
<TH>Comestible</TH><TH>Size</TH><TH>Year</TH>
</TR>
etc.
</TABLE>
```

Including a Caption

The last basic table element is the caption. A *caption* is a short description (a sentence or two) that tells the reader the purpose of the table. You define the caption with the <CAPTION> tag:

```
<CAPTION ALIGN=where>Caption text goes here.</CAPTION>
```

Here, *where* is either TOP or BOTTOM; if you use TOP, the caption appears above the table; if you use BOTTOM, the caption appears—you guessed it—below the table. Here's the <CAPTION> tag from the example (for the complete document, look for BIGPLANT.HTM on the disc):

```
<TABLE BORDER>
<CAPTION ALIGN=TOP>Table 1. Bernard Lavery's humungofoods.</CAPTION>
etc.
</TABLE>
```

Table Refinishing—More Table Tidbits

The tags we've eyeballed so far are enough to enable you to build tables that are sturdy, if not altogether flashy. If that's all you need, you can safely ignore the rest of the dreck in this chapter. However, if you'd like a tad more control over the layout of your tables, the next few sections take you through a few refinements that can give your tables that certain *je ne sais quoi*.

Aligning Text Within Cells

The standard-issue alignment for table cells is left-aligned for data (<TD>) cells and centered for header (<TH>) cells. Not good enough? No sweat. Just shoehorn an ALIGN attribute inside the <TD> or <TH> tag and you can specify the text to be left-aligned, centered, or right-aligned. Here's how it works:

```
<TD ALIGN=alignment>
<TH ALIGN=alignment>
```

In both cases, *alignment* can be LEFT, CENTER, or RIGHT. That's not bad, but there's even more alignment fun to be had. You can also align your text vertically within a cell. This comes in handy if one cell is quite large (because it contains either a truckload of text or a relatively large image), and you'd like to adjust the vertical position of the other cells in the same row. In this case, you use the VALIGN (vertical alignment) attribute with <TD> or <TH>:

```
<TD VALIGN=vertical>
<TH VALIGN=vertical>
```

Here, *vertical* can be TOP, MIDDLE (the default alignment), or BOTTOM. Here's an example document (tblalign.htm on the CD) that demonstrates each of these alignment options:

```
<HTML>
<HEAD>
<TITLE>Table Alignment</TITLE>
</HEAD>
<BODY>
<TABLE BORDER>
<CAPTION>Aligning Text Within Cells:</CAPTION>
<TR>
<TD></TD>
<TD ALIGN=LEFT>Left</TD>
<TD ALIGN=CENTER>Center</TD>
<TD ALIGN=RIGHT>Right</TD>
</TR>
<TR>
<TD><IMG SRC="constru1.gif">
<TD VALIGN=TOP>Top o' the cell</TD>
<TD VALIGN=MIDDLE>Middle o' the cell</TD>
<TD VALIGN=BOTTOM>Bottom o' the cell</TD>
</TR>
</TABLE>
</BODY>
</HTML>
```

Figure 9.2 shows how the table looks in the browser.

Spanning Text Across Multiple Rows or Columns

The data we've entered into our table cells so far has been decidedly monogamous. That is, each hunk of data has used up only one cell. But it's possible (and perfectly legal) for data to be bigamous (take up two cells) or even polygamous (take up three or more cells). Such cells are said to *span* multiple rows or columns, which can come in quite handy for headers and graphics.

Figure 9.2

The various and sundry cell alignment options.

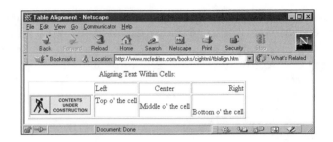

Running Cells on Empty

Did you notice that the top-left corner of the table is empty? I did this just by placing a <TD> tag and </TD> tag side by side, with nothing inbetween. Note that, in the browser, the cell appears "filled in." If you want a truly empty cell, use this tag combo instead: <TD>
</TD>.

Let's start with spanning multiple columns. To do this, you need to interpose the COLSPAN (column span) attribute into the <TD> or <TH> tag:

```
<TD COLSPAN=cols>
<TH COLSPAN=cols>
```

In this case, *cols* is the number of columns you want the cell to span. Here's a simple example (tblspan1.htm on the CD) that shows a cell spanning two columns:

```
<HTML>
<HEAD>
<TITLE>Spanning Text Across Multiple Columns</TITLE>
</HEAD>
<BODY>
<TABLE BORDER>
<CAPTION>The Spanning Thing — Example #1 (COLSPAN)</CAPTION>

<TR>
<TD COLSPAN=2>This item spans two columns</TD>
<TD>This one doesn't</TD>
</TR>
```

```
<TR>
<TD>The 1st Column</TD>
<TD>The 2nd Column</TD>
<TD>The 3rd Column</TD>
</TR>

</TABLE>
</BODY>
</HTML>
```

Figure 9.3 shows how the table looks in Internet Explorer.

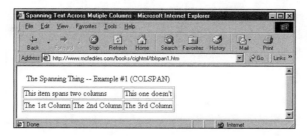

Figure 9.3

A cell that spans two columns.

Spanning multiple rows is similar, except that you substitute ROWSPAN for COLSPAN in <TD> or <TH>:

```
<TD ROWSPAN=rows>
<TH ROWSPAN=rows>
```

The *rows* value is the number of rows you want the cell to span. Here's an example (tblspan2.htm on the CD) that shows a cell spanning two rows:

```
<HTML>
<HEAD>
<TITLE>Spanning Text Across Multiple Rows</TITLE>
</HEAD>
<BODY>
<TABLE BORDER>
<CAPTION>The Spanning Thing — Example #2 (ROWSPAN)</CAPTION>

<TR>
<TD ROWSPAN=2>This item spans two rows</TD>
<TD>The 1st Row</TD>
</TR>

<TR>
<TD>The 2nd Row</TD>
</TR>
```

```
<TR>
<TD>This one doesn't</TD>
<TD>The 3rd Row</TD>
</TR>

</TABLE>
</BODY>
</HTML>
```

Figure 9.4 shows the result.

Figure 9.4

A cell that spans two rows.

A Whack of Table Attributes

For our next table trick, we pull a few more table attributes out of our HTML hat. There are all kinds of wild extras, but the following are the most useful ones:

The background color You learned in Chapter 6, "A Picture Is Worth a Thousand Clicks: Working with Images," that you can adjust the background color of your entire Web page. However, you can also assign a custom color to just the background of a table. To do this, you add the BGCOLOR=#*rrggbb* attribute to the <TABLE> tag, where *rrggbb* is a value that specifies the color you want (see Chapter 3, "From Buck-Naked to Beautiful: Dressing Up Your Page"). For example, the following tag gives your table a light gray background:

```
<TABLE BGCOLOR=#CCCCCC>
```

A background image Internet Explorer enables you to set a background image instead of just a background color for a table. This is just like setting a background image for a Web page. In this case, you toss the BACKGROUND attribute inside the <TABLE> tag and set the attribute equal to the name of the image file you want to use, like so:

```
<TABLE BACKGROUND="tablebg.gif>
```

Tables Backgrounds and Netscape

Keep in mind that Netscape hasn't always supported table background images. It only understood them beginning with version 4.0.

The border size   To change the thickness of the table border, you can assign a value to the <TABLE> tag's BORDER attribute. (Note that this applies only to the part of the border that surrounds the outside of the table; the inner borders aren't affected.) For example, to display your table with a border that's five units thick, you use the following:

```
<TABLE BORDER=5>
```

The width of the table   The browser usually does a pretty good job of adjusting the width of a table to accommodate the current window size. If you need your table to be a particular width, however, use the WIDTH attribute for the <TABLE> tag. You can either specify a value in pixels or, more likely, a percentage of the available window width. For example, to make sure your table always usurps 75% of the window width, you use this version of the <TABLE> tag:

```
<TABLE WIDTH=75%>
```

The width of a cell   You can also specify the width of an individual cell by adding the WIDTH attribute to a <TD> or tag. Again, you can either specify a value in pixels or a percentage of the entire table. (Note that all the cells in the column will adopt the same width.) In this example, the cell takes up 50% of the table's width:

```
<TD WIDTH=50%>
```

The amount of space between cells   By default, browsers allow just two units of space between each cell (vertically and horizontally). To bump that up, use the CELLSPACING attribute for the <TABLE> tag. Here's an example that increases the cell spacing to 10:

```
<TABLE CELLSPACING=10>
```

The amount of space between a cell's contents and its border   Browsers like to cram data into a cell as tightly as possible. To that end, they leave a mere one unit of space between the contents of the cell and the cell border. (This space is called the *cell padding*.) To give your table data more room to breathe, use the <TABLE> tag's CELLPADDING attribute. For example, the following line tells the browser to reserve a full ten units of padding above, below, left, and right of the content in each cell:

```
<TABLE CELLPADDING=10>
```

Here's a Web page that shows you a for-instance for most of these attributes (see tblattr.htm on the CD):

```
<HTML>
<HEAD>
<TITLE>Some Table Extensions</TITLE>
```

```
</HEAD>
<BODY>

<B>&lt;TABLE BGCOLOR=#CCCCCC&gt;</B>
<TABLE BORDER BGCOLOR=#CCCCCC>
<TR>
<TD>Dumb</TD>
<TD>Dumber</TD>
<TD>Dumbest</TD>
</TR>
</TABLE>

<P><B>&lt;TABLE BORDER=5&gt;</B>
<TABLE BORDER=5>
<TR>
<TD>One</TD>
<TD>Two</TD>
<TD>Buckle my shoe</TD>
</TR>
</TABLE>

<P>
<B>&lt;TABLE WIDTH=75%&gt;</B>
<TABLE BORDER WIDTH=75%>
<TR>
<TD>Three</TD>
<TD>Four</TD>
<TD>Shut the door</TD>
</TR>
</TABLE>

<P>
<B>&lt;TD WIDTH=50%&gt;</B>
<TABLE BORDER>
<TR>
<TD WIDTH=50%>WIDTH=50%</TD>
<TD>Normal width</TD>
<TD>Normal width</TD>
</TR>
</TABLE>

<P>
<B>&lt;TABLE CELLSPACING=10&gt;</B>
<TABLE BORDER CELLSPACING=10>
<TR>
<TD>Eeny</TD>
```

```
<TD>Meeny</TD>
<TD>Miney</TD>
<TD>Mo</TD>
</TR>
</TABLE>

<P>
<B>&lt;TABLE CELLPADDING=10&gt;</B>
<TABLE BORDER CELLPADDING=10>
<TR>
<TD>Veni</TD>
<TD>Vidi</TD>
<TD>Vici</TD>
</TR>
</TABLE>

</BODY>
</HTML>
```

When you load this file into Internet Explorer, you see the tables shown in Figure 9.5.

Figure 9.5

Examples of some useful table attributes.

Using a Table to Set Up a Page with a Margin

Many Web sites use a background image that displays a margin down the left side of the page. That margin can be either purely decorative or it can contain links and other info. For example, Figure 9.6 shows a page on my site that uses a margin.

129

Figure 9.6

This page features a margin down the side.

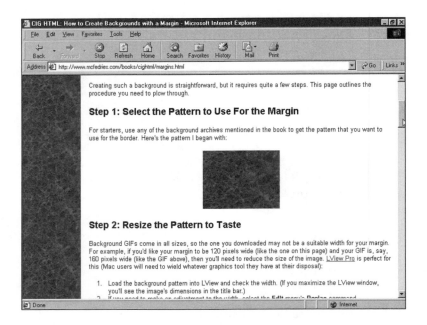

To get the full benefit of a margined background, you need to be able to control where the various Web page elements appear. In most cases, you want to make sure that the page's text and graphics appear to the right of the margin in the white space (as in the previous figure). Alternatively, you might want to place a few icons in the margin.

To control this, you need to use a table. In fact, what you do is turn your entire page into one giant table that has either two or three columns. Why two or three? Because it depends on whether you want to include text and other elements inside the margin. If you won't be populating your margin, you can get away with a simple, two-column setup. Otherwise, you need a three-column setup.

Here's the basic structure of the simple two-column design:

Creating a Margined Background

If you'd like to learn the steps for creating such a margined background, head for the following page on my Web site:

`http://www.mcfedries.com/books/cightml/margins.html`

➤ The first column is the margin.

➤ The second column is the whitespace in which you put all your Web page text and graphics.

With this arrangement, the table ensures that the Web page elements line up nicely along the margin. The tricky part is setting up the first column so that it's at least as wide as the margin. To ensure that this column remains the same size no matter what the size of the browser window, you include our old friend the "pixel shim" image. Recall from Chapter 6 that this is a transparent, 1×1 pixel image that you can size at will. (It's the spacer.gif file on the CD.) In the example page shown in the figure, the margin is 120 pixels wide, and I want to leave a little extra space so that the text doesn't sit too close to the margin. Therefore, I want the left column to be 125 pixels wide, so I put the following <IMG> tag in the first column:

```
<IMG SRC="spacer.gif" WIDTH=125 HEIGHT=1>
```

Here's the basic layout for the Web page (see margin.htm on the CD):

```
<HTML>
<HEAD>
<TITLE>Your Title</TITLE>
</HEAD>
<BODY BACKGROUND="Your Margined Background Image">

<TABLE>
<TR>

<TD WIDTH=Your width VALIGN=TOP>
<IMG SRC="spacer.gif" WIDTH=Your width HEIGHT=1>
</TD>

<TD VALIGN=TOP>
The rest of your Web page stuff goes here
</TD>

</TR>
</TABLE>
</BODY>
</HTML>
```

Web designers commonly use the margins to insert text, links, images, and other stuff. Figure 9.7 shows an example of a page that does this.

To do this, you need a three-column design:

➤ The first column is the margin.

➤ The second column is a "gutter" that acts as a buffer zone between the margin and the rest of the page.

➤ The third column is the whitespace in which you put all your Web page text and graphics.

Figure 9.7

This page crams some text and links inside the margin.

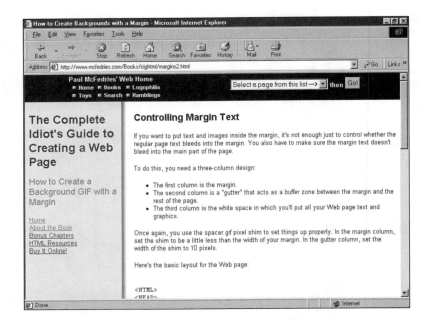

If you want to include text, links, and other goodies in the margin, it's not enough just to control whether the regular page text bleeds into the margin. You also have to make sure the margin text doesn't bleed into the main part of the page.

Once again, you use the spacer.gif pixel shim to set things up properly. In the margin column, set the shim to be a little less than the width of your margin. In the gutter column, set the width of the shim to 10 pixels.

Here's the basic layout for the Web page (see margin2.htm on the CD):

```
<HTML>
<HEAD>
<TITLE>Your Title</TITLE>
</HEAD>
<BODY BACKGROUND="Your Margined Background Image">

<TABLE>
<TR>

<TD WIDTH=A little less than the margin VALIGN=TOP>
<IMG
    SRC="spacer.gif"
    WIDTH=A little less than the margin
    HEIGHT=1>
The margin text and images go here
</TD>
```

```
<TD WIDTH=10 VALIGN=TOP>
<IMG SRC="spacer.gif" WIDTH=10 HEIGHT=1>
</TD>

<TD VALIGN=TOP>
The rest of your Web page stuff goes here
</TD>

</TR>
</TABLE>

</BODY>
</HTML>
```

The Least You Need to Know

This chapter showed you the ins and outs of creating Web page tables using HTML. Admittedly, tables are a bit more convoluted than the simple tags we've looked at so far, but they get easier with practice.

In the next chapter, I reach deep into the bag of Web page wonders and pull out a few multimedia marvels, including animated images and sounds.

Chapter 10

Making Your Web Pages Dance and Sing

In This Chapter

➤ Combining multiple images into a single, animated GIF

➤ Animating text with the <MARQUEE> tag

➤ Adding beeps, boops, burps, and other sounds to your Web page

➤ Delivering video-on-demand from your Web page

➤ How to turn a Web page into a full-fledged entertainment center

Web pages are no longer restricted to static displays of text and graphics, but instead they're dynamic, kinetic, and truly interactive environments. Instead of mere documents to read and look at, pages have become programs that you can manipulate and play with. We are witnessing a rapid transformation away from the simple type-it-and-send-it world of forms to a world in which pages have started performing the Web equivalent of singing and dancing.

This chapter shows you a few techniques for enhancing your own pages with this HTML technology. You learn how to turn your Web site into a multimedia marvel that includes animated GIF images, moving text, sounds, and more.

Do-It-Yourself Disney: Animated GIF Images

In Chapter 6, "A Picture is Worth a Thousand Clicks: Working with Images," I talked about how you can spruce up an otherwise-drab Web page by adding an image or two. However, if you *really* want to catch the eye of a busy Web surfer, why not go one step further and add animations to your page?

Sound impossible? It's actually a lot easier than you might think. Netscape Navigator and Internet Explorer support an interesting variation on the GIF file theme: an *animated GIF*. This format actually incorporates several GIF images into a single package. By using a special program, you can specify that these images be displayed sequentially, thus creating an animation! And the really great news is thatthe program you need—it's called GIF Animator—resides right on this book's disc, so you don't have to bother hunting it down and suffering through an endless download. (Please note that GIF Animator is shareware. If you plan on using it regularly, be sure to fork over the measly US$39.95 it costs to register the program.)

To get started, first use Paint, Paint Shop Pro, or some other drawing program to create the individual image files that will comprise your animation. (It doesn't matter which format you use to save the files; GIF Animator can use most graphic formats, including the BMP files created by Paint. There is one caveat, though: To ensure a smooth animation, make each image the same size.) Figure 10.1 shows the images I'm using as an example. (These images are on the CD as well. They're named aninew1.gif through aninew5.gif. The resulting animated GIF is called aninew.gif.) As you can see, all I've done is change the coloring of the letters from image to image. For your own animations, you can change colors, shapes, text, or whatever else you need to create the effect you're looking for.

Figure 10.1

These images can be combined into a single animated GIF.

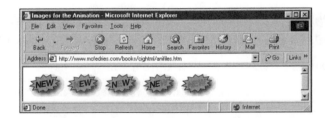

Launch GIF Animator and you eventually see the Startup Wizard dialog box. Now follow these steps:

1. Click the **Animation Wizard** button to launch the Animation Wizard (shown in Figure 10.2).

Figure 10.2

Use the Animation Wizard to construct your animated GIF.

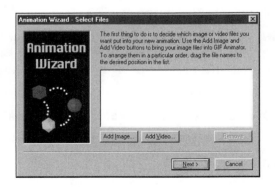

2. Click **Add Image**. GIF Animator hauls the Open dialog box onto the screen.

3. Open the folder that contains the image or images you want to use.

4. You now have two ways to proceed:

   ➤ If all the image files you need for the animation are in the folder, hold down the **Ctrl** key and click each filename. Click **Open** when you're done.

   ➤ If you only need a single image from the folder, click it to highlight it and then click **Open**. You need to repeat steps 4 and 5 until you've selected all the image files for the animation.

5. In the Animation Wizard dialog box, click **Next**. The wizard asks you to choose the "source type."

6. If your images are line drawings or text, activate the **Text-oriented** option; if your images are scanned photos or other high-resolution images, activate the **Photo-oriented** option. Click **Next**. The wizard now asks for the amount of time to display each image (this is called the *delay*).

7. To set the delay, use the **Delay time** spinner to enter a value in 100ths of a second. (You might need to experiment with this value to get your animation just right. A value of 25 is a good place to start.) Click **Next**.

8. In the final wizard dialog box, click **Finish**.

9. Select the **File** menu's **Save** command, enter a name for the new GIF file, and then click **Save**.

10. To check out your animation, click the **Preview** tab, or select **View, Start Preview**.

That's it! Your animated GIF is ready for action. Now you can add it to a Web page simply by setting up a regular <IMG> tag where the SRC attribute points to the GIF file that you just created.

Just a Few Animations Will Do

GIF Animator makes it a breeze to create your own animations. There's also no shortage of ready-to-roll animated GIFs on the Web (see Chapter 24, "Some HTML Resources on the Web"), and I've even included a few on this book's CD. So this is probably as good a place as any to caution you against using too many animated images on your pages. One or two animations can add a nice touch to a page, but any more than that is distracting at best, and downright annoying at worst.

Netscape? Not!

The <MARQUEE> tag is only supported by Internet Explorer, so it doesn't work in Netscape or any other browser. If you want scrolling text that works in most browsers, you can use JavaScript, as described in Chapter 17, "More JavaScript Fun."

Creating a Marquee

Internet Explorer offers Webmeisters an easy way to insert a chunk of animated text on a page. Specifically, you can display a word or phrase that enters the browser screen on the right, scrolls all the way across the screen, and then exits on the left. You can repeat this any number of times and even change the direction of the text. Because this is somewhat reminiscent of text on a theater marquee, the tag you use to control is called the <MARQUEE> tag. In its basic, no-frills guise, this tag has the following structure:

```
<MARQUEE>Put your scrolling text
here.</MARQUEE>
```

The text you cram between the <MARQUEE> and </MARQUEE> tags is what scrolls across the screen. To gain a little more control over the scrolling, the <MARQUEE> tag supports quite a few attributes. Here are a few of the most useful ones:

ALIGN=*Alignment* Determines how the surrounding text is aligned vertically with the marquee. For *Alignment*, you can use either TOP or BOTTOM.

BEHAVIOR=*Type* Determines how the text behaves within the marquee. For *Type*, use SCROLL to get the standard scroll-across movement; use SLIDE to make the text scroll in and then stop when it reaches the opposite side; use ALTERNATE to make the text "bounce" back and forth within the marquee.

BGCOLOR=*Color* Sets the color of the marquee background.

DIRECTION=*WhichWay* This attribute tells the browser which way to scroll the text. *WhichWay* can be either LEFT or RIGHT.

LOOP=*Times* This attribute specifies the number of times you want the text to scroll. If you set *Times* to INFINITE or –1, the text will scroll until kingdom come.

SCROLLDELAY=*Time* This attribute sets the delay in milliseconds between each loop.

SCROLLAMOUNT=*Pixels* This attribute determines how many pixels the text jumps with each iteration. The higher the value for *Pixels*, the faster the text scrolls.

HEIGHT=*Value* Specifies the marquee height either in pixels or as a percentage of the screen.

WIDTH=*Value* Specifies the marquee width either in pixels or as a percentage of the screen.

Here's an HTML file (look for marquee.htm on the CD) that uses several of these attributes. Figure 10.3 shows how it looks in Internet Explorer.

```
<HTML>
<HEAD>
<TITLE>Marquee Malarkey</TITLE>
</HEAD>
<BODY>
Welcome Web <MARQUEE WIDTH=50 ALIGN=BOTTOM BGCOLOR=SILVER
SCROLLAMOUNT=4>
maker.........master..........meister..........
spinner.........weaver.........welder..........
</MARQUEE>!
</BODY>
</HTML>
```

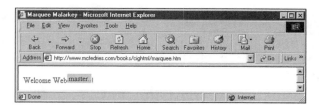

Figure 10.3

At the moment, only Internet Explorer supports the <MARQUEE> tag.

Sound Advice: Adding Sounds to Your Page

The Web is alive with the sounds of, well, you name it! There's music, poetry, special effects, and sound snippets of every stripe. So now that you've labored long and hard to make your Web page pleasing to the eye, perhaps you'd like to add a few extras to appeal to your viewers' ears, as well. It's actually pretty easy to do, and you hear all about it in this section.

First, Some Mumbo-Jumbo About Sound Formats

If you read Chapter 6, "A Picture Is Worth a Thousand Clicks: Working with Images," you were no doubt traumatized by all those graphic formats and their incomprehensible TLAs (three-letter acronyms). The bad news is that the world's audio geeks (yes, these are the same guys who were the audio/visual nerds back in high school) also derive great pleasure in creating a constant stream of new sound formats. However, like graphic formats, the good news is that there are just a few audio formats that the Web has ordained as standards:

AU   This is a common format in the Web soundscape. It's supported by both Netscape Navigator and Internet Explorer.

WAV   This is the standard format used with Windows, which means it's the standard format on the Web. It's supported by all versions of Internet Explorer

139

and by Netscape Navigator 3.0 and up. If you have an earlier version of Netscape, you have to set up a "helper" application to play WAV files (see the next section, "Sounding Off with Sound Links," for details).

MP3   This is an incredibly popular format for digital music. The latest versions of Internet Explorer and Netscape use the Windows Media Player as the helper application for playing MP3 files. You can also get MP3 players from the MP3.com site (http://www.mp3.com/).

MIDI   This is the Musical Instrument Digital Interface format, and it's used to represent electronic music created with a MIDI synthesizer. This format is supported by Internet Explorer and Netscape Navigator 4.0 (for Navigator 3.0, you need the appropriate helper application set up).

I provide a list of some sites that serve sound files in Chapter 24.

Sounding Off with Sound Links

After you have your mitts on a sound file, adding the sound to your Web page is a no-brainer. All you have to do is copy the file to your Web site and then set up a link that points to that file, like so:

```
<A HREF="burp.wav">Click here for a special greeting!</A>
```

Assuming the viewer's browser is set up to handle the sound format you're using, the sound file downloads and then plays without further ado.

Embedding Sound Files

If you want to add MIDI music or other sounds files to your pages, one way to go is the <EMBED> tag, which is supported by both Netscape Navigator and Internet Explorer. At its simplest, you use the SRC attribute to specify the name of the sound file, like so:

```
<EMBED SRC="playme.mid">
```

Here's an example page (see midi.htm on the CD), and Figure 10.4 shows the Internet Explorer interpretation.

```
<HTML>
<HEAD>
<TITLE>MIDI</TITLE>
</HEAD>
<BODY>

Click the Play button to hear some cool jazz music:<BR>
<EMBED SRC="jazz.mid"

</BODY>
</HTML>
```

Figure 10.4

The <EMBED> tag adds a "player" to the Web page.

The <EMBED> tag also supports the following extras:

AUTOSTART=TRUE   If you add this attribute, the browser starts playing the sound file automatically as soon as the user surfs to your page.

LOOP=*Value*   The LOOP attribute tells the browser how many times to play the sound. If you set *Value* to 2, for example, the browser runs through the sound twice. If you really want to drive your visitors away, set *Value* to INFINITE to tell the browser to play the sound indefinitely.

HIDDEN=TRUE   If you add this attribute, the browser hides the controls.

Another Way to Add a Background Sound

With Internet Explorer, the <EMBED> tag isn't the only way to wire your site for sound. Specifically, Internet Explorer supports the <BGSOUND> tag that enables you to specify a sound that plays automatically when someone surfs to your site. (Much like the <EMBED> tag's AUTOSTART=TRUE attribute.) Here's the generic format:

```
<BGSOUND SRC="Filename" LOOP=Times>
```

The *Filename* part is the name of the sound file that you want to play (you can use AU, WAV, or MIDI files). The *Times* part tells the browser how many times to play the sound. You can either enter some positive number or use LOOP=INFINITE to play the sound until the surfer puts their fist through the screen. (Note that you can put this tag anywhere you like in the page.) Here's an example:

```
<BGSOUND SRC="NewAgeTouchyFeely.mid" LOOP=1>
```

141

Lights! Camera! Click! Adding Video to Your Pages

For our next Web multimedia marvel, this section shows you how to add video links to your pages. However, I should add a cautionary note here; this isn't a subject you should treat lightly. Video files tend to be huge and your visitors have to be surfing the Web with a fast connection to bother waiting for a file that's hundreds of kilobytes in size to download. If you're a budding video director, you can make life easier for Web wanderers by producing videos that are small and don't use too many colors.

Video Formats: More @#$%! Acronyms

As you might have guessed, the video technophiles couldn't let the graphics and audio geeks have all the format fun. So, yes, there's no shortage of video file formats available. Sigh. Once again, though, we're lucky that only a few have caught on for Web work:

MOV   This QuickTime format was developed originally for the Macintosh. At the moment, this is probably the most popular video format on the Web.

AVI   This format was introduced with Video for Windows and is now standard in Windows 95 and Windows 98.

MPG   This new format performs the neat trick of creating smaller files with higher video quality. However, you need a fast machine to run these files.

As far as browser support is concerned, there are two distinct camps at the moment:

➤ Internet Explorer can handle all the video formats right out of the box (so to speak) by including support for a few <IMG> tag extensions.

➤ For Navigator and other browsers, you (or your readers) need to install the appropriate plug-in.

The Video Nitty-Gritty

As with sounds, you have a choice of two ways to proceed when adding video to your page. You can either use the <A HREF> tag to set up a link to the video file, or you can use the following form of the <IMG> tag with Internet Explorer:

```
<IMG DYNSRC="Filename" LOOP=Times START=When>
```

Filename is a pointer to the video file you want to play. *Times* specifies how many times the video should play (use LOOP=INFINITE to play the video continuously). *When* tells the browser when to play the video—use START=FILEOPEN to play the video as soon as the user loads the Web page or use START=MOUSEOVER to play the video whenever the user moves their mouse pointer over the video box.

Figure 10.5 shows an example of an HTML file (look for video.htm on the disc) that presents a video clip as shown in the Internet Explorer screen.

```
<HTML>
<HEAD>
<TITLE>Lights! Camera! Click!</TITLE>
</HEAD>
<BODY>
To play the clip, move your mouse pointer over the video image.
<P>
<IMG DYNSRC="moonman.avi" LOOP=2 START=MOUSEOVER>
</BODY>
</HTML>
```

Figure 10.5

Internet Explorer makes it easy to insert video footage in your Web pages.

Redirecting Browsers with Client Pull

If you move your site—or if you rename a page—it's best (when possible) to create a page in the old location that includes a link to the new site or page. (This is known as a *Century-21* page.) Surfers can then click the link to get where you want them to go.

However, you can also use a nifty feature called *client pull* to send visitors to your new page automatically. To see an example, dial the following address into your browser:

```
http://www.mcfedries.com/books/cig-html/
```

This is the old address of this book's home page. When you go there, the page loads and—magic!—two seconds later you're whisked automatically to the book's current home page. Here's the header for the page you loaded:

```
<HTML>
<HEAD>
<TITLE>This page has moved!</TITLE>

<META
   NAME="REFRESH"
   CONTENT="2; URL=http://www.mcfedries.com/books/cightml/">

</HEAD>
```

The secret is the extra <META> tag in the header. The guts of the tag is the CONTENT attribute, which uses the following format:

```
CONTENT="seconds; URL=NewPage"
```

Here, *seconds* is the number of seconds the browser waits before loading the page specified with URL.

The Least You Need to Know

This chapter took you on a Web-based magical multimedia mystery tour that covered animated images, sounds, marquees, and more.

The fun continues in the next chapter where I'll show you how to build forms to get feedback from your surfers.

Need Feedback? Create a Form!

Back in Chapter 5, "Making the Jump to Hyperspace: Adding Links," and Chapter 8, "Images Can Be Links, Too," I showed you how to use hypertext links to add a semblance of interactivity to your pages. However, beyond this basic level of interaction lies a whole genre of Web pages called *forms*. This chapter tells you what forms are all about and takes you step-by-step through the creation of a basic form. I even point out a few resources that you can turn to for processing forms (including a special resource designed just for readers of this book).

What Is a Form, Anyway?

Most modern programs toss a dialog box in your face if they need to extract some information from you. For example, selecting a program's Print command most likely results in some kind of Print dialog box showing up. The purpose of this dialog box is to pester you for information, such as the number of copies you want, the pages you want to print, and so on.

A form is simply the Web-page equivalent of a dialog box. It's a page populated with text boxes, drop-down lists, and command buttons to get information from the user. For example, Figure 11.1 shows a form from my Web site. This is a search form that people can use to search the archives of my Word Spy site. As you can see, it's possible to create forms that look just like dialog boxes.

Figure 11.1

A form used for searching.

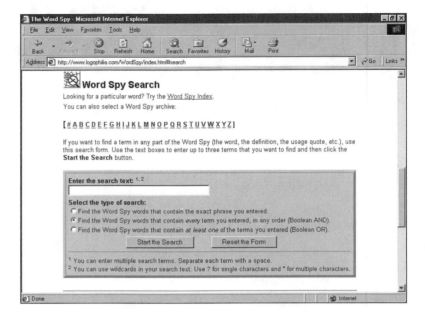

Of course, there are lots of possible uses for forms. If you put out a newsletter or magazine, you can use forms to gather information from subscribers. If your Web site includes pages with restricted access, you can use a form to get a person's user name and password for verification. If you have information in a database, you can use a form to have people specify what type of information they want to access.

Creating a Form

You create forms using special HTML tags, and it's pretty easy to set up a form. (The problem, however, is getting hold of the information that the reader types into the form. Unfortunately, this requires some programming, so it's well beyond the scope of a humble book such as this. So what's a poor, programming-challenged Web wizard to do? Check out the section titled "Oh Say, Can You CGI?" later in this chapter.)

To get started, enter the <FORM> and </FORM> tags. These tags can be inserted anywhere inside the body of the page. You place all the other form-related tags (which I show you in the rest of this chapter) between <FORM> and </FORM>.

The <FORM> tag always includes a couple of extra goodies that tell the Web server how to process the form. Here's the general format:

146

```
<FORM ACTION="url" METHOD=METHOD>
</FORM>
```

Here, the ACTION attribute tells the browser where to send the form's data. This is almost always a program (or *script*, as they're often called) that processes the data and then performs some kind of action (hence the name). The *url* is the URL of the Web page that contains the program.

The METHOD attribute tells the browser how to send the form's data to the URL specified with ACTION. You have two choices here for *METHOD*: POST and GET. Although both work in most cases, GET tends to cause errors in large forms. Therefore, you should always use the POST method.

Let's bring all this gobbledygook down to earth with a concrete example. You can test your forms by using a special script that I host on my server. Here's how to use it:

```
<FORM ACTION="http://www.mcfedries.com/cgi-win/formtest.exe"
METHOD=POST>
```

What this script does is return a page that shows you the data that you entered into the form. You can try this out after you build a working form. Speaking of which, the next few sections take you through the basic form elements.

Making It Go: The Submit Button

Most dialog boxes, as you probably know from hard-won experience, have an OK command button. Clicking this button says, in effect, "All right, I've made my choices. Now go put everything into effect." Forms also have command buttons, and they come in two flavors: submit buttons and reset buttons.

A *submit button* (I talk about the reset button in the next section) is the form equivalent of an OK dialog box button. When the reader clicks the submit button, the form data is shipped out to the program specified by the <FORM> tag's ACTION attribute. Here's the simplest format for the submit button:

```
<INPUT TYPE=SUBMIT>
```

As you'll see, most form elements use some variation on the <INPUT> tag and, as I said before, you place all these tags between <FORM> and </FORM>. In this case, the TYPE=SUBMIT attribute tells the browser to display a command button labeled Submit Query (or, on some browsers, Submit or Send). Note that each form can have just one submit button.

If the standard Submit Query label is a bit too stuffy for your needs, you can make up your own label, as follows:

```
<INPUT TYPE=SUBMIT VALUE="Label">
```

Here, *Label* is the label that appears on the button. In the following example (submit.htm on the CD), I've inserted a submit button with the label Make It So!, and Figure 11.2 shows how it looks in a browser.

```
<HTML>
<HEAD>
<TITLE>Submit Button Custom Label Example</TITLE>
</HEAD>
<BODY>
<H3>An example of a custom label for a submit button:</H3>

<FORM ACTION="http://www.mcfedries.com/cgi-win/formtest.exe"
METHOD=POST>
<INPUT TYPE=SUBMIT VALUE="Make It So!">
</FORM>

</BODY>
</HTML>
```

Figure 11.2

A submit button with a custom label.

Using an Image As a Submit Button

Rather than using a boring command button to submit a form, you might prefer to have the user click an image. That's no sweat. What you need to do is use TYPE=IMAGE for the <INPUT> tag, and add a SRC attribute that specifies the name of the graphics file (much like you do with the <IMG> tag). Here's an example:

```
<INPUT TYPE=IMAGE SRC="go.gif">
```

You should know, too, that when you use an image as a submit button, the test script returns two extra values named "x" and "y". These give you the coordinates of the spot on the image that you clicked. They can be safely ignored.

Starting Over: The Reset Button

If you plan on creating fairly large forms, you can do your readers a big favor by including a reset button somewhere on the form. A reset button clears all the data from the form's fields and re-enters any default values that you specified in the fields. (I explain how to set up default values for each type of field as we go along.) Here's the tag you use to include a reset button:

```
<INPUT TYPE=RESET>
```

This creates a command button labeled Reset. Yes, you can create a custom label by tossing the VALUE attribute into the <INPUT> tag, as in the following example:

```
<INPUT TYPE=RESET VALUE="Start From Scratch">
```

Using Text Boxes for Single-Line Text

For simple text entries, such as a person's name or their favorite Beatle, use text boxes. These are just rectangles within which the reader can type whatever she likes. Here's the basic format for a text box:

```
<INPUT TYPE=TEXT NAME="Field Name">
```

In this case, *Field Name* is a name you assign to the field that's unique among the other fields in the form. For example, to create a text box the reader can use to enter their first name (let's call it First), you'd enter the following:

```
<INPUT TYPE=TEXT NAME="First">
```

For clarity, you also want to precede each text box with a label that tells the reader what kind of information to type in. For example, the following line precedes a text box with First Name: so the reader knows to type in her first name:

```
First Name: <INPUT TYPE=TEXT
NAME="First">
```

Here's some HTML code (textbox.htm on the CD) that utilizes a few text boxes to gather some information from the reader:

```
<HTML>
<HEAD>
<TITLE>Text Box Example</TITLE>
</HEAD>
<BODY>
```

Make 'Em Unique!

It's crucial to remember that every form control must have a unique name. The only exception to this is that a group of related radio buttons (discussed a bit later) must have the same name.

```
<H3>Please tell me about yourself:</H3>

<FORM ACTION="http://www.mcfedries.com/cgi-win/formtest.exe"
METHOD=POST>
First Name: <INPUT TYPE=TEXT NAME="First">
<P>
Last Name: <INPUT TYPE=TEXT NAME="Last">
<P>
Nickname: <INPUT TYPE=TEXT NAME="Nickname">
<P>
Stage Name: <INPUT TYPE=TEXT NAME="Stage">
<P>
<INPUT TYPE=SUBMIT VALUE="Just Do It!">
<INPUT TYPE=RESET VALUE="Just Reset It!">
</FORM>

</BODY>
</HTML>
```

Figure 11.3 shows how it looks in Internet Explorer.

Figure 11.3

A form with a few text boxes.

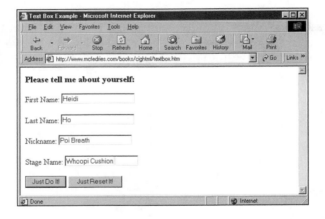

If you run this form (that is, if you click the Just Do It! button), the data is sent to my test script. Why? Because I included the following line:

```
<FORM ACTION="http://www.mcfedries.com/cgi-win/formtest.exe"
➡METHOD=POST>
```

You'd normally replace this ACTION attribute with one that points to a program that does something useful to the data. You don't have such a program right now, so it's safe just to use my script for testing purposes. Remember that this script doesn't do much of anything except send your data back to you. If everything comes back okay (that is, there are no error messages), you know your form is working properly. Just so you know what to expect, Figure 11.4 shows an example of the page that gets returned to you. Notice how the page shows the names of the fields followed by the value the user entered.

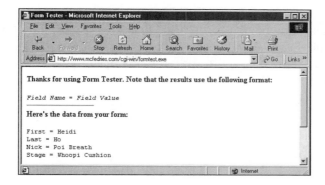

Figure 11.4

An example of the page that's returned when you send the form data to my text script.

Text boxes also come with the following bells and whistles:

Setting the default value If you'd like to put some pre-fab text into the field, include the VALUE attribute in the <INPUT> tag. For example, suppose you want to know the URL of the reader's home page. To include *http://* in the field (because most URLs begin with this), you'd use the following tag:

```
<INPUT TYPE=TEXT NAME="URL" VALUE="http://">
```

Setting the size of the box To determine the length of the text box, use the SIZE attribute. (Note that this attribute affects only the size of the box and not the length of the entry; for the latter, see the MAXLENGTH attribute in the following paragraph.) For example, the following tag displays a text box that's 40 characters long:

```
<INPUT TYPE=TEXT NAME="Address" SIZE=40>
```

Limiting the length of the text In a standard text box, the reader can type away until their fingers are numb. If you'd prefer to restrict the length of the entry, use the MAXLENGTH attribute. For example, the following text box is used to enter a person's age and sensibly restricts the length of the entry to three characters:

```
<INPUT TYPE=TEXT NAME="Age" MAXLENGTH=3>
```

Using Text Areas for Multi-Line Text

If you want to give your readers lots of room to type their hearts out, or if you need multi-line entries (such as an address), you're better off using a *text area* than a text box. A text area is also a rectangle that accepts text input, but text areas can display two or more lines at once. Here's how they work:

```
<TEXTAREA NAME="Field Name" ROWS=TotalRows COLS=TotalColumns WRAP>
</TEXTAREA>
```

Here, *Field Name* is a unique name for the field, *TotalRows* specifies the total number of lines displayed, and *TotalColumns* specifies the total number of columns displayed. The WRAP attribute tells the browser to wrap the text onto the next line whenever the user's typing hits the right edge of the text area.

Note, too, that the <TEXTAREA> tag requires the </TEXTAREA> end tag. (If you want to include default values in the text area, just enter them—on separate lines, if necessary—between <TEXTAREA> and </TEXTAREA>.)

The following HTML tags (textarea.htm on the CD) show a text area in action, and Figure 11.5 shows how it looks in a browser.

```
<HTML>
<HEAD>
<TITLE>Text Area Example</TITLE>
</HEAD>
<BODY>
<H3>Today's Burning Question</H3>
<HR>

<FORM ACTION="http://www.mcfedries.com/cgi-win/formtest.exe"
METHOD=POST>
First Name: <INPUT TYPE=TEXT NAME="First Name">
<p>Last Name: <INPUT TYPE=TEXT NAME="Last Name">
<p>Today's <I>Burning Question</I>: <B>Why is Jerry Lewis so popular
in France?</B>
<p>Please enter your answer in the text area below:
<BR>
<TEXTAREA NAME="Answer" ROWS=10 COLS=60 WRAP>
</TEXTAREA>
<p><INPUT TYPE=SUBMIT VALUE="I Know!">
<INPUT TYPE=RESET>
</FORM>

</BODY>
</HTML>
```

Figure 11.5

An example of a text area.

Toggling an Option On and Off with Check Boxes

If you want to elicit yes/no or true/false information from your readers, check boxes are a lot easier than having the user type in the required data. Here's the general format for an HTML check box:

```
<INPUT TYPE=CHECKBOX NAME="Field Name">
```

As usual, *Field Name* is a unique name for the field. You can also add the CHECKED attribute to the <INPUT> tag, which tells the browser to display the check box "pre-checked." Here's an example:

```
<INPUT TYPE=CHECKBOX NAME="Species" CHECKED>Human
```

Notice in the preceding example that I placed some text beside the <INPUT> tag. This text is used as a label that tells the reader what the check box represents. Here's a longer example (checkbox.htm on the CD) that uses a whole mess of check boxes. Figure 11.6 shows how it looks (I've checked a few of the boxes so you can see how they appear):

```
<HTML>
<HEAD>
<TITLE>Check Box Example</TITLE>
</HEAD>
<BODY>
<H3>Welcome to Hooked On Phobics!</H3>
```

```
<HR>

<FORM ACTION="http://www.mcfedries.com/cgi-win/formtest.exe"
METHOD=POST>
What's <I>your</I> phobia? (Please check all that apply):
<P>
<INPUT TYPE=CHECKBOX NAME="Ants">Myrmecophobia (Fear of ants)<BR>
<INPUT TYPE=CHECKBOX NAME="Bald">Peladophobia (Fear of becoming
bald)<BR>
<INPUT TYPE=CHECKBOX NAME="Beards">Pogonophobia (Fear of beards)<BR>
<INPUT TYPE=CHECKBOX NAME="Bed">Clinophobia (Fear of going to bed)<BR>
<INPUT TYPE=CHECKBOX NAME="Chins">Geniophobia (Fear of chins)<BR>
<INPUT TYPE=CHECKBOX NAME="Flowers">Anthophobia (Fear of flowers)<BR>
<INPUT TYPE=CHECKBOX NAME="Flying">Aviatophobia (Fear of flying)<BR>
<INPUT TYPE=CHECKBOX NAME="Purple">Porphyrophobia (Fear of the color
purple)<BR>
<INPUT TYPE=CHECKBOX NAME="Teeth">Odontophobia (Fear of teeth)<BR>
<INPUT TYPE=CHECKBOX NAME="Thinking">Phronemophobia (Fear of
thinking)<BR>
<INPUT TYPE=CHECKBOX NAME="Vegetables">Lachanophobia (Fear of
vegetables)<BR>
<INPUT TYPE=CHECKBOX NAME="Fear">Phobophobia (Fear of fear)<BR>
<INPUT TYPE=CHECKBOX NAME="Everything">Pantophobia (Fear of
everything)<BR>
<P>
<INPUT TYPE=SUBMIT VALUE="Submit">
<INPUT TYPE=RESET>

</FORM>
</BODY>
</HTML>
```

Check Box Return Values

When you submit a form with a check box, the data returned by the test script is a bit different than with the other controls. For one thing, the script only returns the values for check boxes that were activated; for another, the value returned for these checked check boxes is "on."

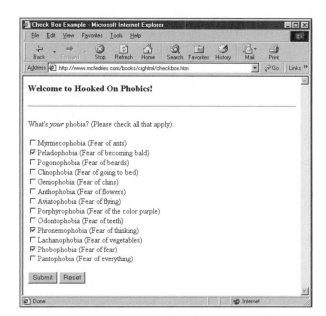

Figure 11.6

Some check box examples.

Multiple Choice Options: Radio Buttons

Instead of yes/no choices, you might want your readers to have a choice of three or four options. In this case, radio buttons are your best bet. With radio buttons, the user gets two or more options, but they can pick only one.

Here's the general format:

```
<INPUT TYPE=RADIO NAME="Field Name"
VALUE="Value">
```

Field Name is the usual field name, except in this case you supply the same name to *all* the radio buttons. That way, the browser knows which buttons are grouped together. *Value* is a unique text string that specifies the value of the option when it's selected. In addition, you can also add CHECKED to one of the buttons to have the browser activate the option by default. The following HTML document (radiobtn.htm on the CD) puts a few radio buttons through their paces, as shown in Figure 11.7.

"Radio" Buttons?

In a rare burst of nerd whimsy, the HTML powers-that-be named these controls after the old car radio buttons that you had to push to select a station.

```
<HTML>
<HEAD>
<TITLE>Radio Button Example</TITLE>
</HEAD>
```

155

```
<BODY>
<H3>Survey</H3>
<HR>

<FORM ACTION="http://www.mcfedries.com/cgi-win/formtest.exe"
METHOD=POST>
Which of the following best describes your current salary level:
<DL><DD>
<INPUT TYPE=RADIO NAME="Salary" VALUE="Poverty" CHECKED>Below the
poverty line<BR>
<INPUT TYPE=RADIO NAME="Salary" VALUE="Living">Living wage<BR>
<INPUT TYPE=RADIO NAME="Salary" VALUE="Comfy">Comfy<BR>
<INPUT TYPE=RADIO NAME="Salary" VALUE="DINK">DINK (Double Income, No
Kids)<BR>
<INPUT TYPE=RADIO NAME="Salary"
VALUE="Rockefellerish">Rockefellerish<BR>
</DL>
Which of the following best describes your political leanings:
<DL><DD>
<INPUT TYPE=RADIO NAME="Politics" VALUE="Way Left" CHECKED>So far
left, I'm right<BR>
<INPUT TYPE=RADIO NAME="Politics" VALUE="Yellow Dog">Yellow Dog
Democrat<BR>
<INPUT TYPE=RADIO NAME="Politics" VALUE="Middle">Right down the
middle<BR>
<INPUT TYPE=RADIO NAME="Politics" VALUE="Republican">Country Club
Republican<BR>
<INPUT TYPE=RADIO NAME="Politics" VALUE="Way Right">So far right, I'm
left<BR>
</UL>
<P>
<INPUT TYPE=SUBMIT VALUE="Submit">
<INPUT TYPE=RESET>
</FORM>

</BODY>
</HTML>
```

Selecting from Lists

Radio buttons are a great way to give your readers multiple choices, but they get unwieldy if you have more than about five or six options. For longer sets of options, you're better off using lists, or *selection lists* as they're called in the HTML world. Selection lists are a wee bit more complex than the other form tags we've looked at, but not by much. Here's the general format:

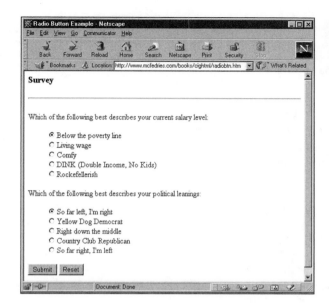

Figure 11.7

A form that uses radio buttons for multiple-choice input.

```
<SELECT NAME="Field Name" SIZE=Items>
<OPTION>First item text</OPTION>
<OPTION>Second item text</OPTION>
<OPTION>And so on...</OPTION>
</SELECT>
```

As I'm sure you've guessed by now, *Field Name* is the unique name for the list. For the SIZE attribute, *Items* is the number of items you want the browser to display. If you omit SIZE, the list becomes a drop-down list. If SIZE is 2 or more, the list becomes a rectangle with scrollbars for navigating the choices. Also, you can insert the MULTI-PLE attribute into the <SELECT> tag. This tells the browser to enable the user to select multiple items from the list.

Between the <SELECT> and </SELECT> tags are the <OPTION></OPTION> tags; these define the list items. If you add the SELECTED attribute to one of the items, the browser selects that item by default.

To get some examples on the table, the following document (lists.htm on the CD) defines no less than three selection lists. Figure 11.8 shows what the Internet Explorer browser does with them.

```
<HTML>
<HEAD>
<TITLE>Selection List Example</TITLE>
</HEAD>
<BODY>
<H3>Putting On Hairs: Reader Survey</H3>
<HR>
```

157

```
<FORM ACTION="http://www.mcfedries.com/cgi-win/formtest.exe"
METHOD=POST>
Select your hair color:<BR>
<SELECT NAME="Color">
<OPTION>Black</OPTION>
<OPTION>Blonde</OPTION>
<OPTION SELECTED>Brunette</OPTION>
<OPTION>Red</OPTION>
<OPTION>Something neon</OPTION>
<OPTION>None</OPTION>
</SELECT>
<P>

Select your hair style:<BR>
<SELECT NAME="Style" SIZE=7>
<OPTION>Bouffant</OPTION>
<OPTION>Mohawk</OPTION>
<OPTION>Page Boy</OPTION>
<OPTION>Permed</OPTION>
<OPTION>Shag</OPTION>
<OPTION SELECTED>Straight</OPTION>
<OPTION>Style? What style?</OPTION>
</SELECT>
<P>

Hair products used in the last year:<BR>
<SELECT NAME="Products" SIZE=5 MULTIPLE>
<OPTION>Gel</OPTION>
<OPTION>Grecian Formula</OPTION>
<OPTION>Mousse</OPTION>
<OPTION>Peroxide</OPTION>
<OPTION>Shoe black</OPTION>
</SELECT>
<P>
<INPUT TYPE=SUBMIT VALUE="Hair Mail It!">
<INPUT TYPE=RESET>
</FORM>

</BODY>
</HTML>
```

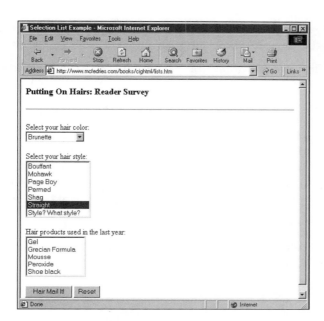

Figure 11.8

A form with a few selection list examples.

Oh Say, Can You CGI?

All this form folderol is fine, but what good is a form if it doesn't really do much of anything? That is, why bother building a fancy form if you have no way to get the data? Unfortunately, as I mentioned earlier, grabbing form data and manipulating it is a programmer's job. Specifically, you have to use something called the *Common Gateway Interface*, or CGI for short. CGI is a method of transferring form data in a manner that makes it relatively easy to incorporate into a program and then massage it all you need. Easy, that is, if you have the requisite nerd skills.

Well, I might not have room to teach you how to program forms, and you might not have the inclination in any case, but that doesn't mean you're totally stuck. The next few sections give you some ideas for getting your forms to do something useful.

A Service Exclusively for Readers

The easy solution to this CGI stuff is to have a helpful author write a program that you can use for submitting your form data. And that's exactly what I've done. I've created a program called MailForm that takes form data and emails it to an address you specify.

To use MailForm, begin by setting up your <FORM> tag as follows:

```
<FORM ACTION="http://www.mcfedries.com/cgi-win/mailform.exe"
➥METHOD=POST>
```

159

Next, create a new Web page that contains some kind of "Thank you" message. This page is displayed to the user after they submit your form.

Finally, return to your form, and somewhere between your <FORM> and </FORM> tags, insert the following lines:

```
<INPUT TYPE=HIDDEN NAME="MFAddress" VALUE="YourEmail">
<INPUT TYPE=HIDDEN NAME="MFSubject" VALUE="Subject">
<INPUT TYPE=HIDDEN NAME="MFReturn" VALUE="ThanksPage">
```

Here, *YourEmail* is the email address to which you want to send the form's data, *Subject* is the Subject line used with the message, and *ThanksPage* is the full address (including the "http://" part) of the thank you page you created earlier.

For example, consider the following lines:

```
<INPUT TYPE=HIDDEN NAME="MFAddress" VALUE="biff@iguana.com">
<INPUT TYPE=HIDDEN NAME="MFSubject" VALUE="Guest Book Entry">
<INPUT TYPE=HIDDEN NAME="MFReturn"
VALUE="http://www.my.com/thanks.htm">
```

When the form is submitted, an email message with the rest of the form's data and the Subject line "Guest Book Entry" is sent to biff@iguana.com, and then the user sees the thanks.htm page.

Here are some pointers for working with MailForm:

➤ **Adding "mailto" automatically**   If your form includes a field for entering an email address, MailForm adds mailto: to the beginning of the address automatically, provided you name the field *email*, like so:

```
<INPUT TYPE=TEXT NAME="email">
```

➤ **Sending form data to another address**   If you like, you can have the form data sent to two different email addresses. To do this, set up your MFAddress value to specify two addresses, which must be separated either by a comma or a semicolon . Here's an example:

```
<INPUT TYPE=HIDDEN NAME="MFAddress"
VALUE="me@here.com;you@there.com">
```

The first address is sent as the To field and the second address is sent as the Cc field.

➤ **Contacting the person who filled in your form**   MailForm has no way of determining the email address of any person who fills in your form. If you want to be able to contact a form user, you must include some kind of text field where the user can enter his email address.

➤ **Don't reply to MailForm messages**
Along similar lines, don't click **Reply**
when you get a MailForm message sent
to you. All this does is send the response
back to my server, which is very annoying!

➤ **Viewing the thanks page within a
frame**   If your MailForm form lies
within a framed page, you probably
want the thank you page displayed
within a particular frame, as well. (I
explain frames in the next chapter.)
Here's how you can do it: include the
TARGET attribute within the <FORM>
tag. For example, if you want the thank
you page to appear within a frame
named "Right," you'd do this:

Check This Out

**Making Form Fields
Mandatory**

To ensure that you can contact a
user, make the email field mandatory. I show you a bit of JavaScript
that can do this in Chapter 17,
"More JavaScript Fun."

```
<FORM ACTION="http://www.mcfedries.com/cgi-win/mailform.exe"
➥METHOD=POST TARGET="Right">
```

➤ **Sorry, MailForm is nontransferable**   The most common MailForm question I
get asked is "Can I get a copy of it to use on my own site?" Nope. MailForm is
set up so that it can only run on my server.

Please remember that I created this service *only* for the readers of *The Complete Idiot's
Guide to Creating a Web Page.* Please do not spread the word to all and sundry that this
service is available. Also, this program is for personal or very light commercial use
only. If you're running a large, commercial site, I urge you to spend the bucks to get
a proper CGI script written. This will help keep the load on my poor server to a
minimum.

Bear in mind as well that your form is dependent on my server for processing the
data. If my server is down for some reason, your form won't work. My server is available most of the time, but you have to expect some downtime. People who abso-
tively, posolutely *must* have reliable service should consider getting a commercial
provider that specializes in this kind of thing.

Ask Your Provider

Many people want to add simple guest books and feedback mechanisms to their sites,
but they don't want to have to bother with the programming aspect. So, in response to their customers' needs, most Web hosting providers make some simple CGI
scripts (programs) available to their customers. For example, one common type of
script grabs form data, extracts the field names and values, and sends them to an
email address you specify (like my MailForm program). Check with the provider's

161

administrator or Webmaster to see if they have any CGI scripts that you can use. And if you haven't settled on a provider yet, you should ask in advance if they have CGI programs available.

The CGI-Joe Route

A more expensive alternative is to hire the services of a CGI wizard (also known as a *CGI-Joe* in Web programming circles) to create a custom program for you. Most Web hosting providers are only too happy to put together a nice little program tailored to your needs. There's also no shortage of hired guns on the Web who create programs to your specifications. As a starting point, check out some of the resources mentioned in the next section.

Check Out the Web's CGI Resources

If your service provider or Web hosting provider doesn't have ready-to-run CGI programs that you can use, there's no shortage of sites on the Net that are willing and able to either teach you CGI or supply you with programs. This section runs through a list of some of these sites (see cgisites.htm on the CD).

Mind Your CGI Program Ps and Qs

Note that if you grab a program or two to use, you need to contact your service provider's administrator to get the full lowdown on how to set up the program. In most cases, the administrator will want to examine the program code to make sure it's up to snuff. If it passes muster, it is put in a special directory (usually called a cgi-bin), and then you can refer to the program in your form.

Bravenet

http://www.bravenet.com/

This site offers lots of free scripts and other Webmaster goodies.

CGI 101

http://www.cgi101.com/

As its name implies, this site offers beginner-level training and tutorials for CGI wanna-be programmers. It also offers CGI hosting, links to other CGI sites, and much more.

The CGI Collection

http://www.itm.com/cgicollection/

This is a nice site with lots of links to scripts, tutorials, mailing lists, books, and much more.

The CGI Directory

http://www.cgidir.com/

This site is bursting at the seams with great CGI info. There are tutorials, book reviews, a FAQ, links to other CGI sites, and hundreds of scripts.

The CGI Resource Index

http://www.cgi-resources.com/

If there's a good CGI resource on the Web, this site knows about it. It has thousands of links to scripts, tutorials, articles, programmers for hire, and much more.

Extropia

http://www.extropia.com/

This site is the brainchild of Selena Sol and Gunther Birznieks, and it's one of the best CGI resources on the Web.

Matt's Script Archive

http://www.worldwidemart.com/scripts/

Matt Wright has written tons of CGI scripts and graciously offers them gratis to the Web community. He has scripts for a guest book, random link generator, animation, and lots more. It's a great site and a must for would-be CGI mavens.

NCSA—The Common Gateway Interface

http://hoohoo.ncsa.uiuc.edu/cgi/

This is *the* place on the Web for CGI info. NCSA (the same folks who made the original Mosaic browser) has put together a great collection of tutorials, tips, and sample programs.

ScriptSearch

http://www.scriptsearch.com/

This site bills itself as "The World's Largest CGI Library," and with thousands of scripts in dozens of categories, I can believe it.

Usenet

comp.infosystems.www.authoring.cgi

This newsgroup is a useful spot for CGI tips and tricks, and it's just a good place to hang around with fellow Web programmers.

Yahoo!'s CGI Index

http://www.yahoo.com/Computers_and_Internet/Internet/World_Wide_Web/
CGI___Common_Gateway_Interface/

This is a long list of CGI-related resources. Many of the links have either CGI how-to info or actual programs you can use.

The Least You Need to Know

This chapter introduced you to the fabulous world of forms. The next chapter tackles yet another HTML "F" word: frames.

WHOO-HOO! YEEE-HA!!

Chapter 12

Fooling Around with Frames

In This Chapter

➤ What frames are all about

➤ How to get a basic frame layout up and running

➤ Tweaking frames to get them just so

➤ How to handle browsers that don't understand frames

➤ A step-by-step approach with the aim to tame the frame game

---

Like most guys, I enjoy technology and take every opportunity to ring the bells and blow the whistles on whatever new techtoy comes my way. Take picture-in-picture (PIP) for instance. I think the engineering genius who came up with PIP should be awarded some kind of Nobel Geeks Prize. For my money, it's just insanely great to be able to leave one channel in view while you surf around to see what else is happening.

Whether you're a PIP fan or foe, you'll be interested to know that you can apply the PIP concept to your Web pages. That is, you can set up your site so that one page remains in view in part of the browser screen and your visitors can use the rest of the screen to trip the link fantastic. The secret to this seemingly miraculous feat is a concept called *frames*, and you learn all about it in this chapter.

What's with All the Frame Fuss?

The competent Web forger always includes a section on each page that enables the user to navigate the important landmarks in their site. This could be a collection of links, a Web page "toolbar" (like the ones I showed you how to whip up back in Chapter 8, "Images Can Be Links, Too"), or an image map (again, see Chapter 8). The problem with these navigation sections, though, is that they end up scrolling off the screen whenever the reader moves down the page. (This is assuming the navigation stuff is sitting at the top of the page.) For example, Figure 12.1 shows a page from my site, and Figure 12.2 shows what happens if you scroll down to read more of the text.

Figure 12.1

A page from my site showing my navigation aids at the top.

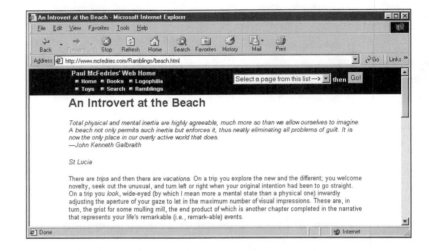

Figure 12.2

Where oh where have my links gone?

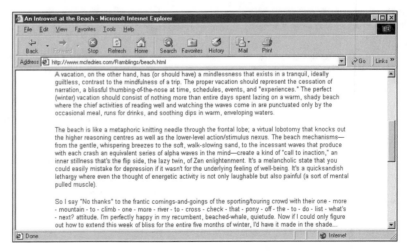

Figure 12.1 shows the various navigation aids that I've plopped onto the top of all the pages on my site. As you can see in the second figure, however, after I scroll down a bit, those navigation doodads are gone like wild geese in winter.

Now have a gander at Figure 12.3. See how I've scrolled down to the same spot, but the navigation section remains conveniently in view. Weird, huh? The window seems to be divided into two sections: The top section holds the navigation knickknacks, and the bottom section shows the regular page text and graphics. What the heck is happening here?

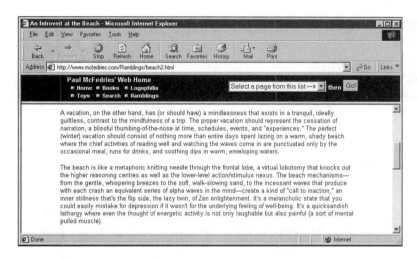

Figure 12.3

This version of the page mysteriously displays the navigation stuff in its own section at the top of the page.

To perform this magic trick, I had to do three things:

➤ I grabbed the HTML tags and text that make up my navigation section, and I put it all into a separate file called header.html.

➤ I grabbed the rest of the page text and put it into another file called beach-f.html.

➤ I created a third page called beach2.html that has a few special tags that serve to divide the browser window into two *frames*. I included in this page the instructions to load the header.html file into the top frame, and the beach-f.html file into the bottom frame.

The big deal is that with this view, surfers can scroll through beach-f.html in the bottom frame until they're blue in the face, and the navigation section remains steadfastly in place. It's even possible to arrange things so that if you click any link, the new page appears in the bottom frame. In other words, the top frame is really the Web equivalent of picture-in-picture!

Okay, now that you know what frames are and why you might want to bother with them, let's see how you go about constructing them.

167

Forging a Frame Page

The good news about frames is that you can build them using just a few not-too-hard-to-master HTML tags. Unfortunately, most frame neophytes get thrown for a loop right off the bat because the first thing you have to create is a Web page that doesn't display anything! *Huh*?

Let me explain. After you enter the frames world, you're faced with not one, but *two* species of Web page:

➤ **Content pages**   A content page is just a regular HTML page like the ones you've dealt with throughout this book. That is, they display text, graphics, and whatever other goodies the author packs into the page.

➤ **Frame pages**   A frame page has only one mission in life: to define the size of each frame and specify which HTML documents are displayed in each frame. Note that you can't add regular text or HTML tags to frame pages. If you try, the browser simply ignores your efforts completely and concentrates solely on the frame information.

In other words, the frame page is really just an empty shell like, say, an ice cube tray. An ice cube tray doesn't do much of anything by itself, and it only becomes useful after you fill in the compartments with water. It's the same with a frame page: It just divvies up the browser screen into two or more frames, and you have to fill these compartments with separate content pages.

The Basic Frame Tags

Building a frame page requires two tag types: <FRAMESET> and <FRAME>. The idea is that you begin with <FRAMESET> and between this tag and its corresponding </FRAMESET> end tag, you add one <FRAME> tag for each frame you want to work with. So, to divide the browser window into two frames, you start like this:

```
<FRAMESET>
<FRAME>
<FRAME>
</FRAMESET>
```

Now you have to tell the browser whether you want the frames to divide the screen horizontally or vertically.

Dividing the Screen Horizontally

If you want the frame divider to run horizontally so that the screen is cleaved into a top part and a bottom part, you toss the ROWS attribute inside the <FRAMESET> tag:

```
<FRAMESET ROWS="Size1,Size2,...">
```

Here, *Size1* and *Size2* are numbers that tell the browser how much screen real estate to give to each frame. There are two types of numbers you can use:

➤ **Percentages** Use percentages to assign a portion of the browser window to each frame. You need to include a percentage value for each frame, and the percentages should add up to 100.

➤ **Pixels** Use pixels if you know exactly how tall you want a frame to be.

For example, suppose you have two frames and you want the top frame to usurp 25% of the screen and the bottom to take the remaining 75%. Here's an HTML file (see frame1.htm on the CD) that does the job:

```
<HTML>
<HEAD>
<TITLE>Horizontal Frames</TITLE>
</HEAD>
<FRAMESET ROWS="25%,75%">
<FRAME>
<FRAME>
</FRAMESET>
</HTML>
```

If you load this sucker into a browser, you see the rather uninspiring screen shown in Figure 12.4. Now you see what I meant earlier when I said that the frame page is just an empty shell!

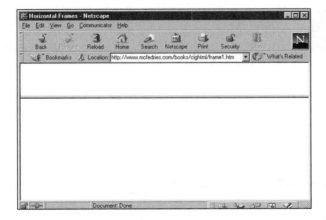

Figure 12.4

A frame page that divides the browser screen horizontally.

Dividing the Screen Vertically

If you'd prefer that the frame divider run vertically to cut the screen into left and right sections, you populate the <FRAMESET> tag with the COLS (columns) attribute and some numbers:

Trying the Asterisk on for Size

It's a common frame scenario to want to give one frame a certain size and to want the second frame to take up whatever room is left in the window. To do the latter, enter an asterisk as the size of the second frame. For example, if you want the top frame's height to be 100 pixels and the bottom frame to take up whatever's left, you'd use this tag:

```
<FRAMESET ROWS="100,*">
```

```
<FRAMESET COLS="Size1,Size2,...">
```

Again, *Size1* and *Size2* tell the browser how much of the window to parcel out to each frame. Here's another HTML file (frame2.htm on the CD) that divides the browser screen into three sections that take up 20%, 60%, and 20% of the screen. Figure 12.5 shows the frames loaded into Internet Explorer.

```
<HTML>
<HEAD>
<TITLE>Vertical Frames</TITLE>
</HEAD>
<FRAMESET COLS="20%,60%,20%">
<FRAME>
<FRAME>
<FRAME>
</FRAMESET>
</HTML>
```

Filling the Frames with Content Pages

The nearly naked frame pages you've seen so far aren't too exciting. What happens if you add some regular text or even an <IMG> tag or two? That's an easy one: not a gosh-darned thing! Feel free to type away until your fingers fall off, but you won't get the browser to show anything but the empty frames.

So how do you fill in the frames? You have to specify a separate content page to show in each frame. You do that by adding an SRC attribute into each of the <FRAME> tags. Here's the general format:

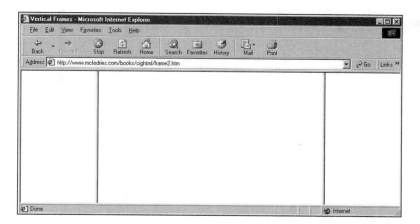

```
<FRAME SRC="URL">
```

As you might expect, the *URL* part is the address of the Web page you want to display in the frame. Here's an example (frame3.htm on the CD):

```
<HTML>
<HEAD>
<TITLE>Horizontal Frames with Content</TITLE>
</HEAD>
<FRAMESET ROWS="25%,75%">
<FRAME SRC="1.htm">
<FRAME SRC="2.htm">
</FRAMESET>
</HTML>
```

Here, 1.htm and 2.htm are just regular HTML Web pages. Figure 12.6 shows how things look in the browser.

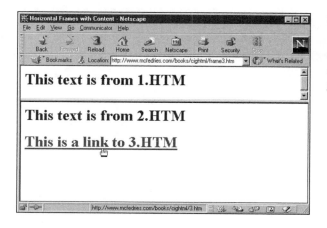

Figure 12.6

To get the frame page to show something useful, specify a separate content page for each frame.

171

Teaching Frames and Links to Get Along

What happens if one of your framed content pages contains a link? Well, clicking the link loads the page as usual, but you can't be sure *where* the page appears. In some browsers, the new page takes over the entire window and your carefully laid out frames are toast. In other browsers, the new page appears in a separate window.

To avoid this random behavior, you need to control exactly where the linked pages show up. The trick is that you first have to assign a name to each frame. After that's done, it becomes an easy matter of modifying your link tags to specify the name of the frame in which you want the page to load.

To assign a name to a frame, you drop the NAME attribute inside the <FRAME> tag, like so:

```
<FRAME SRC="something.htm" NAME="Whatever">
```

For example, here's an updated frame page (frame4.htm on the CD) that includes names for the upper and lower frame:

```
<HTML>
<HEAD>
<TITLE>Named Horizontal Frames</TITLE>
</HEAD>
<FRAMESET ROWS="25%,75%">
<FRAME SRC="1.htm" NAME="Upper">
<FRAME SRC="2.htm" NAME="Lower">
</FRAMESET>
</HTML>
```

With your frames named, you can make any link load inside a particular frame by adding a TARGET attribute to the <A HREF> tag. For example, here's the <A HREF> tag from 2.HTM:

```
<A HREF="3.htm" TARGET="Lower">This is a link to 3.HTM</A>
```

As you can see, the TARGET attribute is set to Lower, which is the name of the bottom frame. Clicking this link, therefore, loads the new page in this frame, as shown in Figure 12.7.

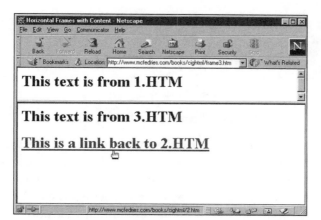

Figure 12.7

Adding TARGET to a link tag forces the new page to load inside the specified frame.

Why Some Folks Say "Fie!" to Frames

You'll notice in the previous figure that even though I clicked a link to load 2.htm into the bottom frame, Netscape's Location box still shows the same URL (that is, the URL of the page containing the <FRAMESET> and <FRAME> tags). That's one of the downsides to frames: The displayed address doesn't change as your readers click from link to link, so the viewers never really know where they are within your site.

Ready-Made Names for Frames

HTML also has three pre-fab frame names that you can specify with the TARGET attribute:

_self	Loads the new page into the same frame that contains the link.
_top	Loads the new page into the entire window.
_blank	Loads the new page into a new browser window.

173

Getting Out of Someone Else's Frames

In frame circles, proper etiquette dictates that links to external sites should either take over the entire screen (TARGET="_top") or should be displayed in a separate browser window (TARGET="_blank"). Unfortunately, many framesters don't follow this etiquette and, instead, greedily display *every* link within their frames. Besides cursing their ancestry, what can you do to make sure that *your* page doesn't get jailed within someone else's frames? Include a link on your page that points to the same page, but uses the TARGET="_top" attribute. For example, if your page is named index.html, add a link like this one:

```
<A HREF="index.html" TARGET="_top">Deframe this page</A>
```

Clicking this link will reload your page without the surrounding frame.

Specifying a Default Target

What do you do if you have a frame that contains tons of links? Do you really have to go through the drudgery of adding the TARGET tag to all those <A> tags? Happily, no, you don't. It's possible to specify a default target, and the browser will send every linked page to whatever frame you specify.

To set the default target, add the following tag to the head section (that is, between the <HEAD> and </HEAD> tags) of the page that contains all the links:

```
<BASE TARGET="Whatever">
```

Frame Frills and Frippery

The frames we've seen so far are serviceable beasts. However, the <FRAME> tag comes with a few extra options that you might need to use. Here's a quick summary of these attributes:

NORESIZE   Stick this attribute inside the <FRAME> tag to prevent surfers from changing the size of the frame. (Otherwise, the frame can be resized by dragging the frame border with the mouse.)

SCROLLING   This attribute determines whether or not a scrollbar appears with a frame. If you set this to YES (that is, SCROLLING=YES) and the content page is too big to fit entirely inside the frame, a scrollbar appears on the right side of the frame. Use SCROLLING=NO to prevent the scrollbar from appearing.

BORDER   Set this attribute to 0 to tell the browser not to display the border between frames. For now, this only works in Netscape version 3.0 and up. For Internet Explorer, try setting FRAMEBORDER to 0, instead.

Handling Frame-Feeble Browsers

I mentioned earlier that you can't add regular text or HTML tags to a frame page. (Actually, you could if you put in a <BODY> tag. However, this would nullify the <FRAMESET> tag, so it would defeat the purpose.) So what happens when a browser that doesn't understand frames comes across your frame page? You guessed it, it doesn't display anything!

This isn't a great way to welcome these surfers to your site, to say the least. However, there is a way to handle these non-frame browsers and at least give them something to chew on. It's called the <NOFRAMES> tag. Any text or HTML tags you insert between this tag and its </NOFRAMES> end tag shows up in a frameless browser. For example, here's the HTML for a page (frame5.htm on the CD) that includes the <NOFRAMES> tag, and you can see the result in Figure 12.8:

```
<HTML>
<HEAD>
<TITLE>Handling Lame Frame Browsers</TITLE>
</HEAD>
<FRAMESET ROWS="25%,75%">
<FRAME SRC="1.htm" NAME="Upper">
<FRAME SRC="2.htm" NAME="Lower">
<NOFRAMES>
<H3>Doh! Looks like you have a browser that is frames-challenged.
<P>
Here's a <A HREF="2.htm">frame-free page</A> that should be more to
your browser's liking.</H3>
</NOFRAMES>
</FRAMESET>
</HTML>
```

Figure 12.8

Frame-ignorant browsers ignore the frame-related tags and just display the other text.

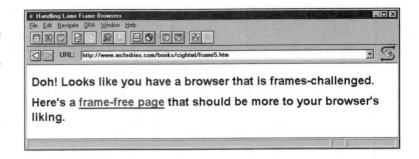

Now wait just a cotton-picking minute! If a browser can't handle frames, how can it know about the <NOFRAMES> tag?

Good question! The answer is that it doesn't. These older browsers are really just bypassing the <FRAMESET> and <FRAME> tags and displaying whatever other text is in the file. The <NOFRAMES> tag actually serves to prevent frame-capable browsers from displaying the text.

Oh.

Frame-Ignorant Browsers Are Rare

Don't sweat this <NOFRAMES> business too much. These days, only a microscopically small percentage of users surf with a browser that doesn't understand frames, so it's probably not worth the hassle to accommodate them. Still, using <NOFRAMES> is good practice and shows how courteous you are.

Fancier Frames

To finish this frames tutorial, let's kick things up a notch and look at a technique that enables you to create some pretty fancy frame effects.

So far, you've only learned how to divide the browser window into horizontal regions or vertical regions. What do you do if you want to combine these types? For example, suppose you define an upper frame and a lower frame and you then want to divide the lower frame into two vertical sections? Well, it turns out that you can use as many <FRAMESET> tags as you like in a single frame page. So you can get your desired layout by defining one <FRAMESET> tag to divide the screen in two horizontally and then insert a second <FRAMESET> tag that divides the lower region vertically. Here's the code for an HTML page (frame6.htm on the CD) that does this:

```
<HTML>
<HEAD>
<TITLE>Nested Frames</TITLE>
</HEAD>
<FRAMESET ROWS="25%,75%">
<FRAME SRC="1.htm" NAME="Upper">
   <FRAMESET COLS="50%,50%">
   <FRAME SRC="2.htm" NAME="Lower">
   <FRAME SRC="3.htm" NAME="Right">
   </FRAMESET>
</FRAMESET>
</HTML>
```

This technique is called *nesting* frames, and you can use it to create whatever layout suits your needs. Figure 12.9 shows how the example looks in the browser.

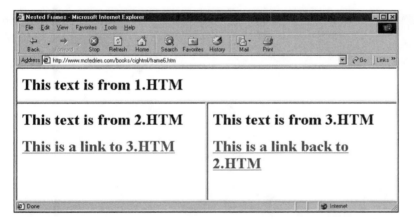

Figure 12.9

You can nest frames to achieve some interesting layouts.

The Least You Need to Know

This chapter cranked up your HTML know-how a notch or two by showing you how to harness the power of frames.

You'll continue breathing some rarefied HTML air in Part 3 when I show you how to use the fancy style sheets that everyone's talking about.

177

Part 3

High HTML Style: Working with Style Sheets

After unveiling a new site to friends, family, and colleagues, you might receive constructive criticisms instead of constant kudos. Grrrr. You mutter a few choice epithets under your breath, but then you realize that, hey, they're right. The changes really would make your pages look better. So, conscientious Webmeister that you are, you begin the long and laborious process of opening all the pages and editing the dozens of tags that determine the look of each page. Sigh. There's got to be a better way.

If making large-scale changes to your Web site is getting you down, I have some good news. There's some HTML technology that will enable you to change fonts, colors, and other features for 2 or 102 pages with only a few keystrokes! This miraculous bit of techno-trickery is called a style sheet and you learn how it works here in Part 3.

Chapter 13

A Beginner's Guide to Style Sheets

In This Chapter

➤ Understanding style sheets

➤ Three methods of using style sheets

➤ Applying styles to sections, words, and phrases

➤ Numerous other style sheet shenanigans

This chapter gets your style sheet education off to an easy start by introducing you ever-so-gently to this brave new Web world. You learn just what styles and sheets are, how they affect your pages, and why they're so darned useful. You also learn the basic methods for incorporating style sheets into your pages. Although I run through a few examples in this chapter, the real style sheet goods can be found in the next two chapters where I delve into the style sheet specifics for things like text, paragraphs, positioning, margins, and more.

What's a Style, and What's a Sheet?

If you've ever used a fancy-schmancy word processor such as Microsoft Word or WordPerfect, then you've probably stumbled over a style or two in your travels. In a nutshell, a style is a combination of two or more formatting options rolled into one nice, neat package. For example, you might have a "Title" style that combines four formatting options: bold, centered, 24-point type size, and an Arial typeface. You can then "apply" this style to any text and the program dutifully formats the text with all four options. If you later change your mind and decide your titles should use an 18-point font, instead, all you have to do is redefine the Title style. The program then trudges through the entire document and updates each bit of text that uses the Title style.

Styles in the HTML Universe

In HTML, a style performs a similar function. That is, it enables you to define a series of formatting options for a given tag, such as <P> or <H1>. Like word processor styles, HTML styles offer two main advantages:

➤ They save time because you create the definition of the style's formatting once, and the browser applies that formatting each time you use the tag.

➤ They make your pages easier to modify because all you need to do is edit the style definition and all the places the style is used within the page get updated automatically.

Let's eyeball an example. The browser window below shows the following HTML file (see ssbefore.htm on the CD), which contains just a single <H1> heading, and you can see the result in Figure 13.1:

```
<HTML>
<HEAD>
<TITLE>Style Sheets: Before</TITLE>
</HEAD>
<BODY>
<H1>Style Sheets: What's the Big Whoop?</H1>
</BODY>
</HTML>
```

Figure 13.1

A simple Web page, showing just a single <H1> heading.

Now suppose you prefer to use bigger text in your heading. You can't change the size of <H1> headings directly, but you could do it by changing the SIZE attribute of the <FONT> tag, like this:

```
<FONT SIZE=7>
Style Sheets: What's the Big Whoop?
</FONT>
```

That's no big deal if you have only one or two headings, but what if you use dozens of them? Not only is it a pain to add those <FONT> tags, but it also makes your HTML source code more difficult to read.

A better solution is to create a style for the <H1> tag that tells the browser to use a larger font size for the <H1> text. The following HTML file (see ssafter.htm on the CD) shows you one way to do it, and Figure 13.2 displays the results (I explain the specifics of this a bit later):

```
<HTML>
<HEAD>
<TITLE>Style Sheets: After</TITLE>

<STYLE>
H1 {font-size: 34pt}
</STYLE>

</HEAD>
<BODY>
<H1>Style Sheets: What's the Big Whoop?</H1>
</BODY>
</HTML>
```

Figure 13.2

Use a style to get a larger heading.

Note the new <STYLE> tag and, in particular, the following line:

```
H1 {font-size: 34pt}
```

What this tells the browser is that, each time it comes across the <H1> tag, it should format the text with a 34-point font size.

And it's easy to make a change if you decide that you want your heading even larger. For example, if you want to use a 72-point font size (what newspaper types called "Second Coming" type), you need only make a single change (see ssafter2.htm on the CD):

```
<HTML>
<HEAD>

<STYLE>
H1 {font-size: 72pt}
```

183

```
</STYLE>

</HEAD>
<BODY>
<H1>Style Sheets: What's the Big Whoop?</H1>
</BODY>
</HTML>
```

Figure 13.3 shows how it looks with Internet Explorer.

Figure 13.3

Styles make it easy to change the formatting in your pages.

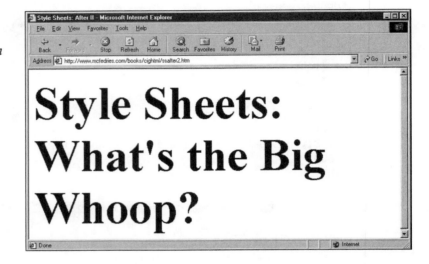

Combining formats into one easy-to-use bundle is a nifty timesaver, and it's worth the price of admission alone. However, style sheets have a few other tricks up their digital sleeves, tricks that enable you to do things that are either difficult or downright impossible with your garden-variety HTML tags. For example, displaying text at a 72-point type size, as shown in Figure 13.3, is impossible under plain HTML. Here's some other style sheet sleight-of-hand you can do:

➤ You can set a background color or image for paragraphs or even single words.

➤ You can define a margin around your page.

➤ You can indent text precisely.

Sheets: Collections of Styles

So far so good, but what the heck is a sheet?

The term *style sheet* harkens back to the days of yore when word processors enabled you to store your styles in a separate document known as a style sheet. This is equivalent to what we would probably call a template, today. As you see later on, it's possible to define all your HTML styles in a separate page and then tell the browser where that page is located, so it's a bit like a style sheet (although *style file* might have been a better—and more fun—name). More generally, an HTML style sheet is any collection of styles, whether it exists in a separate page or within the current page (as in the previous example).

What About Browser Support?

Style sheets have come a long way in the past couple of years. Once an obscure section of the HTML 4.0 standard, style sheets are now a much-traveled part of the Web design landscape. The reason style sheets have come into their own is simple: most modern browsers support them.

Technically, style sheet support is built into Internet Explorer versions 3.0 and later, and Netscape Navigator versions 4.0 and later. However, that accounts for the bulk of browser traffic today. For example, my Web pages for this book (`http://www.mcfedries.com/books/cightml/`) have a Browser Stats section that shows the percentage of visitors who use different versions of Internet Explorer and Netscape Navigator. It also tracks Style Sheet-Friendly Browsers. As I write this, that number is 95.8%, and it's growing steadily.

Therefore, it's perfectly safe to go ahead and start learning and using style sheets right away. Those few style sheet-ignorant browsers that visit your pages ignore the extra tags (and you can use HTML comment tags to block out other style-related text), so no harm comes to your pages.

Some Style Basics

Before I show you how to implement style sheets, let's take a second to get a grip on just what a style looks like. As an example, let's put the style we used earlier under the microscope. Here it is again:

```
H1 {font-size: 34pt}
```

This is called a *style definition*, and here's a rundown of the various parts:

➤ The definition always begins with the HTML tag that you want the style to modify, without the usual angle brackets (< and >).

➤ The rest of the definition is ensconced inside those curly brackets—{and}—which are known officially as *braces*.

➤ The first thing inside the braces is the name of the property you want to set, followed by a colon (:) . In our example, the property is called `font-size`.

➤ Finally, after the colon, you type the value you want to assign to the property (34pt, in the example, where "pt" is short for "points").

As a different example, suppose you want all your <TT> text to appear in a gray font. In style sheet land, font color is governed by the color property, so you'd set this style like so:

```
TT {color: gray}
```

Finally, you can set multiple properties in a single style by separating each property and value with a semi-colon (:). In the following example, <H2> tags are displayed with purple, 20-point text:

```
H2 {color: purple; font-size: 20pt}
```

Applying a Style to Multiple Tags

Besides applying multiple styles to a single tag, it's also possible to apply a single style to multiple tags. All you do is list the tags you want affected, separated by commas, before the opening brace ({) . Here's an example:

```
P, OL, UL, DT, DD {font-size: 10pt}
```

Three Sheets to the Web: Style Sheets and HTML

One of the most confusing things about style sheets is the sheer number of methods you can use to implement them. To help alleviate the confusion, this section shows you just three methods and explains exactly when you should use each method.

Method #1: The <STYLE> Tag

Probably the most straightforward way to implement a style sheet is to use the <STYLE> tag you saw in the earlier example. The idea is that you plop a <STYLE> tag and a </STYLE> tag into your document, and then insert all your style definitions in between. (Style sheet mavens call this an *embedded* style sheet.) The best place to put all this stuff is within the page header, like so:

```
<HTML>
<HEAD>

<STYLE TYPE="text/css">
<!--
```

```
Your style definitions go here
-->
</STYLE>

</HEAD>
<BODY>
The visible Web page stuff goes here
</BODY>
</HTML>
```

Note, too, that I tossed in the HTML comment tags, for good measure. This hides your style definitions from older browsers that don't know a style sheet from a rap sheet.

This method is best when you only want to apply a particular set of style definitions to a single page.

Method #2: Linking to an External Style Sheet

Style sheets get insanely powerful when you use an "external" style sheet. This is a separate file that contains your style definitions. To use these definitions within any Web page, you simply add a special <LINK> tag inside the page header. This tag specifies the name of the external style sheet file, and the browser then uses that file to grab the style definitions.

Here are the steps you need to follow to set up an external style sheet:

1. Use your favorite text editor to create a shiny new text file.
2. Add your style definitions to this file. Note that you don't need the <STYLE> tag or any other HTML tags.
3. Save the file in the same directory as your HTML files, and use a "css" extension (for example, "mystyles.css"). This helps you remember down the road that this is a style sheet file. (The "css" stands for cascading style sheet.)
4. For every page in which you want to use the styles, add a <LINK> tag inside the page header. Here's the general format to use (where *filename.css* is the name of your external style sheet file):

    ```
    <LINK REL="stylesheet" TYPE="text/css" HREF="filename.css">
    ```

For example, suppose you create a style sheet file named mystyles.css and that file includes the following style definitions:

```
H1 {color: red}
TT {font-size: 16pt}
```

You'd then refer to that file by using the <LINK> tag shown in the following example:

```
<HTML>
```

```
<HEAD>
<LINK REL="stylesheet" TYPE="text/css" HREF="mystyles.css">
</HEAD>
<BODY>
<H1>This Heading Will Appear Red</H1>
<TT>This text will be displayed in a 16-point font</TT>
</BODY>
</HTML>
```

Why is this so powerful? Well, you can add the same <LINK> tag to any number of Web pages and they'll all use the same style definitions. This makes it a breeze to create a consistent look and feel for your Web site. And if you decide that your <H1> text should be green, instead, all you have to do is edit the style sheet file. Automatically, every single one of your pages that link to this file will be updated with the new style!

Using Remote Links

The HREF part of the <LINK> tag doesn't have to be a simple filename. You can use a full URL, if need be. This is handy if you've set up your Web site with multiple directories, or if you want to link to an external style sheet file on another Web site. (I don't recommend the latter, however, because the browser has to go fetch the file, forcing your pages to take a bit longer to load.)

Method #3: Inline Styles

In the two style sheet methods we've looked at so far, the browser applies the style to *every* instance of whatever tag you specify in the definition. This is good because it ensures a consistent look throughout a page. But what in tarnation do you do if you want a particular instance of a tag to use a different style? For example, suppose you want all your <H1> headings to appear in a 24-point font, but you want the *first* <H1> heading to appear in a 36-point font. You can accomplish this by shoehorning the STYLE attribute right inside the tag you want to work with. (Among style sheet wonks, this is known as an *inline* style.) Here's an example (see ssinline.htm on the CD):

```
<HTML>
<HEAD>
```

```
<TITLE>Style Sheets: Inline Styles</TITLE>
</HEAD>

<STYLE TYPE="text/css">
<!--
H1 {font-size: 24pt}
-->
</STYLE>

<BODY>
<H1 STYLE="font-size: 36pt">This Heading Uses 36-Point Type</H1>
<H1>This One Uses 24-Point Type</H1>
</BODY>
</HTML>
```

As before, I use the <STYLE> tag in the header to define a style for the <H1> tag.
Notice, however, that the first <H1> tag includes a STYLE attribute that specifies a different font size. (Notice, too, that you define the style slightly differently. That is, you
use quotation marks instead of braces.) Figure 13.4 shows the results.

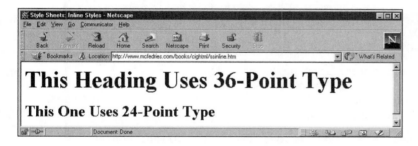

Figure 13.4

*Using inline styles lets
you to set a style for
individual tags and thus
override the default style.*

Applying a Style to a Section

The <DIV> tag is used to divide your page into separate sections. It doesn't do a
whole lot by itself, although the browser usually inserts a line break (equivalent to a

 tag) before the <DIV> tag and after the </DIV> end tag. However, by including
the STYLE attribute inside the <DIV> tag, you can apply an inline style to everything
that's inside one of these sections. Here's an example:

```
<DIV STYLE="font-size: 16pt">
<H1>This Is a 16-Point Heading</H1>
This here sentence will appear in a 16-point font.
<H2>So Will This Heading</H2>
</DIV>
```

In this case, everything between <DIV> and </DIV> gets formatted with the 16-point
font size style.

Applying a Style to a Word or Phrase

What if you only want to apply a style to a particular word or phrase? In most cases, you won't want to use <DIV> because it adds line breaks before an after the defined section. The solution is to use the new <SPAN> tag defined in HTML 4.0. The idea is that you surround your word or phrase with <SPAN> and </SPAN>, and then toss the STYLE attribute inside the <SPAN> tag. Here's an example:

```
Apply the style right <SPAN STYLE="font-size: 20pt">now</SPAN>.
```

Working with Style Classes

Although I promised you earlier that I'd only show you three methods for implementing styles in your pages, I can't resist telling you about a fourth method that can be really handy: the *style class*. The style class was created to solve a common problem: What if you want to apply a specific style to a number of different tags and sections throughout the document?

Couldn't you just use inline styles?

Absolutely. However, what if you decide to change the style? Then you'd have to go though the entire page and edit all those inline styles. An easier approach is to set up a style class within your main style sheet (that is, either within the <STYLE> tag or within an external style sheet file). Here's the basic format to use:

```
.ClassName {style definitions go here}
```

Here, *ClassName* is a unique name (without any spaces) that you use for the class. Here are a couple of examples:

```
.TitleText {font-size: 20pt; color: Navy; text-align: center}
.SubtitleText {font-size: 16pt; color: Gray; text-align: center}
```

The TitleText class uses a font size of 20 points, navy text, and a center alignment; the SubtitleText class uses a font size of 16 points, gray text, and a center alignment.

To use these classes, add a CLASS attribute to the tags you want the styles applied to, and set it equal to the class name (without the dot). Here's a for instance:

```
<DIV CLASS="TitleText">This is the Title of the Document</DIV>
```

The advantage here is that if you decide to change this style, you need only edit the style class; after that, every tag that uses the class changes automatically.

Here's a page (see ssclass.htm on the CD) that offers up a complete example.

```
<HTML>
<HEAD>
<TITLE>Style Sheets: Styles Classes</TITLE>
</HEAD>
```

```
<STYLE TYPE="text/css">
<!--
.TitleText {font-size: 20pt; color: Navy; text-align: center}
.SubtitleText {font-size: 16pt; color: Gray; text-align: center}
-->
</STYLE>

<BODY>
<DIV CLASS="TitleText">This is the Title of the Document</DIV>
<DIV CLASS="SubtitleText">This is the Subtitle of the Document</DIV>
</BODY>
</HTML>
```

Figure 13.5 shows how Internet Explorer interprets the classes.

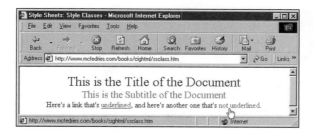

Figure 13.5

Use style classes for even more control over your styles.

The Least You Need to Know

This chapter gave you an introduction to using style sheets to enhance the look of your Web pages without doing a lot of work. You learned what style sheets are and how to implement them in your Web pages.

The next chapter makes things a bit more concrete by taking you through style sheet examples for text, colors, and backgrounds.

Chapter 14

Sheet Music: Styles for Fonts, Colors, and Backgrounds

In This Chapter

➤ Fiddling with font sizes, families, and weights

➤ Indenting and aligning text

➤ Dealing with text formatting such as underlining and strikethrough

➤ Working with style sheet colors

➤ Getting a handle on background styles

➤ Lots of ways to use styles to gussy up your pages

Okay, now that you know how to sew styles into your HTML creations, it's time to examine the specifics of the various styles available. This chapter examines style definitions for fonts, text, colors, and backgrounds.

Using Styles to Control Fonts

Earlier in the book (Chapter 3, "From Buck-Naked to Beautiful: Dressing Up Your Page," to be exact) I showed you how to use the <FONT> tag to adjust font properties such as the size and typeface. Well, anything the <FONT> tag can do, style sheets can do better. The next few sections show you why.

Font Size Styles

The <FONT> tag's control over the size of the font is limited, at best. Style sheets are vastly superior because they enable you to set the size of your text to just about anything you want.

Just so you know, the *font size* is a measure of the relative height used for each character. Although style sheets give you several ways to specify these heights, it's probably best to stick with *points* (where there are 72 points to an inch). To set the size, use the font-size style and set it to a number that ends with pt, like so:

```
P {font-size: 14pt}
```

The following HTML file (see ss-size.htm on the CD) tries a few different values on for, uh, size, and Figure 14.1 shows how the browser interprets them:

```
<HTML>
<HEAD>
<TITLE>Style Sheets: Font Sizes</TITLE>

<STYLE TYPE="text/css">
<!--
H1 {font-size: 30pt}
-->
</STYLE>

</HEAD>
<BODY>

<H1>Font Size Styles:</H1>
You can size your text to
<SPAN STYLE="font-size: 10pt">10 points</SPAN>,
<SPAN STYLE="font-size: 12pt">12 points</SPAN>,
<SPAN STYLE="font-size: 14pt">14 points</SPAN>,
<SPAN STYLE="font-size: 18pt">18 points</SPAN>,
<SPAN STYLE="font-size: 24pt">24 points</SPAN>,
or whatever.

</BODY>
</HTML>
```

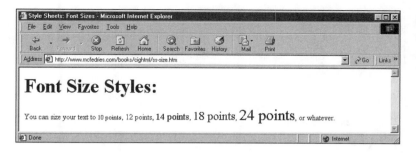

Figure 14.1

Styles enable you to set all kinds of different font sizes.

Font Family Styles (the Typeface)

The *font family* represents the overall look associated with each character (it's more commonly known as the *typeface*). Unlike the other styles, there are no set values you can use. Instead, you normally specify several possibilities and the browser uses the first one that's installed on the user's computer. Here's an example:

```
TT {font-family: Courier, "Courier New"}
```

Notice that multiple-word family names must be enclosed in quotation marks. The following HTML file (it's ssfamily.htm on the CD) puts a few families to the test, and Figure 14.2 shows how they look with Netscape:

```
<HTML>
<HEAD>
<TITLE>Style Sheets: Font Families</TITLE>

<STYLE TYPE="text/css">
<!--
H1 {font-size: 18pt; font-family: "Times New Roman"}
H2 {font-size: 18pt; font-family: Arial}
H3 {font-size: 18pt; font-family: "Comic Sans MS"}
H4 {font-size: 18pt; font-family: Impact}
H5 {font-size: 18pt; font-family:
"Courier New"}
-->
</STYLE>

</HEAD>
<BODY>

<H1>Times New Roman</H1>
<H2>Arial</H2>
<H3>Comic Sans MS</H3>
<H4>Impact</H4>
<H5>Courier New</H5>

</BODY>
</HTML>
```

Check This Out

Font Family Values

As with the <FONT> tag's FACE attribute (see Chapter 3), the reader only sees your specified typefaces if they are installed on the reader's computer.

195

Figure 14.2

A few font families.

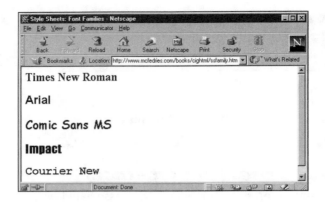

Font Weight Styles (Bolding)

The font weight controls the thickness of text. For example, the <B> tag renders text as bold by displaying thicker letters. As usual, however, style sheets give you much greater control. In this case, you use the font-weight style:

```
{font-weight: value}
```

Here, *value* can be either of the following:

➤ **A predefined weight**   Use either normal or **bold**.

➤ **A specific weight**   Use one of the following: 100, 200, 300, 400 (normal), 500, 600, 700 (bold), 800, or 900.

Here's an example file (it's ssweight.htm on the CD) that puts the font-weight style through its paces (Figure 14.3 shows what happens in Internet Explorer):

```
<HTML>
<HEAD>
<TITLE>Style Sheets: Font Weights</TITLE>
</HEAD>
<BODY>

<DIV STYLE="font-size: 18pt">
The <SPAN STYLE="font-family: 'Courier New',Courier">font-
weight</SPAN> style uses the following values:
<SPAN STYLE="font-weight: 100">100</SPAN>,
<SPAN STYLE="font-weight: 200">200</SPAN>,
<SPAN STYLE="font-weight: 300">300</SPAN>,
<SPAN STYLE="font-weight: 400">400</SPAN>,
<SPAN STYLE="font-weight: 500">500</SPAN>,
<SPAN STYLE="font-weight: 600">600</SPAN>,
<SPAN STYLE="font-weight: 700">700</SPAN>,
<SPAN STYLE="font-weight: 800">800</SPAN>,
<SPAN STYLE="font-weight: 900">900</SPAN>,
```

```
</DIV>

</BODY>
</HTML>
```

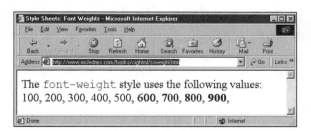

The font-weight style uses the following values:
100, 200, 300, 400, 500, **600**, **700**, **800**, **900**,

Figure 14.3

The various values for the font-weight style.

Font Style Styles (Italics)

If font-weight is the style sheet equivalent of the <B> tag, you might be wondering if there's an equivalent style for the <I> tag. Yup, there is, but it has the confusing name of font-style. Yeah, that's *real* descriptive. Anyway, it's very simple:

```
{font-style: italic}
```

Textstyles: More Ways to Format Text

Besides fiddling with fonts, style sheets offer a few other ways to format your page text. This section looks at four of them: indentation, alignment, underlining, and casing.

Font Wait

Unfortunately, while I write this, neither Internet Explorer 5.0 nor Netscape Navigator 4.7 do much of anything when confronted with font weight values from 100 to 500 (as you can see in the figure). I guess we'll just have wait for them to get this right in future versions.

Oblique Fonts

Some fonts have an *oblique* style that looks sort of like *italic*, but it's really just the letters slanted to one side. If a particular font has an oblique version, you can use the following style to specify it:

```
{font-style: oblique}
```

197

Indenting Entire Paragraphs

If you want the entire paragraph indented instead of just the first line, you need to work with the various margin styles. I tell you about them in Chapter 15, "The Box Model: Styles for Dimensions, Borders, Margins, and More."

Indenting the First Line of a Paragraph

Many professionally-typeset pages indent the beginning of each paragraph. The only way to do that in regular HTML is to string together a series of non-breaking spaces ( ) at the start of each paragraph. With style sheets, however, it's no sweat because you just use the `text-indent` style. For example, the following page (see ssindent.htm on the CD) includes a style sheet that tells the browser to indent the first line of every paragraph by half an inch, as shown in Figure 14.4.

```
<HTML>
<HEAD>
<TITLE>Style Sheets: Text Indents</TITLE>

<STYLE TYPE="text/css">
<!--
P {text-indent: 0.5in}
-->
</STYLE>
</HEAD>
<BODY>

<H1>Textstyles: More Ways to Format Text</H1>
<P>Besides fiddling with fonts, style sheets offer a few other
ways to format your page text. This section looks at four of them:
indentation, alignment, underlining, and casing.
<H2>Controlling Indents</H2>
<P>Many professionally-typeset pages indent the beginning of each
paragraph. The only way to do that in regular HTML is to string
together a series of non-breaking spaces (<TT>&#38;nbsp;</TT>) at
the start of each paragraph. With style sheets, however, it's no
sweat because you just use the <TT>text-indent</TT> style. For
example, the following page includes a style sheet that tells the
browser to indent the first line of every paragraph by half an inch.

</BODY>
</HTML>
```

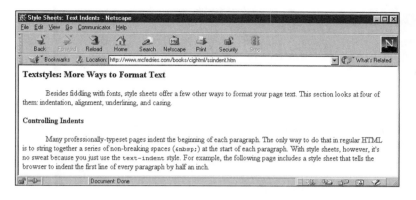

Figure 14.4

Use text-indent to indent the first line of a paragraph.

Aligning Text

To set the alignment of a section of text, use the `text-align` style:

    {text-align: *alignment*}

alignment can be one of the following four values:

➤ **left** Aligns the text with the left side of the browser window.

➤ **center** Centers the text within the browser window.

➤ **right** Aligns the text with the right side of the browser window.

➤ **justify** Aligns the text with both the left and right sides of the browser window.

Neat freaks in the crowd will love the `justify` value because it makes longish paragraphs look nice and tidy. I use it a lot on my site, as you can see in Figure 14.5.

Figure 14.5

The justify value makes paragraphs looks their best.

Using the Text Decoration Styles

One of the most common questions that readers ask me is "How can I display my links without an underline?" And my answer is "Use the `text-decoration` style on the <A> tag and set it to `none`":

```
A {text-decoration: none}
```

That's a nice trick, but the text-decoration style has a few others up its sleeve. Here's a complete list of the values you can use with this style:

➤ **blink**   This is a Netscape-only (version 4.0 and up) value, and it's the equivalent of the dumb <BLINK> tag.

➤ **line-through**   Formats text with a line through the middle (this is usually called *strikethrough* text). Most people use this style to represent text that's been "deleted" from a document.

➤ **none**   Formats text without any decoration.

➤ **overline**   Formats text with a line over the top. (Note that Netscape doesn't yet support this value.)

➤ **underline**   Formats text with an underline.

Here's some sample code that uses a few text decoration values (see ssdecor.htm on the CD):

```
<HTML>
<HEAD>
<TITLE>Style Sheets: Text Decoration</TITLE>
</HEAD>
<BODY>
<H2 STYLE="text-decoration: none">None</H2>
<H2 STYLE="text-decoration: line-through">Line-through</H2>
<H2 STYLE="text-decoration: overline">Overline</H2>
<H2 STYLE="text-decoration: underline">Underline</H2>
</BODY>
</HTML>
```

Figure 14.6 shows how they look in Internet Explorer.

Working with Uppercase and Lowercase Letters

You can format text as all-uppercase, all-lowercase, or with only the first letter of each word as uppercase (this is often called *title case*). The style that accomplishes this goes by the unlikely name of `text-transform`. (Sheesh. Only a major league geek could come up with such a non-obvious name.) This style comes equipped with four values for your style pleasure:

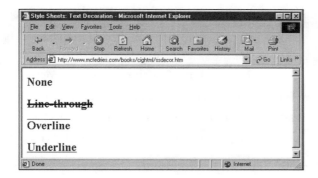

Figure 14.6
Some text-decoration style examples.

➤ **capitalize** Converts the first letter of every word to uppercase.

➤ **lowercase** Converts every letter to lowercase.

➤ **none** Leaves the text as is.

➤ **uppercase** Converts every letter to uppercase.

Here's some code that demonstrates the various text-transform values (check out sstrans.htm on the CD), and Figure 14.7 shows how it looks in Netscape.

```
<HTML>
<HEAD>
<TITLE>Style Sheets: Text Transform</TITLE>
</HEAD>
<BODY>
<H2 STYLE="text-transform: capitalize">
I left my heart in Truth or Consequences, New Mexico</H2>
<H2 STYLE="text-transform: lowercase">
I left my heart in Truth or Consequences, New Mexico</H2>
<H2 STYLE="text-transform: none">
I left my heart in Truth or Consequences, New Mexico</H2>
<H2 STYLE="text-transform: uppercase">
I left my heart in Truth or Consequences, New Mexico</H2>
</BODY>
</HTML>
```

Coloring Your Web World with Color Styles

Using color within a style sheet is more or less the same as using the <FONT> tag's COLOR attribute (discussed in Chapter 3). In this case, you use the color style and set it to one of the weird six-digit RGB values, as in this example:

```
<SPAN STYLE="color: #FF0000">This text is red</SPAN>
```

201

Figure 14.7

Examples of the ill-named text-transform *style.*

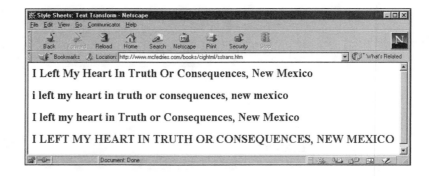

The big advantage you get with style sheet colors is that you can finally get those unintuitive RGB values out of your life. That's because color names are part of the style sheet specification. These color names—semi-officially known as the *X11 color set*—enable you to use friendly monikers such as "red" and "yellow" instead of the obscure RGB values. There are 140 names in all and they cover most of the color spectrum, from AliceBlue to WhiteSmoke. In between are all kinds of fun names, such as PapayaWhip, DodgerBlue, and PeachPuff. Here's an example:

```
Try my <SPAN STYLE="color: LemonChiffon">Lemon Chiffon</SPAN> pie!
```

To help you get a handle on this riot of colors, I've put together a table of the various color names (along with the RGB equivalents, so you'll remember how much easier the names are to use). The file is called x11color.htm, and you'll find it on the CD. Figure 14.8 shows part of the file.

Figure 14.8

Use the x11color.htm page to check out the wild colors (and their even wilder names) that you can use with style sheets.

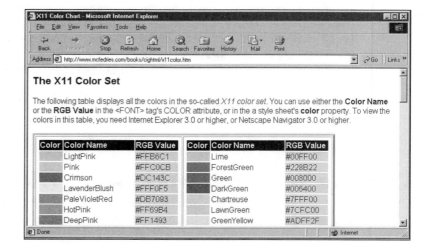

Using Background Styles

As you learned back in Chapter 6, "A Picture Is Worth a Thousand Clicks: Working with Images," you can use the <BODY> tag to set up your page with either a background color (using the BGCOLOR attribute) or a background image (using the BACKGROUND attribute). Either way, the attribute you set applies to the entire page.

With style sheets, however, you can apply a background color or image to sections of your page, or even to individual words. The secret to this lies in two styles: `background-color` and `background-image`.

To set a background color, use either a color name or an RGB value:

```
{background-color: blue}
{background-color: #0000FF}
```

To specify a background image, use the following syntax:

```
{background-image: URL(filename)}
```

Here, *filename* is the name of the graphics file you want to use (or an URL that points to the file). The HTML code below shows a few examples of these styles (see ssback.htm on the CD).

```
<HTML>
<HEAD>
<TITLE>Style Sheet Backgrounds</TITLE>
</HEAD>
<BODY>

<DIV STYLE="background-color: black; color: white">
The background style is great for setting off entire sections
of text using a different color. For example, this section
uses a black background with white text.
</DIV>

<DIV STYLE="background-color: skyblue; color: navy">
On the other hand, this section achieves a slightly different
effect by using a pleasant Sky Blue background with Navy text.
</DIV>

<P>You can also use the background style to
<SPAN STYLE="background-color: yellow">highlight individual
words</SPAN>.
<P>

<DIV STYLE="background-image: URL(bg03.gif); font-size: 16pt">
<B>One of the most interesting ways to use the background style
is to specify a background image. The browser will tile the
```

```
image so that it fills the entire section, like this.</B>
</DIV>

</BODY>
</HTML>
```

Figure 14.9 shows this file displayed in both Internet Explorer (on the left) and Netscape Navigator (on the right). Notice that Explorer paints the background color right across the screen (which looks nice), but Navigator just follows the text (which looks kind of ragged). To get the full effect, load the page ssback.htm into both Internet Explorer and Navigator on your own machine.

Figure 14.9

Some background styles. Explorer and Navigator display background colors slightly differently.

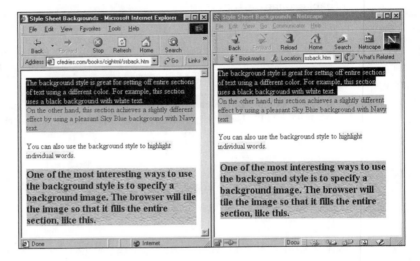

Two Other Background Styles

Another background style you might want to check out is background-repeat, which controls whether (and how) the browser tiles the background image to fill the window. There are four possible values:

repeat	Tiles the background image to cover the entire browser window.
repeat-x	Tiles the background image horizontally, only.
repeat-y	Tiles the background image vertically, only.
no-repeat	Doesn't tile the background image.

Also, Internet Explorer supports the background-attachment style. If you set this style to fixed, the background image remains in place when the user scrolls up and down the page. Set this style to scroll to revert to the usual background behavior (that is, the background image scrolls along with the text).

The Least You Need to Know

This chapter continued your style sheet education by examining specific styles for fonts, text, colors, and backgrounds.

Chapter 15 takes you even further by looking at the style sheet box model and its associated styles for dimensions, borders, margins, positioning, and lots more.

The Box Model: Styles for Dimensions, Borders, Margins, and More

---

In This Chapter

➤ Knocking some sense into the box model

➤ Setting the box dimensions

➤ Putting extra padding around the content

➤ Adding borders to the box

➤ Messing with the box margins

➤ Positioning the box precisely on the page

➤ How to wrap your page boxes in the style sheet equivalent of paper, bows, and ribbons

---

So far, you've learned what style sheets are and how to implement them (Chapter 13), and you've learned some specific styles for fonts, text, colors, and backgrounds (Chapter 14). Style sheets are pretty useful little beasts, aren't they? They just give you so much more control over what your pages look like than plain old HTML.

This chapter takes this control up a notch by eyeballing quite a few more styles that cover things like dimensions (the height and width of things), padding and margins (the amount of space around things), borders (lines around things), and position (where things appear on the page).

Thinking Outside the Box: Understanding the Box Model

Everything in this chapter is based on something called the style sheet *box model*. So let's begin by figuring out just what this box model thing is all about and why it's important.

In the geeky world known as Style Sheet Land, stuff inside a page is broken down into separate *elements*. In particular, there's a class of elements called *blocks*, and it includes those tags that start new sections of text: <P>, <BLOCKQUOTE>, <H1> through <H6>, <DIV>, <TABLE>, and so on.

In this strange world, each of these block elements is considered to have an invisible box around it (okay, it's a *very* strange world). This box has the following components:

➤ **Content**   This is the stuff inside the box (the text, the table, yadda, yadda, yadda).

➤ **Dimensions**   This is the height and width of the box.

➤ **Padding**   This is the space around the content. It's similar to the <TABLE> tag's CELLPADDING attribute that I told you about in Chapter 9, "Table Talk: Adding Tables to Your Page."

➤ **Border**   This is a line that surrounds the box and that marks the edges of the box.

➤ **Margin**   This is the space outside of the border. It separates the box from other boxes to the left and right, as well as above and below.

➤ **Position**   This is the location of the box within the page.

Figure 15.1 illustrates the basic structure of the box. The shaded area is the box itself.

Figure 15.1

The style sheet box model.

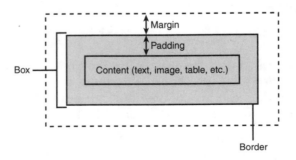

All the styles that you learned about in Chapter 14 dealt with formatting the box content. The rest of this chapter covers the five components that comprise the rest of the box: the dimensions, padding, border, margin, and position.

Inline Elements

Page knickknacks that don't create blocks—things like <B> and <I>—are called *inline elements*. You can use many of the style properties that I discuss in the rest of the chapter on inline elements, but I don't recommend it. The big problem is that Netscape tends to convert inline elements to block elements if you try to apply block styles (such as a margin).

Box Blueprints: Specifying the Dimensions

The dimensions of the box are straightforward: the width property specifies how wide the box is, and the height property specifies how tall the box is. Note, however, that as of this writing, Netscape doesn't support the height property.

Here's some simple HTML code that tries out these two styles (see ssdimens.htm on the CD). Note that I included a <STYLE> tag that sets the border property for the <P> tag so that you can easily see the dimensions of the resulting paragraphs (I discuss the border property in detail a bit later). Figure 15.2 shows what Internet Explorer makes of the whole thing.

```
<HTML>
<HEAD>
<TITLE>Style Sheet Dimensions</TITLE>

<STYLE TYPE="text/css">
<!--
P {border: thin solid}
-->
</STYLE>

</HEAD>
<BODY>

<P>This is a regular paragraph.
<P STYLE="height: 50px">This is a paragraph that's 50 pixels high.
<P STYLE="width: 100px">This is a paragraph that's 100 pixels wide.

</BODY>
</HTML>
```

209

Figure 15.2

Some paragraphs with different dimensions.

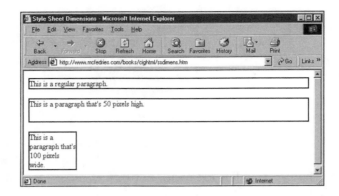

Cushy Content: Adding Padding to the Inside of the Box

If you look at the previous figure, you can see that the text tends to slide right up against the border of the box, particularly on the left and right. If your text is feeling claustrophobic, you can give it some extra elbowroom by increasing the amount of padding that surrounds the content within the box. Style sheets give you four padding properties to play with:

➤ **padding-left**   Adds space to the left of the content.

➤ **padding-right**   Adds space to the right of the content.

➤ **padding-top**   Adds space on top of the content.

➤ **padding-bottom**   Adds space below the content.

It's usually easiest to specify a value in pixels (*px*), like so:

```
P {padding-left: 10px}
```

Here's some code (see sspaddng.htm on the CD) that tries out each padding property on a couple of <DIV> sections. Figure 15.3 shows the result in Netscape.

```
<HTML>
<HEAD>
<TITLE>Style Sheet Padding</TITLE>

<STYLE TYPE="text/css">
<!--
DIV {border: thin solid;
     width: 100px;
     margin-bottom: 5px}
-->
</STYLE>
```

```
</HEAD>
<BODY>

<DIV STYLE="padding-top: 10px; padding-bottom: 10px">
This section has 10 pixels of padding on the top and bottom.</DIV>
<DIV STYLE="padding-left: 15px; padding-right: 15px">
This section has 15 pixels of padding on the left and right.</DIV>

</BODY>
</HTML>
```

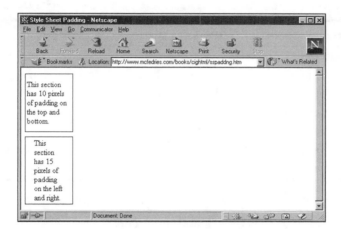

Figure 15.3

Trying out the padding properties.

The Box Revealed: Setting Borders

In the last couple of examples, I included borders so you could explicitly see the box in each element. So it's high time we checked out this border stuff to see what kind of fun you can have with it. The various border properties come in three flavors: width, style, and color.

The border width is controlled by the following five properties:

➤ **border-width** Specifies the width of all the borders.

➤ **border-left-width** Specifies the width of the left border.

➤ **border-right-width** Specifies the width of the right border.

➤ **border-top-width** Specifies the width of the top border.

➤ **border-bottom-width** Specifies the width of the bottom border.

In each case, you can set the width to either a specific value (such as 5px) or to one of the following: thin, medium, or thick.

The border style has five similar properties:

➤ **border-style**   Specifies the style of all the borders.

➤ **border-left-style**   Specifies the style of the left border.

➤ **border-right-style**   Specifies the style of the right border.

➤ **border-top-style**   Specifies the style of the top border.

➤ **border-bottom-style**   Specifies the style of the bottom border.

The following table outlines the various values you can use for each property.

Table 15.1   Values for the Various Border Style Properties

Enter...	To Get a Border That Uses...
double	A double line
groove	A V-shaped line that appears to be etched into the page
inset	A line that appears to be sunken into the page
none	No line (that is, no border is displayed)
outset	A line that appears to be raised from the page
ridge	A V-shaped line that appears to be coming out of the page
solid	A solid line

As you might have guessed, the border color is controlled by five properties:

➤ **border-color**   Specifies the color of all the borders.

➤ **border-left-color**   Specifies the color of the left border.

➤ **border-right-color**   Specifies the color of the right border.

➤ **border-top-color**   Specifies the color of the top border.

➤ **border-bottom-color**   Specifies the color of the bottom border.

You can set each property to one of the usual color values.

Check This Out

Be Sure to Set the Style

For borders to work properly, make sure you set at least the style.

The following page (it's ssborder.htm on the CD) demonstrates some of the border-width and border-style values. Figure 15.4 shows how they look in Internet Explorer.

```
<HTML>
<HEAD>
<TITLE>Style Sheet Padding</TITLE>

<STYLE TYPE="text/css">
<!--
TABLE {margin-bottom: 5px}
-->
```

```
</STYLE>

</HEAD>
<BODY>

<TABLE STYLE="border-width: thin; border-style: solid"><TR><TD>
This table uses a thin border with a solid style.
</TD></TR></TABLE>

<TABLE STYLE="border-width: medium; border-style: groove"><TR><TD>
This table uses a medium border with a groove style.
</TD></TR></TABLE>

<TABLE STYLE="border-width: medium; border-style: inset"><TR><TD>
This table uses a medium border with an inset style.
</TD></TR></TABLE>

<TABLE STYLE="border-width: thick; border-style: ridge"><TR><TD>
This table uses a thick border with a ridge style.
</TD></TR></TABLE>

<TABLE STYLE="border-width: thick; border-style: outset"><TR><TD>
This table uses a thick border with an outset style.
</TD></TR></TABLE>

</BODY>
</HTML>
```

Figure 15.4

Internet Explorer trying some border styles on for size.

213

Room to Breathe: Specifying Margins Around the Box

For our next style sheet trick, I show you how to use styles to specify margins. The default margins used by the browser depend on what element you're dealing with. For example, each new paragraph creates a bit of margin space above itself, and you always get a little bit of space at the top and bottom of the page, and on the left and right sides of the page. On the other hand, <DIV> sections don't use margins.

To control all this, use any of the following margin properties:

➤ `margin-left`   Specifies the size of the left margin.

➤ `margin-right`   Specifies the size of the right margin.

➤ `margin-top`   Specifies the size of the top margin.

➤ `margin-bottom`   Specifies the size of the bottom margin.

In each case, set the width to a specific value (such as 0px for no margin).

The following HTML code (ssmargin.htm on the CD) sets two different margins (see Figure 15.5):

➤ A <STYLE> block sets the margins of the <BLOCKQUOTE> tag to be 100 pixels on the left and right.

➤ The <BODY> tag's STYLE attribute sets the overall margins of the page to 0 for the left, top, and right. (Note, however, that Netscape doesn't seem to like this.)

214

```
<HTML>
<HEAD>
<TITLE>Style Sheet Margins</TITLE>
</HEAD>

<STYLE TYPE="text/css">
<!--
BLOCKQUOTE {margin-left: 100px;
            margin-right: 100px;
            font-size: 14pt;
            font-family: Arial}
-->
</STYLE>

<BODY STYLE="margin-left: 0px;
             margin-top: 0px;
             margin-right: 0px;">

<DIV STYLE="background: black;
            color: white;
            text-align: center">
<H1>The Browser Displays This Heading with No Margins</H1>
</DIV>

<BLOCKQUOTE>
A pun does not commonly justify a blow in return. But if a blow
were given for such cause, and death ensued, the jury would be
judges both of the facts and of the pun, and might, if the
latter were of an aggravated character, return a verdict of
justifiable homicide.<BR>
&#151;Oliver Wendell Holmes, Sr.
</BLOCKQUOTE>

</BODY>
</HTML>
```

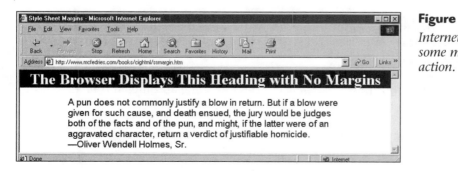

Figure 15.5

Internet Explorer showing some margin styles in action.

Where the Box Goes: Working with Position Styles

Now that you've determined the structure and layout of your box, the last thing you have to decide is where to put it on the page. This might seem like a strange thing. After all, don't elements such as paragraphs and headings always go exactly where you put them on the page? In regular HTML they do, but style sheets, as you've seen so often, give you much more flexibility.

Your first chore is to decide how you want your element positioned. This is determined by, appropriately enough, the position property, which can take any of the following three values:

➤ **position: absolute**   When you use this value, you can toss the element anywhere you like on the page. For example, you could tell the browser to display a heading 100 pixels from the left and 50 pixels from the top.

➤ **position: relative**   This value first positions the element according to where it would normally appear in regular HTML. It then offsets the element horizontally and vertically, according to values you specify.

➤ **position: static**   This value positions the element according to where it would normally appear in regular HTML.

If you decide to set position to either absolute or relative, you then need to specify the exact position you want. For this you need to use some or all of the following four properties:

➤ **left**   The element's position from the left side of the browser window (if you're using position: absolute) or to the left of the element's natural position in the page (if you're using position: relative).

➤ **top**   The element's position from the top of the browser window (if you're using position: absolute) or below the element's natural position in the page (if you're using position: relative).

➤ **right**   The element's position from the right side of the browser window, if you're using position: absolute. Note that this value has no effect if you're using position: relative.

➤ **bottom**   The element's position from the bottom of the browser window, if you're using position: absolute. This value has no effect if you're using position: relative.

The following page (ssposit.htm on the CD) tries out some absolute and relative positioning, and Figure 15.6 shows what happens in Internet Explorer.

```
<HTML>
<HEAD>
<TITLE>Style Sheet Positioning</TITLE>
```

```
</HEAD>

<STYLE TYPE="text/css">
<!--
DIV {font-family: Arial;
     font-size: 16pt}
-->
</STYLE>

<BODY>

<DIV STYLE="position: absolute; left: 600px; top: 150px">Section
1</DIV>
<DIV STYLE="position: absolute; left: 100px; top: 100px">Section
2</DIV>
<DIV STYLE="position: absolute; left: 500px; top: 50px">Section
3</DIV>
<DIV STYLE="position: absolute; left: 50px; top: 0px">Section 4</DIV>
This is regular text. Even though it comes after all those &lt;DIV&gt;
tags, it still appears at the top of the page. That's because elements
that are positioned absolutely aren't part of the regular document
flow.
<P STYLE="position: relative; left: 200px">
This paragraph is shoved left from its normal position by 200 pixels
using relative positioning.

</BODY>
</HTML>
```

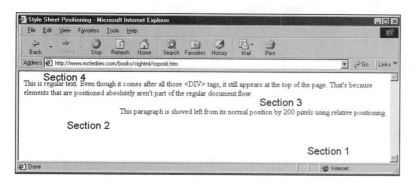

Figure 15.6

Use position styles to toss elements all over your page.

Positioning in the Third Dimension

Style sheets understand not just the usual 2D positioning, but also positioning in the third dimension. It sounds like science fiction, but all it really means is that you can "stack" elements on top of each other for interesting effects. The style property that controls this is called z-index. An element with a higher z-index value is displayed "on top" of an element with a lower z-index value. Here's an example (see sszindex.htm on the CD):

```
<IMG
   SRC="home2.gif"
   STYLE="z-index: 0; position: absolute; left: 100px; top:
10px">
<DIV STYLE="z-index: 1; position: absolute; left: 10px; top:
30px">
<B>This text appears on top of the image.</B>
</DIV>
```

The Least You Need to Know

This chapter closed out your look at style sheets by examining various properties related to the box model. You learned about dimensions, padding, borders, margins, and positioning.

Things take a turn for the radical from here as you learn how add JavaScripts and Java applets to your pages in Part 4, "Working with JavaScripts and Java Applets."

Part 4
Working with JavaScripts and Java Applets

At this point on your HTML learning curve, you know pretty much everything there is to know about making your page look its best. From fonts to images to tables to style sheets, you've got the know-how to turn out well-buffed Web pages. The problem, though, is that your pages just kind of sit there. Outside of adding a few animated GIFs, how can you make your pages seem more dynamic? You find at least part of the answer here in Part 4. These three chapters show you how to add a bit of "software" to your pages in the form of JavaScripts and Java applets. You'll see just how easy it is to display messages to the user, validate for content, store data about the user, and much more.

Chapter 16

The Programmable Page: Adding JavaScripts to Your Pages

In This Chapter

➤ How to insert scripts into a page

➤ Using scripts to display messages to the surfer

➤ Writing text to the page on-the-fly

➤ Detecting the user's browser

➤ Everything you need to know to use JavaScripts on your pages

---

Way, way, back in Chapter 1, "A Brief HTML Web Page Primer," I took great pains to ensure you that the "Language" part of "Hypertext Markup Language" in no way meant that you had to learn a programming language to create a Web page. You've seen so far that, thankfully, I wasn't lying.

Now, however, it's time to get ever so slightly acquainted with a *real* programming language. It's called *JavaScript* and you use it to add tiny little programs called *scripts* to your pages. You can use these scripts to pop up a welcome message whenever someone visits your site, display the current time, find out which browser a visitor is using, and tons more.

Does this mean you have to learn how to program in JavaScript? Well, no, not if you don't want to. You can always go the "black box" route where you simply add a script to your page without understanding exactly how the script does its thing. That's the approach I take in this chapter. You won't learn any programming here. Instead, I show you how to add a script to your page, and I run through a few examples of some useful scripts. (You'll see even more examples in the next chapter.)

Using the <SCRIPT> Tag

JavaScript code goes right inside the Web page, just like HTML tags. When a JavaScript-savvy browser (such as Netscape 2.0 and later and Internet Explorer 3.0 and later) accesses the page, the JavaScript code is executed and the program does its thing. For example, the program might check the time of day and display an appropriate welcome message, or you could embed a calculator right on the page.

JavaScripts reside between the <SCRIPT> and </SCRIPT> tags and always take the following form:

```
<SCRIPT LANGUAGE="JavaScript">
<!--
The script commands go here.
//-->
</SCRIPT>
```

Note the use of HTML comment tags. These ensure that JavaScript-feeble browsers don't try to read the JavaScript commands.

JavaScript Comments

In the same way that HTML has comment tags that tell the browser to ignore the text and tags between them, programmers can also add comments to scripts. To do so, they insert two slashes (//) at the beginning of each line they want ignored. A common example is the line just above the </SCRIPT> end tag:

```
//-->
```

You have to put the comment slashes at the beginning to prevent JavaScript from trying to "execute" the end tag of the HTML comment (-->).

Inserting the Script

Where you store the script in your page depends on what it does:

➤ If the script writes text to the page, you position the script where you want the text to appear.

➤ Otherwise, you position the script between the </HEAD> and <BODY> tags.

Using an External JavaScript File

Besides having your scripts snuggle up to your regular page tags, it's also possible in some cases to plop the scripts into a separate file. Although this is really only for advanced users who know what they're doing, it's worthwhile because it has three benefits:

Check This Out

Skipping the External Stuff

This section on using an external JavaScript file is advanced stuff, so don't worry if it makes no sense to you now. Just skip over it and come back to it later, after you've had some experience working with JavaScripts.

➤ It makes it easier to reuse a script because you only need to tell the browser the name and location of the separate file. You don't have to insert the script itself into all your pages.

➤ If you need to adjust the script, you only have to adjust it in the separate file. Every page that accesses the script automatically uses the edited version.

➤ It makes your page's source code look less cluttered, so it's easier to read.

The key thing about all this is that you can only put what are known as *functions* in the external file. A JavaScript function looks like this:

```
function Name()
{
A bunch of programming statements go here.
}
```

Here, *Name* is the name of the function.

To tell the browser about the external file, add the SRC attribute to the <SCRIPT> tag. For example, if your functions are all in a file named scripts.js (it's traditional to use the .js extension for these files; they're just text files, however), you'd put the following into your page between </HEAD> and <BODY>:

```
<SCRIPT LANGUAGE="JavaScript" SRC="scripts.js">
</SCRIPT>
```

Some JavaScript Examples

The real purpose of this chapter isn't so much to show you how to insert scripts (although that's clearly important). No, what I really want to do is give you a good supply of scripts to use, at no extra charge, in your own pages. To that end, the next few sections take you through quite a few JavaScripts that perform all manner of interesting and useful functions. (Remember, too, that you get even more script examples in the next chapter.)

Displaying a Message to the User

Let's begin with the simplest of all JavaScript functions: displaying a message to the user in a simple dialog box (also called a *pop-up box* or an *alert box*). Here's the JavaScript code that does the job:

```
alert("Insert your message here")
```

For example, suppose you want to have a message pop up each time a user visits your home page. You can do that by inserting the following script between the </HEAD> and <BODY> tags (see jsalert1.htm on the CD):

```
<SCRIPT LANGUAGE="JavaScript">
<!--
alert("Welcome to my Web site!")
//-->
</SCRIPT>
```

Figure 16.1 shows what happens when the user loads your page.

Figure 16.1

The JavaScript alert() statement displays a little dialog box like this one.

Writing Data to the Page

After displaying a dialog box message to the user, the second most common JavaScript chore is to write some data to the page. This is really powerful because it means that you can display *dynamic* text on your page. For example, you could write the current date and time (see the next section to learn how to do this).

The JavaScript statement that performs this magic is document.write(), which looks like this:

```
document.write("The stuff you want to write goes here.")
```

The idea is that you place this statement at the spot within your page that you want the text to appear.

For example, many Web spinners like to include in their page the date and time that the page was last modified. This helps the surfer know whether they're dealing with

recent data. Fortunately, JavaScript has a special statement called document
.lastModified that returns the date and time that the file was last edited. Here's
a script (see jswrite1.htm on the CD) that shows you one way to use it with docu-
ment.write():

Stay on the Case

JavaScript is *really* finicky about uppercase versus lowercase letters. Therefore, when
entering JavaScript statements, always use precisely the same combination of uppercase and lowercase letters that I show you. For example, you must use document.
lastModified and not Document.LastModified or document.lastmodified.

```
<SCRIPT LANGUAGE="JavaScript">
<!--
document.write("This page was last edited on " +
document.lastModified)
//-->
</SCRIPT>
```

Figure 16.2 shows how things shake out in Netscape.

Figure 16.2

Use document.write()
*to add text to your page
on-the-fly.*

The text shown in the previous example is a bit plain. Can you put some fancy pants on it?

No problem. You can easily add HTML tags within the document.write() statement.
Here's a revised script (see jswrite2.htm on the CD) that does just that:

```
<SCRIPT LANGUAGE="JavaScript">
<!--
document.write("<FONT FACE='Arial' SIZE=+1><B>This page was last
[ic:ccc]edited on <TT>" + document.lastModified) + "</TT></B></FONT>"
//—-->
</SCRIPT>
```

I added the <FONT>, <B>, and <TT> tags to produce the effect shown in Figure 16.3.

225

Figure 16.3

There's no problem adding tags within your `document.write()` *statements.*

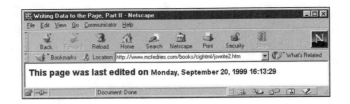

Quotes Within Quotes

One thing you have to watch out for in `document.write()` (and, indeed, in most JavaScript statements) is when you use quotation marks within quotation marks. In the previous example, I had to use <FONT FACE='Arial'> instead of <FONT FACE="Arial"> because `document.write()` already has its own double quotation marks , and it would seriously confuse things to use <FONT FACE="Arial">. Therefore, always use single quotation marks within JavaScript statements such as `document.write()`.

Hiding Your Email Address from a Spam Crawler

As you might know, *spam* is the whimsical name given to a non-whimsical thing: unsolicited commercial email messages. If you put up a Web page and include your email address on it somewhere, I'll bet you dollars to doughnuts that you'll start receiving more spam in your inbox. Why? Because programs called "spam crawlers" troll the Web looking for pages containing email addresses that they can harvest for their evil intentions. They look for "@" signs and "mailto" links.

You can foil spam crawlers by using a simple bit of JavaScript code to write your email address to the page. Here's the code (see jsnospam.htm on the CD):

```
<SCRIPT LANGUAGE="JavaScript">
<!--
var addr1 = "mailto:"
var addr2 = "paul"
var addr3 = "@"
var addr4 = "mcfedries.com"
document.write('<A HREF="' + addr1 + addr2 + addr3 + addr4 + '">')
```

```
document.write('Email Me!</A>')
//-->
</SCRIPT>
```

Place this script at the spot in the page where you want your mailto link to appear. Of course, you need to edit things for your own email address. As you can see in Figure 16.4, what you end up with is a mailto link that works normally, as far as the surfer is concerned.

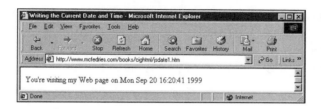

Figure 16.4

The JavaScript code creates a standard mailto link.

Putting the Date and Time into a Page

A similar example involves putting the current date and time into the page. The current date and time is produced by JavaScript's Date() statement. Here's a simple example that uses Date() (see jsdate1.htm on the CD). Figure 16.5 shows Internet Explorer's interpretation.

```
<SCRIPT LANGUAGE="JavaScript">
<!--
document.write("You're visiting my Web page on " + Date
//-->
</SCRIPT>
```

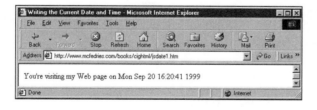

Figure 16.5

This simple script inserts the current date and time.

That's not bad, but the date and time display is a bit ugly. To get more control, you need to break out the various components of the date and time: the day of the week, the month, the hours and minutes, and so on.

Here's a quick summary of the JavaScript statements that do this:

➤ **getDay()**   Returns a number between 0 and 6, where 0 is Sunday, 1 is Monday, and so on.

➤ **getMonth()**   Returns the number of the current month, where 1 is January, 2 is February, and so on.

➤ **getYear()** Returns the current year. If the year is before 2000, it returns a two-digit year (such as 99); if it's in 2000 or later, it returns the four-digit year.

➤ **getSeconds()** Returns the seconds in the current time.

➤ **getMinutes()** Returns the minutes in the current time.

➤ **getHours()** Returns the hours in the current time. Note that this is military time, so if it's 5:00 in the afternoon, it returns 17.

To use these statements, you must first store the current date in what programmers call a *variable*, like so:

```
d = new Date()
```

You can then apply one of the statements to this variable. Here's how you'd get the current day:

```
d.getDay()
```

Note, too, that after you go to all this trouble, then it becomes relatively easy to display a custom message to the user based on the current time. For example, you might want to add "Good morning!" if the current date and time is before noon.

Here's a long script that takes advantage of all this (see jsdate2.htm on the CD).

```
<SCRIPT LANGUAGE="JavaScript">
<!--
// Store the date in a variable
d = new Date()
dateText = ""

// Get the current day and convert it to the name of the day
dayValue = d.getDay()
if (dayValue == 0)
    dateText += "Sunday"
else if (dayValue == 1)
    dateText += "Monday"
else if (dayValue == 2)
    dateText += "Tuesday"
else if (dayValue == 3)
    dateText += "Wednesday"
else if (dayValue == 4)
    dateText += "Thursday"
else if (dayValue == 5)
    dateText += "Friday"
else if (dayValue == 6)
    dateText += "Saturday"

// Get the current month and convert it to the name of the month
```

```
monthValue = d.getMonth()
dateText += " "
if (monthValue == 0)
    dateText += "January"
if (monthValue == 1)
    dateText += "February"
if (monthValue == 2)
    dateText += "March"
if (monthValue == 3)
    dateText += "April"
if (monthValue == 4)
    dateText += "May"
if (monthValue == 5)
    dateText += "June"
if (monthValue == 6)
    dateText += "July"
if (monthValue == 7)
    dateText += "August"
if (monthValue == 8)
    dateText += "September"
if (monthValue == 9)
    dateText += "October"
if (monthValue == 10)
    dateText += "November"
if (monthValue == 11)
    dateText += "December"

// Get the current year; if it's before 2000, add 1900
if (d.getYear() < 2000)
    dateText += " " + d.getDate() + ", " + (1900 + d.getYear
else
    dateText += " " + d.getDate() + ", " + (d.getYear

// Get the current minutes
minuteValue = d.getMinutes()
if (minuteValue < 10)
    minuteValue = "0" + minuteValue

// Get the current hours
hourValue = d.getHours()

// Customize the greeting based on the current hours
if (hourValue < 12)
    {
    greeting = "Good morning!"
    timeText = " at " + hourValue + ":" + minuteValue + " AM"
```

```
    }
else if (hourValue == 12)
    {
    greeting = "Good afternoon!"
    timeText = " at " + hourValue + ":" + minuteValue + " PM"
    }
else if (hourValue < 17)
    {
    greeting = "Good afternoon!"
    timeText = " at " + (hourValue-12) + ":" + minuteValue + " PM"
    }
else
    {
    greeting = "Good evening!"
    timeText = " at " + (hourValue-12) + ":" + minuteValue + " PM"
    }
// Write the greeting, the date, and the time to the page
document.write(greeting + " It's " + dateText + timeText)
//-->
</SCRIPT>
```

Whew! That's some script! It works quite nicely, though, as you can see in Figure 16.6.

Figure 16.6

This page uses JavaScript to display the date and time and an appropriate message based on the time of day.

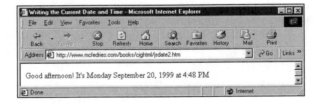

Understanding JavaScript Functions

In the examples you've seen so far, how did the browser know that it was supposed to run the JavaScript statements? Because the browser routinely scours the page for a <SCRIPT> and </SCRIPT> combo. If it sees one, it goes right ahead and runs whatever JavaScript statements are stuffed in there.

The exception to this is when the statements reside inside a JavaScript function. In that case, the browser ignores the function's statements. So how do they get executed? You have to put in a statement that says to the browser, "Hey, you! Run this function for me, will ya!" In geekspeak, this is known as *calling* the function.

Let's see a simple example. Instead of displaying a dialog box when the user loads your page, what if you want to display a message when the user *leaves* your page? The browser has already processed your page, so it doesn't do anything to it when the user leaves. Therefore, to execute some JavaScript code at that point, you have to create a function and then call it. Here's an example function called SayGoodbye():

```
function SayGoodbye()
{
    alert("Thanks for visiting my Web site!")
}
```

Here's how it looks within the page (see jsalert2.htm on the CD):

```
<HTML>
<HEAD>
<TITLE>Displaying a Message to the User, Part 2</TITLE>
</HEAD>

<SCRIPT LANGUAGE="JavaScript">
<!--
function SayGoodbye()
{
    alert("Thanks for visiting my Web site!")
}
//-->
</SCRIPT>

<BODY onUnload="SayGoodbye()">
</BODY>
</HTML>
```

The thing to notice here is the special onUnload statement in the <BODY> tag. This tells the browser to execute the SayGoodbye() function when the user leaves ("unloads") the page.

So, to summarize, here's how the browser executes JavaScript statements:

➤ If the statements aren't within a function, the browser executes them as soon as the page loads.

➤ If the statements are within a function, the browser doesn't execute them until the function is called.

Displaying Messages in the Status Bar

Rather than tossing a dialog box-based message at the user, many HTMLists prefer a more subtle approach: displaying the message in the browser's status bar. To do this, use the self.status statement:

```
self.status = "Put your message here"
```

Here, *self* refers to the browser window. Here's a simple example (see jsstatus.htm on the CD).

```
<SCRIPT LANGUAGE="JavaScript">
<!--
self.status = "Welcome to my Web site!"
//-->
</SCRIPT>
```

Figure 16.7 shows how things look after the page is loaded into Internet Explorer.

Figure 16.7

Use the self.status statement to display a message in the browser's status bar.

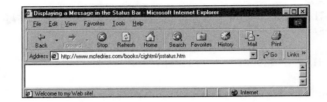

One of the most requested JavaScript examples is a script that not only displays a message in the browser's status bar, but also scrolls the message from right to left. This is a complex procedure, as you can see below, but you can safely ignore most of the code. You'll find everything on the CD in the file named jsscroll.htm, which also provides instructions for customizing the status bar message. Figure 16.8 shows the page in Netscape.

```
<SCRIPT LANGUAGE="JavaScript">
<!--
// Use the following three variables to set up the message:
var msg = "Enter your status bar message here"
var delay = 50
var startPos = 100

// Don't touch these variables:
var timerID = null
var timerRunning = false
var pos = 0

// Crank it up!
StartScrolling()

function StartScrolling(){
    // Make sure the clock is stopped
    StopTheClock()

    // Pad the message with spaces to get the "start" position
    for (var i = 0; i < startPos; i++) msg = " " + msg
```

```
        // Off we go...
        DoTheScroll()
    }

    function StopTheClock(){
        if(timerRunning)
            clearTimeout(timerID)
        timerRunning = false
    }

    function DoTheScroll(){
        if (pos < msg.length)
            self.status = msg.substring(pos, msg.length);
        else
            pos=-1;
        ++pos
        timerRunning = true
        timerID = self.setTimeout("DoTheScroll()", delay)
    }
    //-->
    </SCRIPT>
```

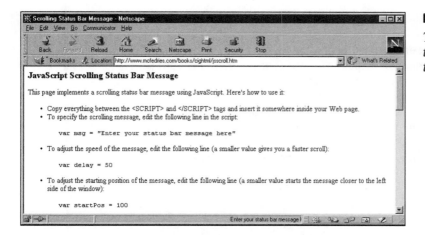

Figure 16.8

This page uses JavaScript to scroll a message along the browser's status bar.

Detecting the User's Browser

For the final example in this chapter, I show you how to determine which browser the user is surfing with. Why would you care? Well, you might want to send the surfer to a page that's been customized for their browser.

More Status Bar Silliness

My JavaScript page is also home to several other status bar scripts that display multiple messages, random messages, and more. See the following page for the appropriate links:

```
http://www.mcfedries.com/JavaScript/
```

JavaScript offers two statements that return browser info:

➤ **navigator.appName**   This returns the name of the browser.

➤ **navigator.appVersion**   This returns the version number of the browser.

Here's a script (see jsbrowsr.thm on the CD) that determines the browser name and version and then displays a custom message (shown in Figure 16.9).

```
<SCRIPT LANGUAGE="JavaScript">
<!--
    var browserName = navigator.appName
    var browserVer = parseInt(navigator.appVersion);
    if (browserName == "Netscape")
        {
        alert("Welcome Netscape Navigator user!" + "\n\n" + "You are
        ➥using version " + browserVer)
        }
    else if (browserName == "Microsoft Internet Explorer")
        {
        var ver = navigator.appVersion
        var start = ver.indexOf("MSIE") + 5
        var end = ver.indexOf(";",start)
        browserVer = parseInt(ver.substring(start,end))
        alert("Welcome Internet Explorer user!" + "\n\n" + "You are
        ➥using version " + browserVer)
        }
    else
        {
        alert("Welcome " + browserName + " user!" + "\n\n" + "You are
        ➥using version " + browserVer)
        }
```

```
//-->
</SCRIPT>
```

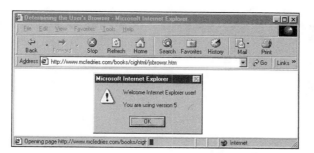

Figure 16.9

This page displays the user's browser info.

Sending the User to Another Page

If you want to modify this script to send the user to another page based on his browser, use the `location.href` statement:

```
location.href = "url"
```

Here, *url* is the name or full URL of the page to which you want to send the surfer.

JavaScript Resources on the Web

If you want to learn how to program in JavaScript, or if you just want to grab a few more scripts for your pages, the Web is stuffed to the gills with great JavaScript sites. Here's a list of my favorites (see js_sites.htm on the CD):

Answers to Common Questions About JavaScript

`http://idm.internet.com/faq/js-faq.shtml`

This site has a slick collection of Frequently Asked Questions about JavaScript.

Ask the JavaScript Pro

http://www.inquiry.com/techtips/js_pro/

This site provides an answer to just about every JavaScript question under the sun.

JavaGoodies

http://www.javagoodies.com/

This site includes a nice collection of scripts and tutorials by Joe "Huh?" Burns.

JavaScript for the Total Non-Programmer

http://www.webteacher.com/javatour/

Like the name says, this site offers a *really* basic JavaScript tutorial.

The JavaScript Source

http://javascript.internet.com/

This side includes lots of "cut and paste" JavaScripts, tutorials, book reviews, and even a help forum.

JavaScripts.com

http://www.javascripts.com/

This EarthWeb site offers thousands of scripts, tutorials, discussion groups, and even a weekly newsletter.

Jscripts.com

http://jscripts.com/

This well-constructed site run by reader Adam Charnock features lots of interesting scripts.

McFedries.com JavaScripts

http://mcfedries.com/JavaScript/

I offer a few scripts on my site.

Netscape's JavaScript Sample Code

`http://developer.netscape.com/docs/examples/javascript.html`

This site offers a great collection of JavaScript examples from the people who invented the darn thing.

Netscape's Online JavaScript Reference Manual

`http://developer.netscape.com/docs/manuals/communicator/jsref/index.htm`

This is the definitive place to learn about JavaScript, although it's not exactly designed for newcomers.

ScriptSearch

`http://www.scriptsearch.com/`

This site boasts a truly huge number of scripts for doing just about anything you can think of (and plenty of things you can't).

Webmonkey

`http://www.hotwired.com/webmonkey/javascript/`

This Wired Magazine-related site has a great name and an even greater collection of JavaScript tutorials, tips, and scripts.

Website Abstraction

`http://www.wsabstract.com/`

This site with a geeky name offers lots of scripts and tutorials for both beginning and advanced programmers.

Web Trixter

`http://www.webtrixter.com/`

This is a nice site put together by reader Chris Miller.

Yahoo! JavaScript Index

```
http://dir.yahoo.com/Computers_and_Internet/Programming_Languages/
JavaScript/
```

This Yahoo! index offers dozens of links to JavaScript sites in the four corners of the Net.

ZDNet JavaScript Library

```
http://www.zdnet.com/devhead/resources/scriptlibrary/javascript/
```

This site offers a nice collection of top-quality scripts, plus a "scripthead" column that discusses JavaScript techniques.

Dynamic HTML

The Web page wave of the future is a not-so-little something called *Dynamic HTML* (or DHTML, for short). This exciting technology marries HTML, style sheets, and JavaScript to enable you to program just about anything and everything on a page. It's an official HTML standard now, so it will be around for years to come. Internet Explorer versions 4.0 and later understand it already but, unfortunately, Netscape doesn't (at least as of version 4.7; note, too, that Netscape has its own version of DHTML, which should be ignored because it's not a standard). Here are some addresses for sites that tell you more about DHTML (see js_sites.htm on the CD for links to these pages):

```
http://www.dhtmlzone.com/index.html
http://msdn.microsoft.com/workshop/author/default.asp
http://dynamicdrive.com/
http://www.stars.com/Authoring/DHTML/
http://www.ruleweb.com/dhtml/index.html
```

The Least You Need to Know

This chapter introduced you to the brave new world of JavaScript. After a quick look at the ins and outs of the <SCRIPT> tag, you got right down to it by running through quite a few example scripts for things like displaying messages and inserting text. I closed with a list of good JavaScript resources for the eager and the curious.

Speaking of the latter, you'll be pleased to know that this book's JavaScripts studies aren't over yet. The next chapter takes you through even more scripts.

More JavaScript Fun

The previous chapter showed you that although programming JavaScript is tough, just inserting a script or two into a page isn't a big deal. If you liked the examples I took you through in that chapter, wait until you see what I have in store for you here. By necessity, these are much more complex scripts, but you'll see that they do much more interesting things. Don't worry if some of the scripts look intimidating. Remember: you don't have to understand their inner workings to get them to work. Just follow my instructions and you'll have your JavaScript-enhanced pages up and at 'em in no time.

A Script for Mouseovers

Have you ever visited a Web site, sat your mouse over an image, and then seen that image magically transform into a different graphic? This neat effect is called a "mouseover" and it's all done with JavaScript.

Browser Support

The mouseover technique I show you in this section works in Netscape version 3.0 and later, as well as in Internet Explorer version 4.0 and later. This accounts for at least 95% of all users.

There are several ways to go about this, but there's one method that's relatively simple and straightforward. You begin by entering a normal <IMG> tag, except that you name it by inserting the NAME attribute:

```
<IMG SRC="whatever.gif" NAME="somename">
```

For the example I'm using, I have two images:

➤ **mouseout.gif** This is the regular image that appears without the mouse pointer over it.

➤ **mouseovr.gif** This is the image that appears when the user puts the mouse pointerover mouseout.gif.

Here's the <IMG> tag (each attribute is on a separate line for easier reading):

```
<IMG SRC="mouseout.gif"
    WIDTH=157
    HEIGHT=39
    BORDER=0
    NAME="mypicture">
```

As you can see, I've used mouseout.gif to start, and I've given the name "mypicture" to the <IMG> tag. Now you construct an <A> tag (mouseovers only work with images that are set up as links):

```
<A HREF="jsmouse1.html"
    onMouseover="mypicture.src='mouseovr.gif'"
    onMouseout="mypicture.src='mouseout.gif'">
```

There are two extra JavaScript attributes here: onMouseover and onMouseout. The onMouseover attribute says, essentially, "When the user moves their mouse pointer over the image named mypicture, change its SRC attribute to mouseovr.gif."

Similarly, the onMouseout attribute says, essentially, "When the user moves their mouse pointer off (out of) the image named mypicture, change its SRC attribute to mouseout.gif."

Here's how the whole thing looks (see jsmouse1.htm on the CD):

```
<A HREF="jsmouse1.html"
    onMouseover="mypicture.src='mouseovr.gif'"
    onMouseout="mypicture.src='mouseout.gif'">
<IMG SRC="mouseout.gif"
    WIDTH=157
    HEIGHT=39
```

```
      BORDER=0
      NAME="mypicture">
  </A>
```

Figure 17.1 offers two Internet Explorer windows showing the same page (jsmouse1.htm). In the top window, I don't have the mouse over the image, so Internet Explorer shows mouseout.gif. In the bottom window, I've put my mouse over the image, so Internet Explorer displays mouseovr.gif.

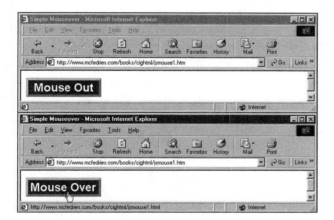

Figure 17.1

Internet Explorer showing the <IMG> tag without the mouse over it (top window) and with the mouse over it (bottom window).

Techno Talk

Where's the <SCRIPT> Tag?

You might be wondering where the heck is the <SCRIPT> tag that I told you in the previous chapter that you had to use for JavaScript. It's nowhere in sight because sometimes you can just enter a JavaScript statement directly, without needing a <SCRIPT> tag. For example, consider the following chunk from the <A> tag in this example:

```
onMouseover="mypicture.src='mouseovr.gif'"
```

The onMouseover part is called an *event*, and the rest of the line is an honest-to-goodness JavaScript statement. In other words, when the onMouseover event occurs (that is, when the user places their mouse over the image), the JavaScript statement is executed automatically.

Here are a few notes to keep handy when working with mouseovers:

➤ If you have a lot of visitors who use Internet Explorer version 3.0, then you'll have trouble because they'll keep getting errors. Another mouseover technique that avoids these Internet Explorer errors is shown here:

```
http://www.mcfedries.com/JavaScript/mouseover2.html
```

➤ Don't use large images for your mouseover effects. When the user puts the mouse over the image for the first time, the browser delays while it downloads the mouseover image. If you use a large image, that delay can be several seconds or longer, which spoils the effect. Mouseovers are best used with images that weigh only a few kilobytes or so.

➤ If you have a larger image that you must use, it's possible to "pre-load" the image (that is, have the browser load the image and keep it waiting in memory when it first opens the page). I show you how this works in the following page:

```
http://www.mcfedries.com/JavaScript/mouseover3.html
```

Creating a Password-Protected Page

Many readers have written to me over the years and asked how they can set up a page that can only be accessed if the user enters the appropriate password. "That depends," I always respond, "on how bulletproof you need your password to be." Here are a couple of things to consider when deciding how much password-protection you need for your page:

➤ If you have sensitive information that must be protected at all costs, ask your Web hosting provider if they can establish a password-protected portion of your site. If that's not possible, you might need to hire a CGI programmer to create a password-protection script. There are also some password scripts available on the Web. (See Chapter 11, "Need Feedback? Create a Form!," for some resources.)

➤ If your needs aren't so grandiose, then you can set up a reasonably strong password system using just a few dollops of JavaScript.

Hold on just a sec, mister! JavaScript stuff sits right inside the page. Won't someone be able to see the password if they look at the page source code?

That's very perceptive of you. However, in the system that I show you, the password never appears in the JavaScript code! Why? Because the password is just the name of the protected page (minus the .htm or .html extension). Because it's just as hard to guess the name of a Web page as it is to guess a password, you get basically the same level of protection.

You Must Have a Default Page!

For this password scheme to work, it's absolutely crucial to have a default page in the same directory as the password-protected page. Why? Well, recall that a default page is the one the server sends out if the user doesn't specify a page. For example, suppose the user enters the following address:

http://www.yourserver.com/finances/

Most servers use index.html as the default page, so the above is equivalent to the following address:

http://www.yourserver.com/finances/index.html

If you don't include the default page in the directory, most Web servers simply return a list of all the files in the directory! This would obviously defeat our password protection scheme.

The system I'm going to show you requires three parts:

➤ A page that has a link to the password-protected part of your site. I use a page titled jspwtest.htm (it's on the CD) for this example.

➤ A page that asks the user for the proper password (this is jspass.htm on the CD).

➤ The password-protected page (this is idiot.htm on the CD). When you name this file, you must use lowercase letters only.

The next couple of sections show you how to set everything up.

Creating a Link to the Password-Protected Part of Your Site

You can send people to the password-protected page by including a link in one or more pages on your site. Other than the password-protected page itself, this is the only thing you need to create yourself. Here's the <A> tag to use:

```
<A HREF="javascript:GetPassword()">
```

As you can see, this link calls a JavaScript function named GetPassword(). Here's the code for that function (place this between the </HEAD> and <BODY> tags in the same page):

```
<SCRIPT LANGUAGE="JavaScript">
<!--
function GetPassword()
{
    window.open("jspass.htm", "","width=225,height=70")
}
//-->
</SCRIPT>
```

All the GetPassword() function does is open a new window that contains the jspass.htm page. Figure 17.2 shows a page that uses this link and function (see jspwtest.htm on the CD) and it shows the window that appears when you click the link.

Figure 17.2

When you click this link, the GetPassword() function displays a window.

Clicking this link... —

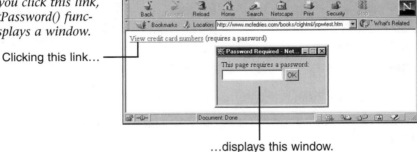

...displays this window.

Understanding the Script That Processes the Password

The little window that shows up contains a simple form that asks the user to enter the password:

```
<FORM>
This page requires a password:<BR>
<INPUT TYPE="TEXT" NAME="pw" SIZE=15>
<INPUT TYPE="BUTTON" VALUE="OK"
onClick="SubmitPassword(this.form)">
</FORM>
```

There are two things to note here for future use:

➤ The text box is named pw.

➤ The button uses the JavaScript onClick event to run a function. That is, when the user clicks the button, the JavaScript function named SubmitPassword() is called.

Here's the code for the SubmitPassword() function:

```
<SCRIPT LANGUAGE="JavaScript">
<!--

function SubmitPassword(frm)
{
    //
    // Get the value entered into the text box
    //
    var password = frm.pw.value
    //
    // Convert it to lowercase
    //
    password = password.toLowerCase()
    //
    // Add the .htm extension
    //
    var loc = password + ".htm"
    //
    // Make sure the user entered something
    //
    if (password != "")
    {
        //
        // If so, send the browser there
        //
        opener.location.href = loc
    }
    //
    // Close this window
    //
    window.close()
}

//-->
</SCRIPT>
```

Here's what happens:

1. The value in the pw text box is stored in the password variable.
2. The password value is changed to all lowercase letters (just in case the user entered any uppercase letters).
3. The .htm extension is tacked on to password. (You might need to change this to ".html" if your pages use that extension.)

4. If password isn't blank, the main browser window is sent to the password-protected page.

5. The little window is closed.

If you try out the example page that's on the CD, enter **idiot** as the password.

JavaScript and Forms

In the previous example, you saw how I used a small form to get the password and then I used JavaScript to process that value. As you see over the next few sections, JavaScript is quite happy to work with forms for all kinds of things.

Making Form Fields Mandatory

One of the problems we Webmasters face when constructing forms is getting our users to fill in all the required fields. We can augment the form with all kinds of notes that warn the user of the dire consequences that can result from leaving a field blank, but users have a way of ignoring these things.

A better approach is to use a little JavaScript know-how to make one or more form fields mandatory. That is, make it so the browser won't submit the form unless the user puts something in those fields.

For example, there isn't any way for my MailForm script (see Chapter 11) to reliably detect the user's email address, which means you have to rely on your readers to enter their email address so that you can contact them. One thing you can do is use JavaScript to make your form's email field mandatory.

To set this up, you first need to make two adjustments to your <FORM> tag:

➤ Add the NAME attribute and set it to whatever you want to name your form.

➤ Add the JavaScript onSubmit attribute, like so (here, *FormName* is the name you gave your form).

```
onSubmit="return validate(FormName)"
```

Here's an example:

```
<FORM
    ACTION="http://www.mcfedries.com/cgi-win/formtest.exe"
    METHOD=POST
    NAME="MyForm"
    onSubmit="return Validate(MyForm)">
```

The onSubmit event means that when the user submits the form, the function specified by onSubmit is executed before the form is sent to the server. This enables you to check that a particular field has been filled in (or whatever). If it hasn't, the JavaScript can tell the browser not to submit the form.

248

You set up the rest of your form in the usual manner. You just need to pay attention to the names you supply each field because you use those names in the JavaScript procedure. Here's the example field I'll use:

```
<B>Please enter your email address:</B><BR>
<INPUT TYPE=TEXT SIZE=35 NAME="Email">
```

Here, at long last, is the script (see jsform1.htm on the CD):

```
<SCRIPT LANGUAGE="JavaScript">
<!--
function Validate(frm)
{
    //
    // Check the Email field to see if any characters were entered
    //
    if (frm.Email.value == "")
    {
        alert("Tsk tsk. Please enter an email address.")
        frm.Email.focus()
        return false
    }
}
//-->
</SCRIPT>
```

What's happening here is that the Validate() function checks the value the user entered into the specified field (Email, in this case). If the value is empty (""), it means the user didn't enter a value. So the script displays an alert (see Figure 17.3), puts the cursor back in the Email field (this is called setting the "focus" in programming parlance), and then returns false, which tells the browser not to submit the form.

Figure 17.3

If the user doesn't enter anything in the text box, they see this message.

To use this script on your own form, there are two things you need to adjust:

➤ The `if` statement checks the length of the form field named Email. When setting this up for your own use, you need to change `Email` to the name of your field.

➤ The same goes for the `frm.Email.focus()` statement. That is, you need to change `Email` to the name of your field.

An Extra Step

The user can easily thwart this script by entering a trivial value (such as a single letter) in the text box. My Web site offers a more sophisticated version of the script that checks to see if the user entered the @ sign (which is part of every email address). See the following page:

```
http://www.mcfedries.com/JavaScript/mandatory.html
```

Confirming Form Data with the User

It's important that the data submitted in a form be as accurate as possible. However, your typical surfer has a short attention span (present company excepted, of course), so he tends to fill in form data haphazardly. To help boost the accuracy of submissions, it's a good idea to display the entered data to the user before submitting it. If everything looks good, he can submit the data; otherwise, he can cancel and make changes.

Before getting to the JavaScript, let's set up a sample form that includes the four main form controls: a text box, an option list, radio buttons, and a check box (see Chapter 11). Here it is (see jscheck.htm on the CD):

```
<FORM
    ACTION="http://www.mcfedries.com/cgi-win/formtest.exe"
    METHOD=POST
    NAME="MyForm"
    onSubmit="return CheckData(MyForm)">
```

```
Please enter your name:<BR>
<INPUT TYPE=TEXT NAME="UserName">
<P>
Who is your favorite Beatle?<BR>
<SELECT NAME="Beatle">
<OPTION VALUE="George" SELECTED>George
<OPTION VALUE="John">John
<OPTION VALUE="Paul">Paul
<OPTION VALUE="Ringo">Ringo
<OPTION VALUE="Pete Best">Pete Best
<OPTION VALUE="Hunh?">Who the heck are the Beatles?
</SELECT>
<P>
Have you ever gotten jiggy with it?<BR>
<INPUT TYPE=RADIO NAME="Jiggy" VALUE="Yes" CHECKED>Yes
<INPUT TYPE=RADIO NAME="Jiggy" VALUE="No">No
<INPUT TYPE=RADIO NAME="Jiggy" VALUE="Shhh">Not Telling
<P>
<INPUT TYPE=CHECKBOX NAME="Spam">Send tons of spam?
<P>
<INPUT TYPE=SUBMIT VALUE="Fire!">
</FORM>
```

Note, in particular, that I added the JavaScript onSubmit attribute to the <FORM> tag:

```
onSubmit="return CheckData(MyForm)"
```

This tells the browser that when the user submits the form, it must run the CheckData() JavaScript function. The return part means that the browser should examine the value returned by CheckData() to see whether the form submission should proceed or be cancelled. Here's the JavaScript:

```
<SCRIPT LANGUAGE="JavaScript">
<!--
function CheckData(frm)
{
    //
    // Get the text box value
    //
    var tb = frm.UserName.value
    //
    // Get the selected option
    //
    var opt = frm.Beatle.options[frm.Beatle.selectedIndex].value
    //
```

251

```
// Get the selected radio button
//
for (var i = 0; i < frm.Jiggy.length; i++)
{
    if (frm.Jiggy[i].checked)
        var rb = frm.Jiggy[i].value
}
//
// Get the check box value
//
if (frm.Spam.checked)
    var cb = "On"
else
    var cb = "Off"
//
// Construct the message to display
//
var msg = "Your name: " + tb + "\n"
    + "Favorite Beatle: " + opt + "\n"
    + "Jiggy with it? " + rb + "\n"
    + "Send spam: " + cb + "\n"
//
// Show the data to the user
//
return confirm("Here is the form data you entered:" + "\n\n"
    + msg + "\n"
    + "Do you want to submit this data?")
}
//-->
</SCRIPT>
```

Adding New Lines

In case you're wondering, all those "\n" things in the script are just the JavaScript code for starting a new line. This makes the displayed message easier to read.

The bulk of the function is spent getting the various form values. After that's done, a message containing all the values is constructed and then shown to the user via the confirm() statement. Figure 17.4 shows the dialog box that pops up. If the user click **Yes**, the confirm() statement returns True, and the form gets submitted; if they click **No**, confirm() returns False and the form doesn't do anything.

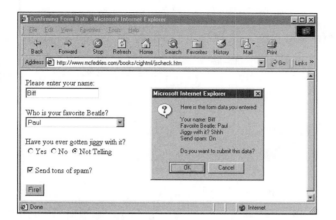

Figure 17.4

When the user submits the form, he sees this confirmation message.

Creating a Drop-Down List of Links

After your Web site grows to a certain size, you run up against a daunting problem: how do you let surfers navigate to the various nooks and crannies of your site without cluttering each page with tons of links or a massive image map? My solution to this problem is the humble option list that you learned about in Chapter 11. Figure 17.5 shows what I mean. As you can see, the list contains all kinds of items that represent pages on my site. The surfer simply picks an item from the list and is immediately whisked to the selected spot. Best of all, it takes up just a small strip of space at the top of each of my pages.

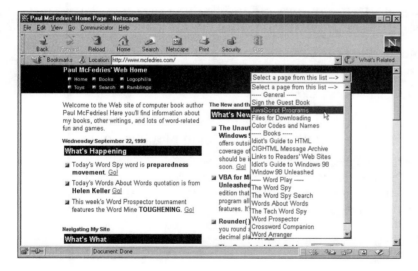

Figure 17.5

Each of my pages uses a drop-down list to help folks navigate my site.

As you've no doubt guessed by now, the secret behind this list legerdemain is JavaScript. This section shows you how it easy it is to set up just such a list on your own site.

Let's begin with the list itself. You start by setting up a more-or-less standard selection list within a form:

```
<FORM>
<SELECT WIDTH=20 onChange="JumpToIt(this)">
</SELECT>
</FORM>
```

There are two things you should note about this structure:

➤ The <FORM> tag is completely naked. That's okay because with this technique you never have to submit any form data to a server. That makes this method as lightning quick as a regular link.

➤ The <SELECT> tag houses the JavaScript onChange attribute. This tells the browser that whenever the list changes (that is, whenever the user selects a different item), it must run the JavaScript function named JumpToIt(). (The this part is a reference to the list itself that gets sent to the function.)

Now you need to populate the list with items that represent your pages. You do that with <OPTION> tags that take the following form:

```
<OPTION VALUE="URL">Item text
```

Here, replace *URL* with the URL of the page, and replace *Item text* with whatever text you want to appear in the list (such as the page title).

If you want to add non-active items to the list (such as a "Select an item from this list" message or headings), use <OPTION> tags that take the following form:

```
<OPTION VALUE="None">Item text
```

Again, replace *Item text* with the text that you want to appear in the list. Here's the list structure with a few items added (there's a larger list in jslist.htm on the CD):

```
<SELECT WIDTH=20 onChange="JumpToIt(this)">
<OPTION VALUE="None">Select a JavaScript resource from this list --->
<OPTION VALUE="http://www.javagoodies.com/">JavaGoodies
<OPTION VALUE="http://www.javascripts.com/">JavaScripts.com
<OPTION VALUE="http://jscripts.com/">Jscripts.com
<OPTION VALUE="http://www.scriptsearch.com/">ScriptSearch
<OPTION VALUE="http://www.wsabstract.com/">Website Abstraction
</SELECT>
```

Here's the JavaScript that is executed when the user selects a list item:

```
<SCRIPT LANGUAGE="JavaScript">
<!--
function JumpToIt(list)
{
    var selection = list.options[list.selectedIndex].value
    if (selection != "None")
        location.href = selection
}
//-->
</SCRIPT>
```

The value of the currently selected list item is stored in the selection variable. If the value isn't "None", then the value is a URL, so the location.href property is set to that value, and away you go.

A Mortgage Calculator

For the final example, I show you a particularly powerful script that sets up a mortgage calculator. Figure 17.6 shows the calculator, which I created using form and table tags.

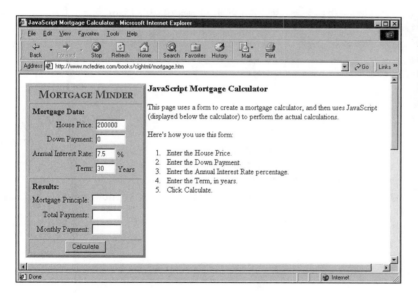

Figure 17.6

A mortgage calculator created using standard form and table tags. JavaScript makes the calculator calculate.

The calculator looks pretty enough, but can it calculate anything? Sure! Using the JavaScript below, you can actually compute the monthly mortgage payment based on the values you input.

```
<SCRIPT LANGUAGE="JavaScript">
<!--
function checkForZero(field)
{
    if (field.value == 0 || field.value.length == 0) {
        alert ("This field can't be 0!");
        field.focus(); }
    else
        calculatePayment(field.form);
}

function cmdCalc_Click(form)
{
    if (form.price.value == 0 || form.price.value.length == 0) {
        alert ("The Price field can't be 0!");
        form.price.focus(); }
    else if (form.ir.value == 0 || form.ir.value.length == 0) {
        alert ("The Interest Rate field can't be 0!");
        form.ir.focus(); }
    else if (form.term.value == 0 || form.term.value.length == 0) {
        alert ("The Term field can't be 0!");
        form.term.focus(); }
    else
        calculatePayment(form);
}

function calculatePayment(form)
{
    princ = form.price.value - form.dp.value;
    intRate = (form.ir.value/100) / 12;
    months = form.term.value * 12;
    form.pmt.value = Math.floor((princ*intRate)/(1-Math.pow(1+
    ➥intRate,(-1*months)))*100)/100;
    form.principle.value = princ;
    form.payments.value = months;
}
//-->
</SCRIPT>
```

That's a complex chunk of code, to be sure, but luckily you don't have to understand how it works. The only thing you need to make sure of when using this script in another page, is that you use the same names for the form controls that I use in the example mortgage.htm file (which is, of course, on the CD).

The Least You Need to Know

This chapter extended your JavaScript know-how by taking you through quite a few examples. You saw useful scripts for doing mouseovers, password-protecting pages, dealing with forms, creating a list of links, and powering a mortgage calculator.

The next chapter introduces you to Java, the bigger and more powerful cousin of JavaScript.

Chapter 18

Caffeinating Your Pages: Adding Java Applets

In This Chapter

➤ A bit of Java background

➤ How to put a Java applet inside a Web page

➤ Some Java resources to check out

➤ A fistful of examples and just a few bad coffee puns

The forms that I told you about back in Chapter 11, "Need Feedback? Create a Form!," are a great way to get feedback and to make your site feel more alive and interactive. However, we're starting to see a trend away from the simple type-it-and-send-it world of forms toward pages that are truly dynamic. Instead of mere documents to read and look at, pages are becoming programs that you can manipulate and play with.

The engine that's propelling this sea change is a technology called Java that's poised to become the biggest thing on the Web since, well, the Web itself. The idea behind Java is blindingly simple, but devilishly clever: When you access a Java-enhanced Web page, your browser gets not only a page containing the usual HTML suspects, but it also receives a program. The browser (assuming it can tell a Java program from a Jackson Pollock) then runs the program right on the Web page. So if the program is, say, a game of Hangman, then you're able to play Hangman right on the page. Now *that's* interactive!

This chapter gives you a bit of background on Java and then shows you how to add Java applets to your Web pages.

Java Versus JavaScript

"Java" and "JavaScript" sound kind of the same, so you might be wondering if they're related. Yes, they are, but only as distant cousins. The only thing they have in common is that the JavaScript programming language is basically a scaled-down version of Java. Other than that, they're completely different. The main difference is that you can construct JavaScript programs using a simple text editor, but creating Java programs requires a separate hunk of software called a *compiler*.

Java: A Piping Hot Mug of Browser-Based Programs

Java programs (or *applets*, as they're usually called) are written using the Java programming language developed by Sun Microsystems. Here are a few advantages that Java programs have over traditional software:

➤ The programs are sent to your browser and are started "behind the scenes." You don't have to worry about installation, setup, or loading because your browser takes care of all that dirty work for you.

➤ The programs are designed to work on just about any system. Whether you're running Windows, a Mac, or a UNIX machine, Java programs run without complaint.

➤ Java is secure. When people hear about Java, their first concern is that some pimple-faced programmer who has succumbed to the dark side of The Force will send them a Java virus. But Java has built-in safeguards to prevent such attacks.

➤ Because you're always sent the latest and greatest version of the program when you access a site, you don't need to worry about upgrades and new releases.

So what do you need to start sipping some of this Java stuff? All you really need is a Web browser that knows what the heck to do with any Java applet that comes its way. The latest versions of most browsers are now Java-jolted. Netscape has been Java-aware since version 2.0, and Internet Explorer has done Java since version 3.0. In other words, you shouldn't have any problems with Java applets, and most of the folks viewing your pages are able to work with whatever applets you purloin for your own use.

Java applets come in all shapes and sizes, from tiny animations (known as *dancing baloney*) to full-blown software packages: word processors, spreadsheets, real-time stock quotes and portfolio management, high-end games, and much more. However, even the simplest Java doohickeys are exciting in their own way. This Java jazz is such a radical departure from typical Web content that interacting with even the humblest applet is a revelation. So, in that spirit, let's visit a few sites that boast some Java functionality.

Our first example is the Random Sentence Generator that I built myself. As you can see in Figure 18.1, you click the **Generate a New Sentence** button and the applet provides you with a new, random (and often hilarious) sentence. If you want to try this out for yourself, head for the following page:

```
http://www.logophilia.com/WordPlay/random-sentence.html
```

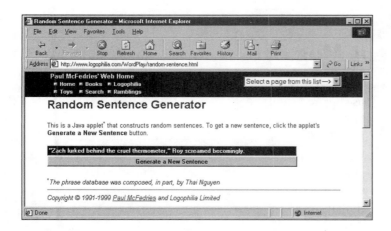

Figure 18.1

See semi-sensible sentences with the Random Sentence Generator Java applet.

Generating random sentences redefines the word "timewaster." If you're looking for more serious fun, there are thousands of Java-based games available. My own day isn't complete without a visit to the Word Game of the Day page on the Merriam-Webster site:

```
http://www.m-w.com/game/
```

This page offers a link to the game, which is one of five Java-fueled word games that rotate each day. Figure 18.2 shows an example.

After you've had your fill of fun, you'll find that there are plenty of practical Java applications just waiting to be downloaded. For example, there are many applets that offer real-time updating of information (such as stock quotes, sports scores, late-breaking news, and the like). Financial applets seem to be a popular category. For example, Figure 18.3 shows the Fidelity Fund Evaluator. This sophisticated Java applet presents you with several options for comparing mutual fund performance. It's available on the Fidelity site:

```
http://fundevaluator.fidelity.com/
```

261

Figure 18.2

There's no shortage of Java games on the Web.

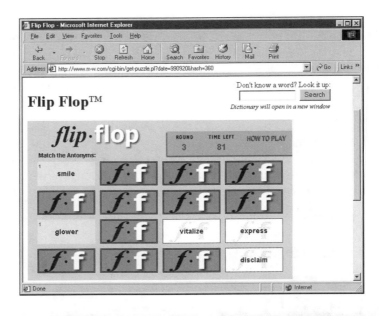

Figure 18.3

This is a Java applet that enables you to compare mutual funds.

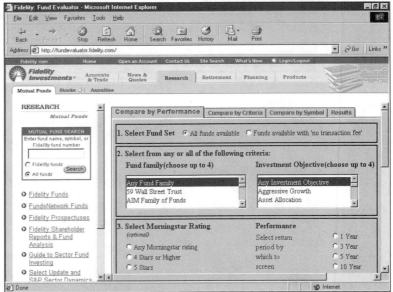

How to Add a Java Applet to a Web Page

If you'd like to give your visitors some Java applets to play with, they're easy enough to add to your pages. The secret is the <APPLET> tag:

```
<APPLET CODE="file" WIDTH=x HEIGHT=y>
Alternative text for non-Java browsers goes here.
</APPLET>
```

The critical chunk in this tag is the CODE attribute. The *file* part is the name of the "class" file that contains the Java code.

Example I: A Java Clock

Here's an example:

```
<APPLET CODE="JavaTime.class"
WIDTH=300 HEIGHT=60>
If you see this text, it means your
browser doesn't support Java.
</APPLET>
```

The JavaTime.class file is a Java application I wrote myself. It implements a digital clock that displays the current date and time, as shown in Figure 18.4.

JavaTime Is on the Disk

The JavaTime applet is on this book's disc in the Chap18 directory. See the javatime.htm file for the full instructions on using this applet.

Figure 18.4

The JavaTime applet serves up the current date and time.

The <APPLET> tag also takes a few other attributes:

ALIGN This attributes sets the alignment of the applet with respect to the text that surrounds it. You can use one of the following values: LEFT, CENTER, RIGHT, TOP, MIDDLE, or BOTTOM.

CODEBASE You use this attribute to specify a different location for the Java files. For example, suppose you create a "classes" directory to store all your Java junk. Then you'd add CODEBASE="classes/" to the <APPLET> tag so that the browser knows where to look for the Java files.

HSPACE This attribute sets a value (in pixels) for the amount of space that appears to the left and right of the applet.

VSPACE This attribute sets a value (in pixels) for the amount of space that appears above and below the applet.

Example II: Using Parameters

Most of the Java applets you abscond with for your own devices will run "as is." In other words, you just copy the class file to your Web site, plop the appropriate <APPLET> tag into your page, and off you go.

However, many applets are customizable. They enable you to specify features such as the colors the applet displays, the contents of some controls, and so on. For these flexible applets, you specify your own custom settings by shoehorning <PARAM> tags between the <APPLET> and </APPLET> tags. The <PARAM> tag (short for *parameter*) uses the following format:

```
<PARAM NAME="name" VALUE="value">
```

Here, *name* is the name of the parameter and *value* is the custom value you want to use for the parameter. Let's make all this more concrete with an example. On the disc, you'll find another Java applet that I built with my bare hands called JavaJump.class. (Look in the javajump directory.) As you can see in Figure 18.5, JavaJump consists of a drop-down list and a command button. The idea is that you select a page from the list and click the **Go!** button. The applet then tells the browser to go to that page.

Figure 18.5

*JavaJump: Select a page from the list and then click **Go!** to jump to that page.*

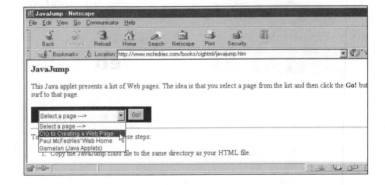

Here's the code that sets up the applet (see javajump.htm on the disc):

```
<APPLET CODE="JavaJump.class" WIDTH=250 HEIGHT=32>
<PARAM NAME="bgcolor" VALUE="0,0,0">
<PARAM NAME="pages" VALUE="3">
<PARAM NAME="url1" VALUE="CIG to Creating a Web
Page;http://www.mcfedries.com/books/cightml">
<PARAM NAME="url2" VALUE="Paul McFedries' Web
```

```
Home;http://www.mcfedries.com/">
<PARAM NAME="url3" VALUE="Gamelan (Java
Applets);http://www.gamelan.com/">
</APPLET>
```

Let's look at each <PARAM> tag in turn. The first one sets the background color of the applet:

```
<PARAM NAME="bgcolor" VALUE="red.green.blue">
```

Here, the VALUE parameter is set to three numbers (*red*, *green*, and *blue*), which are values between 0 and 255.

The second <PARAM> tag specifies the number of items that appear in the list:

```
<PARAM NAME="pages" VALUE="total">
```

The rest of the <PARAM> tags specify the list items and they use the following format:

```
<PARAM NAME="urlx" VALUE="Name;URL ">
```

Here, *x* is the item number (so your parameter names will be url1, url2, and so on), *Name* is the page name that appears in the list, and *URL* is the full URL of the Web page.

Java Resources on the Web

If this short chapter has tickled your Java fancy and you want more, don't sweat it. The Web is brim full to bursting with Java sites. Some of them are just so-so, but there are plenty of good ones. Here are some of my favorites (see javasite.htm on the CD).

Arcade Games Online

```
http://www.arcadegamesonline.com/
```

If you want Java-based games, this site's got 'em in spades.

CodeGuru

```
http://www.codeguru.com/java/
```

This site has a nice collection of applets that's augmented by forums, a Web-based newsgroup interface, and more.

Developer's Daily

http://www.devdaily.com/

Designed with the Java programmer in mind, this site has links to tons of tutorials, FAQs, and applets.

FreewareJava.com

http://freewarejava.com/

This site includes hundreds of applets, Java courses, links to other sites, and much more.

Gamelan

http://www.gamelan.com/

This is "The Official Directory for Java" and remains one of the premier Java sites on the Web.

JARS.COM

http://jars.com/

This site bills itself as "The #1 Java Review Service," and I have no reason to doubt it. You'll find thoughtful reviews of hundreds of applets in dozens of categories.

The Java Boutique

http://javaboutique.internet.com/

This is a first-rate site with lots of applets, programming tutorials, Java news, articles, forums, and more.

Netscape's Java Developer Central

http://developer.netscape.com/tech/java/index.html

If you think you want to learn Java, this comprehensive site is a great place to start.

ScriptSearch

http://www.scriptsearch.com/

As I'm sure you've come to expect, this site has the Java goods, as well, with hundreds and hundreds of applets to play with.

Sun Microsystems

http://java.sun.com/

I mentioned earlier that Sun invented Java, so their site's a must-visit for news, documentation, discussions, and lots and lots of high-quality applets.

Webmonkey

http://www.hotwired.com/webmonkey/java/

The famously simian site has a few nice Java tutorials and articles that are worth checking out.

Yahoo! Java Index

http://dir.yahoo.com/Computers_and_Internet/Programming_Languages/Java/

This site contains a great listing of Java resources.

The Least You Need to Know

This chapter used only a few bad coffee puns to help you understand the whole Java phenomenon and to show you how to add Java applets to your Web pages.

Now that you've got a nice caffeine buzz going, you're ready to tackle the next topic: Easier methods for cobbling together pages, which is the subject of the chapters in Part 5 "Painless Page Production: Easier Ways to Do the HTML Thing."

Part 5

Painless Page Production: Easier Ways to Do the HTML Thing

HTML certainly isn't brain surgery, or even rocket science, for that matter. You just slap up some text, toss in a few well-placed tags, and you're laughing. However, it does have a sort of primitive feel to it, as though we've taken a step backwards in electronic evolution. This is especially true for those of us who've grown accustomed to (even codependent on) the fancy-schmanciness of a graphical environment, such as Windows or the Mac. We find it a little odd to be cobbling Web pages together by hand when we'd normally convince a mouse and a few menus and dialog boxes to do our bidding.

If you're looking for a more modern way to build Web pages, you've come to the right place. The chapters in this section take you through a few programs and resources that can ease the drudgery of Web page production. We look at a few HTML editors, which are programs that let you insert HTML tags using a civilized pull-down-menu-and-dialog-box interface. I also tell you about a few Net-based resources that can make it easier to create your Web masterpieces.

Chapter 19

Netscape Composer and the Well-Tempered Web

In This Chapter

➤ Starting Composer

➤ Various methods for creating new Web pages

➤ Using Composer to format characters and paragraphs

➤ Inserting lists, images, links, and tables

➤ How you and Composer can make beautiful HTML music together

---

With the release of Netscape Communicator, Netscape made its bid to become the all-purpose, everything-but-the-kitchen-sink-but-wait-until-you-see-what-we-have-in-store-for-version-5, "Swiss Army knife" of the Internet. Besides containing one of the best Web browsers around (Navigator 4.*x*), Communicator is also stuffed with an email program, a Usenet newsreader, a discussions feature, the capability to handle most other Net services, including FTP and Gopher, and much more. You can even stick in a few extra utensils by taking advantage of plug-ins such as Live3D and many others.

But that wasn't enough for the Web's resident greedy-guts. Oh no. They shouted, "Give us more! Give us more!" So, the eager-to-please souls at Netscape obliged by bringing out Netscape Composer. This is a program that enables HTML nuts like us to not only see a Web page in all its glory (more or less), but also to edit the darn thing at the same time! This chapter gets you up to speed with Composer and shows you how to use it to edit your HTML creations.

Composer Version

Just so you know, this chapter was written using Communicator version 4.7.

Conducting Composer onto Your Screen

Assuming you've got Netscape Communicator installed on your system (if not, you can grab it from Netscape's Web site: `http://home.netscape.com/`), it's time to take a closer look at its Composer component. You have a trio of ways to proceed:

➤ Double-click the Composer icon that the setup program created.

➤ In Navigator, pull down the Communicator menu and select the Composer command. (Pressing Ctrl+4 also works.)

➤ If you prefer to edit the Web page that's currently displayed in Navigator, pull down the File menu and select the Edit Page command.

You should now see the Composer window, as shown in Figure 19.1.

Figure 19.1

The main Composer window.

Cranking Out a New HTML Document

When you invoke Netscape Composer, the program loads a new HTML document for you, no questions asked. However, you can start a fresh HTML file any time you jolly well feel like it. Composer actually gives you three choices for minting a fresh file:

➤ You can create a file using one of Netscape's prefab templates.

➤ You can use Netscape's online Page Wizard.

➤ You can create a blank file.

The next three sections give you the scoop on each method.

Using Templates to Get a Head Start

Type-A types and other folks in a hurry might not want to waste time building a new Web page from the ground up. To get you up to speed a little more quickly, Netscape has a decent collection of Web page *templates* on its Web site. These are pre-built HTML files you can customize to suit your style.

To choose one of these templates, follow these steps:

1. Select the **File**, **New**, **Page from Template** command. You can also click the **New** toolbar button to display the Create New Page dialog box, and then click the **From Template** button.

2. In the New Page From Template dialog box, click **Netscape Templates**. Composer fires up Navigator and sends it to a special page on Netscape's Web site.

3. If you scroll down this page a bit, you stumble across a list of template pages in various categories, as shown in Figure 19.2. To use one of these templates, click the link.

4. When the template page appears, use either of the following techniques:

   ➤ Select the **File** menu's **Edit Page** command. This loads the page into Composer. Note, however, that this is a *new* Composer window; the Composer window you used to start this whole process is still open (and now sad and alone).

   ➤ Select the **File** menu's **Save As** command and use the Save As dialog box to save the page to an HTML file on your computer. You can then return to Composer and open the file for editing (by selecting the **File** menu's **Open** command).

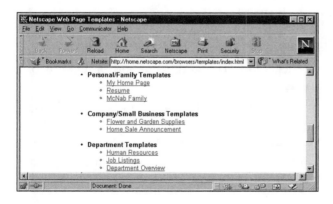

Figure 19.2

The kind and generous nerds at Netscape have put together a few HTML templates for your convenience.

Step-by-Step HTML: The Page Wizard

In your travels through the computing landscape, you've no doubt made the acquaintance of more than a few "wizards." These are program features that normally lead you step-by-step through procedures that would otherwise take a Ph.D. in electrical engineering to figure out on your own. However, the wizard concept is also being applied to procedures that are merely tedious and time-consuming. Because building a Web page sometimes falls into this category, it should come as no surprise that there are a few Web page wizards floating around.

The Netscape folks have one of these wizards, and it's handy if you want to create a professional-looking Web page, but you don't have the time or the inclination to fiddle with Composer's HTML bells and whistles.

To wake the wizard, use either of the following techniques:

➤ Select the **File**, **New**, **Page from Wizard** command.

➤ Click the **New** toolbar button to have the Create New Page dialog box report for duty, and then click the **Page From Wizard** button.

Composer fires up Navigator once again, but this time you're hurled to the Netscape Page Wizard page. Scroll down a bit and then click the **Start** button to get the show on the road.

The Page Wizard screen is divided into three frames:

Preview   The frame on the right shows the current state of your page.

Instructions   The frame on the left provides instructions for building the page and using the Wizard.

Choices   The frame at the bottom enables you to enter text and other items that you want to appear on the page.

Here are the basic steps to follow to fill in the particulars of your page:

1. In the Instructions frame, click a link. This adds some sort of text box or other control to the Choices frame.
2. Enter your text (or whatever) in the Choices frame and then click **Apply**. This updates your page in the Preview frame. Figure 19.3 shows an example.
3. Lather. Rinse. Repeat Steps 1 and 2 until you're done.
4. Click the **Build** button at the bottom of the Instructions frame. This loads your shiny new page into Navigator.

5. As with the templates, you can now get the page into Composer either by selecting the **File** menu's **Edit Page** command, or by selecting the **File** menu's **Save As** command to save the page to your computer and then opening it in Composer.

Clicking this link...

...adds the text box text to the page preview.

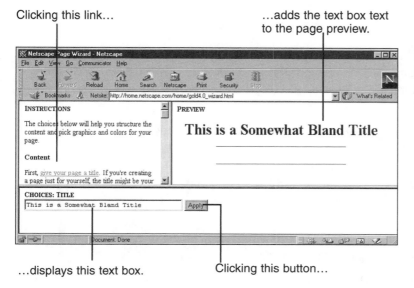

Figure 19.3

Netscape's Page Wizard steps you through the creation of a page.

...displays this text box.

Clicking this button...

Creating a Blank File

If you want to start from scratch, Composer is only too happy to oblige. Once again, there are two routes to take:

➤ Select the **File**, **New**, **Blank Page** command (you can also press **Ctrl+Shift+N**).

➤ Click the **New** toolbar button to display the Create New Page dialog box, and then click the **Blank Page** button.

Note that you're not really starting from scratch when you peel off a blank file. Composer is decent enough to add the basic HTML skeleton of the page automatically. This includes the <HTML>, <HEAD>, and <BODY> tags (and their corresponding end tags, natch). However, Composer hides these details from you so you can concentrate on page content (more on this a bit later).

Don't Forget to Save!

To make sure nothing untoward happens to your HTML creations, make sure you save your work constantly. You save stuff in Composer either by selecting the **File** menu's **Save** command, by pressing **Ctrl+S**, or by clicking the **Save** button in the toolbar.

If you keep forgetting to save, why not get Composer to handle this chore for you automatically? All you have to do is pull down the **Edit** menu, select **Preferences**, and then click **Composer**. Make sure the **Automatically save page every** check box is activated, and then enter the save interval (in minutes) in the text box provided. I recommend changing this value to **1**.

Populating Your Document with Tags (Sort Of)

When you're playing around with Composer, bear in mind that you aren't working with HTML tags directly. Rather, you type in your document text and then use Composer's menu commands and toolbar buttons to "format" the text. This formatting is the same as adding tags, but Composer doesn't display the HTML nuts and bolts. Instead, it just shows you how your text looks in the browser. (More accurately, it shows what the page looks like in Navigator; with other browsers your mileage may vary). In other words, Composer is a WYSIWYG display. (That is, What You See Is What You Get, although some wags prefer When You See It, Won't You Gag?) Here are the basic steps you follow for each document:

1. Type in your document text.
2. If you want to format some text, highlight the text you want to work with; if you're inserting an HTML object such as a link or an image, position the editor's cursor where you want the object to appear.
3. Choose the appropriate menu command or toolbar button (I go through the available commands and buttons in the rest of this chapter).
4. Save the file from time to time, as described earlier.
5. Check how the page looks in Netscape by selecting the **File, Browse Page** command, or by clicking the **Preview** button in the Composition toolbar.
6. Repeat steps 1–5 until you're done.

The next few sections expand on step 3 by showing you how to work with Composer's menus and toolbars.

Summoning the Source

After all that time spent playing with HTML tags earlier in this book, you might feel the need to see what's happening under the Composer surface. No problemo. Simply select the **View** menu's **Page Source** command, and Composer loads the tags into a separate window. Note, however, that you can't edit the tags.

Tweaking the Title and Other Header Info

As I mentioned earlier, Composer adds the basic tags to your new pages. However, it doesn't add the <TITLE> and </TITLE> tags, until you provide the page with a title. To do that, you need to pull down the **Format** menu and select the **Page Colors and Properties** command. In the Page Properties dialog box that appears (see Figure 19.4), use the **Title** text box to enter a new title for the page.

Figure 19.4

In the Page Properties dialog box, use the General tab to enter your page title.

The General tab sports a few other text boxes for your typing pleasure:

➤ **Author**   Enter your name. This creates an "Author" <META> tag that goes in the header.

➤ **Description**   Enter a brief description of your site. This generates a "Description" <META> tag that search engines use to describe your site. (I described this <META> tag in Chapter 7, "Publishing Your Page on the Web.")

➤ **Keywords**   Enter one or more words or phrases, separated by commas, that capture the essence of your site. This generates a "Keywords" <META> tag that search engines use to see if your site matches search text entered by a user. (Again, see Chapter 7.)

Click **Apply** to put the settings into effect. (Don't close the dialog box because you need it in the next section.)

Setting the Background and Text Colors

While you've got the Page Properties dialog box on stage, this is as good a time as any to specify the page background, as well as the default colors for text and links. To do so, display the Colors and Background tab, as shown in Figure 19.5. You have the following controls at your disposal:

Use custom colors   Activate this option to specify your page's default text colors. Click the buttons to pick out colors for **Normal Text**, **Link Text**, **Active Link Text**, and **Followed Link Text**. Click the **Background** button to set the background color.

Background Image   If you want to use an image as your background, activate the **Use Image** check box and then enter the name and location of the graphics file (or click **Choose File** to pick put the file using a dialog box).

Save these settings for new pages   If you activate this check box, Composer remembers your settings and uses them as the default for future pages that you create.

When you're done, click **OK**.

Working with Paragraphs

Remember way back in Chapter 2, "Laying the Foundation: The Basic Structure of a Web Page," when I told you about the <P> tag? At the time, I mentioned that pressing Enter to start a new paragraph didn't work in HTML because you had to use the <P> tag, instead. Well, you can forget all that, because in Composer, pressing Enter really does start a new paragraph.

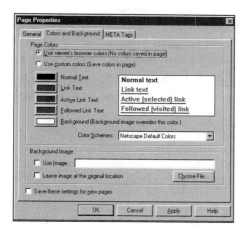

Figure 19.5
Use the Colors and Background tab to pick out your page's text colors and to set the page background.

No, Netscape hasn't rewritten the HTML specifications (although, with all those darned Netscape extensions, it sometimes seems that way). Instead, pressing Enter in Composer adds the following tags *behind the scenes*:

➤ If you press **Enter** once, Composer inserts a <BR> tag.

➤ If you press **Enter** twice, Composer inserts a <P> tag.

If you want to set the alignment of a paragraph, select **Format**, **Align** and then choose either **Left** (or press **Ctrl+L**), **Center** (or press **Ctrl+E**), or **Right** (or press **Ctrl+R**).

 You can also click the Alignment button.

Formatting Characters

Composer is loaded for bear with all kinds of character formatting options. (Most of which I droned on and on about back in Chapter 3, "From Buck-Naked to Beautiful: Dressing Up Your Page.") You can work with these options using either of the following methods:

➤ If the text you want to mark already exists, highlight the text and then apply the option.

➤ If the text doesn't exist, just apply the option where the text will appear and then start typing.

To try out these options, pull down the **Format** menu, select **Style**, and choose one of the commands listed in the following table (or you can use the toolbar buttons or keyboard shortcuts shown in the following table).

Table 19.1   Toolbar Buttons and Shortcut Keys for Text Formatting

Style	Command	Button	Shortcut
Bold	Bold	A	**Ctrl+B**
Italic	Italic	A	**Ctrl+I**
<u>Underlined</u>	Underline	A	**Ctrl+U**
Superscript	Superscript	None	None
Subscript	Subscript	None	None
Blinking	Blink	None	None
~~Strikethrough~~	Strikethrough	None	None

If it's a different font you want, you have two choices:

➤ Select **Format**, **Font** and then pick a typeface from the submenu that slides out. To get monospaced characters (the <TT> tag), activate the **Format**, **Font**, **Fixed Width** command.

➤ Pull down the Font drop-down list in the Formatting toolbar (see Figure 19.6).

Need to change the font size? That's easier done than said:

➤ Select **Format**, **Size** and then choose a size from the submenu.

➤ Pull down the Size drop-down list in the Formatting toolbar (see Figure 19.6).

Netscape also supports different colors for fonts. You might recall from Chapter 9 that specifying a color meant figuring out an obscure 6-digit hexadecimal code. Yuck! With Composer, however, choosing your colors is easy. Once again, you have two ways to proceed:

➤ Select the **Format**, **Color** command. A palette of colors appears, as shown in Figure 19.6. Now just click the color you want.

➤ Drop down the Font Color list in the Formatting toolbar.

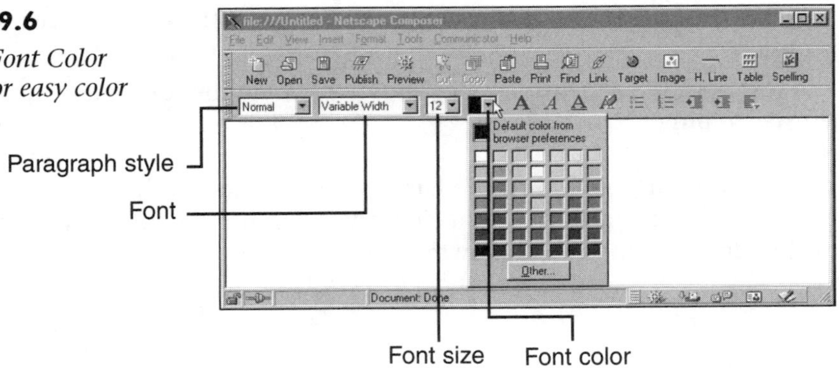

Figure 19.6

Use the Font Color palette for easy color selection.

Paragraph style

Font

Font size   Font color

If you change your mind and decide you don't want your text formatted, use either of the following techniques to remove all the formatting from the highlighted text:

➤ Select **Format, Remove All Styles** (or press **Ctrl+Shift+K**).

 ➤ Click the **Remove All Styles** toolbar button.

Working with Headings

To change the heading style (as described in Chapter 3), you have two ways to proceed:

➤ Select the **Format, Heading** command, and then choose the heading you want from the submenu. For example, to get the <H1> heading, you select the **1** command.

➤ Pull down the Paragraph Style list in the toolbar, and then select a heading style (such as Heading 1 to get the <H1> heading).

Working with Lists

If you need to add a list to your document (be it a bulleted list or a numbered list), Composer can cope. (I took you through all this list lunacy back in Chapter 4, "A Fistful of List Grist for Your Web Page Mill.")

To insert the container for the list (in the HTML world, this means <UL> and </UL> for a bulleted list or <OL> and </OL> for a numbered list), pull down the **Format** menu, select the **List** command, and then select either **Bulleted** or **Numbered**. Mouse types can also simply click either the Bulleted List button or the Numbered List button in the Format toolbar.

 The Bulleted List button.

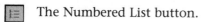 The Numbered List button.

Composer inserts the appropriate container and adds the first item. Type in the item text and then press **Enter** to generate the next bullet or number automatically. To end the list, select the **Format, List, None** command.

Inserting an Image

Looking to add an image or two to give your page some added oomph? (I gave you the big picture on images in Chapter 6, "A Picture Is Worth a Thousand Clicks: Working with Images.") Let's see how it's done in Composer.

First, position the cursor where you want the image to appear and then pull down the **Insert** menu and select the **Image** command. You can also click the **Image** button in the Composition toolbar.

The dialog box that appears (see Figure 19.7) is loaded with all sorts of options and seems to be an exercise in bad interface design. Fortunately, there are only a few controls you need to deal with:

Image location   Enter the name of the graphics file, or else click **Choose File** to pick out the file from a dialog box.

Text alignment and wrapping around images   Click one of these buttons to select how surrounding text is aligned with the image.

Height   Enter the image's height, in pixels.

Width   Enter the image's width, in pixels.

Alt. Text/LowRes   Click this button to enter a text alternative (the ALT attribute) for non-graphical browsers.

If you'd like to turn the image into a link, activate the **Link** tab and then enter the URL you want to use in the **Link to a page location or local file** text box. When you're done, click **OK** to insert the <IMG> tag with the options you specified.

Figure 19.7

Use this dialog box to plop an image into your page.

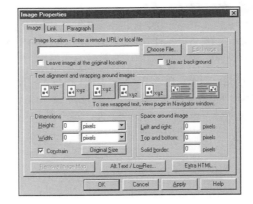

Inserting Links

Back in Chapter 5, "Making the Jump to Hyperspace: Adding Links," I showed you how to add some dynamism to your documents by inserting hypertext links. If you always have trouble remembering the proper syntax for the <A> tag, fret no more, because Composer makes it easy. Here are the steps to follow to insert a link in your document:

1. To turn existing text into a link, highlight the text.
2. Pull down the **Insert** menu and select the **Link** command. (Alternatively, press **Ctrl+Shift+L** or click the **Link** button in the Composition toolbar.) Composer displays the Link tab of the Character Properties dialog box, as shown in Figure 19.8.

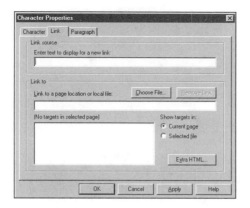

Figure 19.8
*Use this dialog box to
enter the description and
URL for the link.*

3. If you didn't highlight any text beforehand, use the **Enter text to display for a new link** box to type in the link text.

4. Use the **Link to a page location or local file** text box to enter the URL of the page you want to display when the user clicks the link. (You can choose a file on your system by clicking the **Choose File** button.)

5. If you want to link to a target (which is the same thing as an anchor; see Chapter 5), click the target in the list provided.

6. Click **OK**. Composer inserts the link.

Inserting a Table

I showed you how to craft HTML tables back in Chapter 9, "Table Talk: Adding Tables to Your Page." If you read that chapter, then you saw that tables are perhaps the most complex of HTML structures. If that complexity is causing you to avoid tables, Composer can help. Here are the steps to follow:

1. Move the cursor to where you want the table to appear.

2. Select **Insert, Table, Table** to fire up the New Table Properties dialog box, shown in Figure 19.9. (For some variety, you can also click the **Table** button in the Composition toolbar.)

3. Enter the **Number of rows** and the **Number of columns** for the new table.

Check This Out

Adding Targets

If you want to add a target or two to your page, either select the **Insert** menu's **Target** command, or click the **Target** toolbar button. Enter the target text in the dialog box that appears, and then click **OK**.

Figure 19.9

Use this dialog box to specify the dimensions of features of your new table.

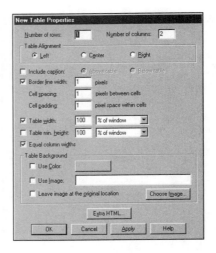

4. Use the **Table Alignment** options to specify the table's horizontal alignment within the page.

5. If you want a caption, activate the **Include caption** check box, and then choose either **Above table** or **Below table**.

6. If you want a border, leave the **Border line width** check box activated and enter the width you want in the text box.

7. Use the **Cell spacing** and **Cell padding** text boxes to specify the spacing you need within and between cells.

8. To specify a table width, leave the **Table width** check box activated, enter a value in the text box, and then choose either **pixels** or **% of window** in the list.

9. To set the table background, activate either **Use Color** or **Use Image**.

10. When you're done, click **OK**.

Publishing Your Page

After your page is polished to a glossy shine, you can also use Composer to toss the page onto your Web server. Here are the steps to follow:

1. Either select the **File**, **Publish** command, or click the **Publish** toolbar button. The Publish dialog box appears (shown in Figure 19.10).

2. Fill in the fields:

Page Title   This is the title of your page.

HTML Filename   This is the name you want the file to have on the server.

HTTP or FTP Location to publish to   This is the location on the server that you use to store your Web page files.

User name and **Password**   Use these text boxes to enter the log in data you need to access your server directory. Activate the **Save password** check box to have Composer remember the password in the future.

Files associated with the page   Activate this option to have Composer send along any other files referenced within your page (such as the image files you specified).

All files in page's folder   Activate this option to have Composer send whatever files reside in the same folder as your Web page.

3. Click **OK**. Composer connects to the server and ships out the files.
4. Click **OK** when Composer lets you know the operation is done.

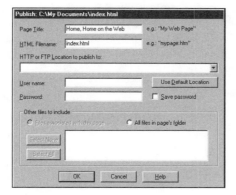

Figure 19.10

Use the Publish dialog box to foist your page on the Web server.

The Least You Need to Know

This chapter showed you how to mine the HTML notes and nuances available in Netscape Composer.

Next on the HTML hit parade, Chapter 20, "Suite Web O' Mine: The Microsoft Office 2000 HTML Tools," takes a look at the various Web page doodads that come in the Microsoft Office suite.

Suite Web O' Mine: The Microsoft Office 2000 HTML Tools

In This Chapter

➤ Saving Office 2000 documents as Web pages

➤ Inserting links in Office documents

➤ Complete coverage of Word's Web page prowess

➤ Publishing pages using data from Excel, PowerPoint, and Access

➤ A few thousand words on a few Office 2000 HTML trinkets

In most respects, Microsoft Office 2000 is a ho-hum update to Office 97. There's just not enough that's new and noteworthy to tempt the average Joe and Josephine into spending their upgrade dollars. The exception is if those Joes and Josephines are into Web page publishing, for that's the one area where Office 2000 really shines.

Entire books could be (and probably have been) written on the Web and HTML knick-knacks in Office 2000. A single chapter is a woefully inadequate amount of space to devote to such a huge topic. So, obviously, my goal here isn't a comprehensive look at all the Office 2000 HTML tools. Instead, I treat this chapter as an overview that gives you some idea of what's inside the Office 2000 box and offers some pointers and techniques for getting started with those tools. In particular, I concentrate mostly on how you can convert your carefully crafted Office documents into a format suitable for Web viewing.

Common Office 2000 HTML Doodads

From a Web spinner's point of view, the most intriguing new feature in Office 2000 is its native support for HTML files. That's right: HTML is a format that most Office 2000 programs are happy to work with. You can even perform the amazing trick of converting an Office document (such as a Word file) into HTML and then converting it back to its natural format, and it will look and behave exactly as it did originally! What's even more amazing, if you use Internet Explorer 5.0, is that you can view the document either in its original format or in its HTML version, and they look identical.

The Secret of Office 2000's Success

How does Office 2000 preserve the look of a document when it's converted into HTML? For the most part, the secret is a combination of style sheets and something called XML—eXtensible Markup Language. The Office 2000 applications use extremely sophisticated styles to make sure documents are rendered precisely the same when converted to HTML. And for those elements that can't be specified with style sheets alone, Office 2000 uses XML. In a nutshell, XML enables you to create entirely new tags, the behavior of which is described by a program. So Office 2000 sometimes uses XML techniques to preserve features that aren't part of HTML (such as VBA macros).

The next couple of sections look at two techniques that are common to all the major Office 2000 programs: saving documents as HTML and inserting links.

Saving Office Documents in HTML Format

In previous editions of Microsoft Office, saving a file as HTML was an often hair-raising, ulcer-inducing experience. There was just no way to tell exactly what you'd end up with after the conversion was complete. As I've said, that's no longer the case with Office 2000, however, so you can convert with confidence. Here's how:

1. Open or create the Office 2000 document you want to convert.
2. Select the **File**, **Save as Web Page** command. The Save As dialog box saunters onto the screen, as shown in Figure 20.1. Note that the **Save as type** list shows **Web Page**.

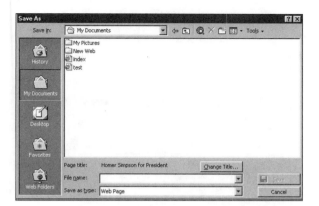

Figure 20.1
This dialog box appears when you run the Save as Web Page command.

3. Click **Change Title** to edit or enter the page title.
4. Select a location for the page.
5. Use the **File name** text box to enter a name for the new file.
6. Click **Save**.

Extra Save As Goodies

The Save As dialog boxes for Excel and PowerPoint have some extra bells to ring and whistles to blow. I talk about them later in this chapter. For Excel, see "Spreadsheeting the Word: Creating Web Pages in Excel." For PowerPoint, see "PowerPoint to the People: Putting Slide Shows on the Web."

Inserting Links in Office 2000

Any Web page worth its salt comes with a few links for surfers to click. If you want to add links to your page but the <A> tag scares the living daylights out of you, the Office 2000 Insert Hyperlink feature gives you a graphical way to go about it. (This feature is available in Word, Excel, PowerPoint, Access, and FrontPage.) Here's how it works:

Links and Access

In an Access table, you can only insert links in fields that use the Hyperlink data type.

1. Type in the link text and then highlight it. If you'd prefer that the link text be the address of the link, don't highlight any text in advance.

2. Select the **Insert** menu's **Hyperlink** command. (Alternatively, either click the **Insert Hyperlink** button on program's Standard toolbar, or press **Ctrl+K**.) The program displays the Insert Hyperlink dialog box, shown in Figure 20.2, so that you can define the particulars of the hyperlink.

Figure 20.2

Use the Insert Hyperlink dialog box to enter your hyperlink particulars.

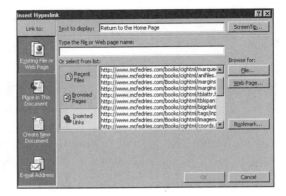

3. Use the **Link to** list to choose an icon for the type of link you want:

   ➤ **Existing File or Web Page**   This is the standard type of link that takes the surfer to a new page.

   ➤ **Place in This Document**   This is a link to an anchor in the current page.

   ➤ **Create New Document**   This is a standard link, but it points to a page that doesn't exist yet.

   ➤ **E-mail address**   This is a mailto link.

4. Use the **Text to display** text box to edit the link text, if necessary.

5. Select the page, anchor, or new document, or enter the email address (depending on which icon you chose in step 3).

6. Click **OK**.

The Word Wide Web: HTML and Word 2000

I think one of the reasons HTML seems so, well, *primitive*, is that most of what you're coding is stuff that even the most brain-dead word processor has been able to handle for years. Formatting characters, creating paragraphs, setting up lists, and working with heading styles, are all old hat to today's crop of word processing programs. Even inline images and tables are *de rigueur* in high-end word pro circles. That leaves only hypertext links as a challenge, and you saw in the previous section that they're no big deal in Office 2000.

In other words, it seems entirely logical that you should be able to chuck the old HTML-tags-in-a-text-editor model out the window and, instead, create top-notch Web pages from the friendly confines of your favorite word processor. And you know what? You can! With Word 2000, you've got a full-fledged HTML machine that lets you create Web pages as easily as you pound out memos and letters. The next few sections show you how to wield Word's Web page tools.

Easy Street I: The Web Page Wizard

If you need to create some professional-looking Web pages, but you don't have the time or the inclination to fiddle with Word's HTML bells and whistles, Word has a handy Web Page Wizard that can automate much of the usual page forging drudgery.

This HTML sorcerer's apprentice is a typical example of the wizard species. Here's how it works:

1. To bring the wizard on stage, select **File**, **New** to display the New dialog box, activate the **Web Pages** tab, click the **Web Page Wizard** icon, and then click **OK**. Word creates a new document and rouses the wizard from its slumbers, as shown in Figure 20.3. Click **Next**.

What's a Wizard?

A *wizard* is a helper program that leads you step-by-step through many arcane and fussy procedures. Really it's just a series of dialog boxes that ask you questions and then act on the answers you provide.

Figure 20.3

The Web Page Wizard takes you step-by-step through the creation of a darned nice Web site.

2. Enter a **Web site title** for your pages. You're creating several pages at once, so this is (usually) the name of the folder in which these files are stored. However, you can also use the **Web site location** text box to specify some other locale. Click **Next**.

3. If you want a framed site, choose either **Vertical frame** or **Horizontal frame**. If you'd prefer to be frame-free, choose **Separate page**, instead. Click **Next**.

4. You now add one or more pages to the site. Click **Add a Blank Page** for an empty page; **Add Template Page** to add one of Word's templates (discussed in the next section); or **Add Existing File** to add an existing HTML file. Click **Next**.

5. The wizard adds navigation links to your other pages on each page. Use the next wizard dialog box to change the order of those links (by highlighting pages and clicking **Move Up** or **Move Down**). Click **Next** when you're done.

6. If you want to give your pages a particular combination of fonts, bullets, and background—what Word calls a *visual theme*—activate the **Add a visual theme** option and click **Browse Themes** to pick one that you like. Click **Next**.

7. In the final wizard dialog box, click **Finish**. Word shuts down the wizard and busies itself creating your pages.

From here, you need to view each page and fill in the content. Turn to "Hand-Crafting Web Pages," later in this chapter, to see a list of techniques for customizing your pages.

Easy Street II: Web Page Templates

If you just want to create a single page, the Web Page Wizard's site-building prowess might be overkill. An easier route is to choose one of Word's pre-fab Web page templates. There are seven in all, and they range from basic layouts with some text and images to fancier constructions that use tables and other tricks.

To choose a template, first select the **File**, **New** command to ask the New dialog box to drop by. Activate the **Web Pages** tab (shown in Figure 20.4) to see the templates. Click the one you want to work with and then click **OK**. When the new page appears, edit the text and customize the page to your liking (as described in the next section).

Figure 20.4

The Web Pages tab is populated with a number of page templates to help you get started.

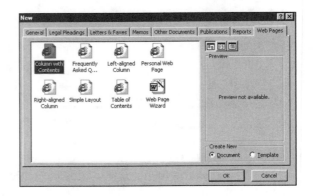

Hand-Crafting Web Pages

Whether you want to improve upon the Web Page Wizard's handiwork, tweak a template, or create a new page from scratch, you have to know how to wield the myriad Web page layout and formatting tools that ship with Word 2000.

Hidden HTML

Note that Word 2000 doesn't show HTML tags onscreen. You use a combination of formatting commands (such as boldfacing), styles (such as headings), and objects (such as links and tables) to produce your Web page. All this fussing creates a document with the correct HTML bric-a-brac, but you don't see any of it. Instead, Word 2000 just shows you what your text looks like in a browser. In other words, it's a WYSIWYG display. (That is, What You See Is What You Get, although some wags prefer Why Your Screen Inadvertently Will Yield Garbage.)

Here are the basic steps you follow for each Web document:

1. Type in your document text.
2. If you want to format some text or apply a style, select the text you want to work with. If you're inserting an HTML object, such as a link or an image, position the insertion point where you want the object to appear.
3. Choose the appropriate menu command or toolbar button.
4. Save the file from time to time (by selecting the **File** menu's **Save** command).
5. Repeat steps 1 through 4 until you're done.

The rest of this section expands on step 3 by showing you how to work with Word 2000's HTML-related menu commands and toolbar buttons:

➤ **Creating a new Web page**   If you didn't bother with the Web Page Wizard or the templates, you can crank up a new, blank page by selecting **File**, **New**, activating the **General** tab, clicking the **Web Page** icon, and clicking **OK**. (Tip: If you're already viewing a Web page, you can also click the **New Web Page** toolbar button.)

➤ **Adjusting the page title**   Select **File**, **Properties**. In the Document Properties dialog box that skates in, use the **Title** text box to enter a new title for the page, and then click **OK**.

➤ **Working with paragraphs**   To start a new paragraph, press **Enter**. Yup, that's it. Word adds the <P> tag behind the scenes. To adjust paragraph alignment, indents, and margins, select the **Format**, **Paragraph** command. You can also control the alignment and indent using buttons on the Formatting toolbar.

➤ **Formatting Web page text**   Thanks to the word processing ground upon which it sits, Word 2000 has no shortage of options for formatting characters.

Most of them can be had by selecting the **Format**, **Font** command. There are also buttons on the Formatting toolbar for one-click formatting.

Hungry for Some HTML?

If you find you miss the HTML tags, it's easy enough to see them. Save the document and then select the **View** menu's **HTML Source** command. This loads the file into the Microsoft Development Environment. Let me just warn you now that what you see looks like *nothing* you've ever seen before in your HTML coding experience. Word populates even the simplest Web page with all kinds of incomprehensible tags and markings. It's a real mess. If you can find your way around to the point where you feel comfortable editing the tags and text, feel free to do so. When you're done, click **File**, **Exit** to return to friendlier confines of Word.

Words Uses Styles to Format Text

By default, most of the text formatting you apply is translated into the style sheet equivalent. For example, if you change the typeface, Word inserts the font-family style. (Part 3, "High HTML Style: Working with Style Sheets," gave you the skinny on font-family and other styles.) That's not so good if your page is viewed by surfers using style–sheet–stupid browsers. To tell Word not to use styles for text formatting, select **Tools**, **Options**, display the **General** tab, and click **Web Options**. In the **General** tab of the Web Options dialog box, deactivate the **Rely on CSS for font formatting** check box. Click **OK** to close each dialog box.

➤ **Creating headings**   If you want to format your text using the various HTML headings (such as <H1>), select **Format**, **Style** and choose the corresponding Word style (such as Heading 1 for <H1>).

➤ **Inserting a list**   To get yourself a list, select the **Format**, **Bullets and Numbering** command and then choose either a bulleted or a numbered list.

➤ **Tossing in a link**   See "Inserting Links in Office 2000," earlier in this chapter.

➤ **Creating an anchor**   If you need to link to an anchor, you can create one by highlighting the anchor text and then selecting **Insert**, **Bookmark**. Enter the name of the anchor in the **Bookmark name** text box and then click **Add**.

➤ **Inserting an image**   Select the **Insert**, **Picture** command. This pushes out a submenu with various choices for grabbing an image: Clip Art, From File, and so on.

➤ **Setting the background**   Select the **Format**, **Background** command, and then click the color you want in the palette that pops out. If you prefer an image as the background, click **Fill Effects** in the palette, display the **Picture** tab, and then click **Select Picture**.

➤ **Choosing a Web page theme**   Select **Format**, **Theme**, use the Theme dialog box to highlight the theme you want, and then click **OK**.

Check This Out

Word Is Style Sheet-Crazy

You might think that adding a bulleted list or a numbered list would insert the standard HTML <UL> and <OL> tags. Nope. Instead, Word 2000 uses some fairly sophisticated style sheet stuff to render the lists.

Constructing Tables

Word has been table-aware for a few years now, and Word's Web files leverage all this table know-how, so you can create HTML tables just as easily as you can create regular Word tables.

If all you need to do is create a simple table for displaying row-and-column data, you can use Word's standard table-creation tools. First, position the cursor where you want the table to appear, and then select the **Table**, **Insert**, **Table** command. In the dialog box that appears, enter the number of rows and columns you want, and then click **OK**.

Most Web page tables are used for more involved tasks, such as organizing the entire page so that text and graphics line up nicely. To accomplish this, fancier tables are needed where rows and columns have varying widths, cells span multiple rows or columns, and so on.

For these more complicated scenarios, Word has a tool that enables you to "draw" the table to the specifications you prefer. Here's how it works:

1. Click the **Tables and Borders** button on the Standard toolbar to display the Tables and Borders toolbar.

2. Click the **Draw Table** button on the Tables and Borders toolbar. (Note that you can combine steps 1 and 2 into a single operation by selecting **Table**, **Draw Table**.)

3. Move the mouse pointer (it should now look like a pencil; see Figure 20.5) to where you want the upper-left corner of the table to appear, and then drag the mouse to create a box that defines the perimeter of the table.

Figue 20.5

In Word 2000 you use your mouse to "draw" tables.

Drag the mouse to create the table.

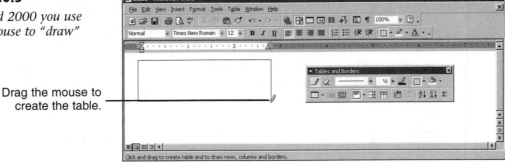

4. Move the mouse pointer inside the table and then drag across to create a row, or drag down to create a column.

5. You can split a cell by moving the mouse pointer inside the cell and then dragging up (to split the cell vertically) or across (to split the cell horizontally). You can also click the **Split Cells** button and use the Split Cells dialog box to enter the number of rows and columns you want inside the cell.

6. To merge two or more cells, click the **Draw Table** button to deactivate it, then drag to select the cells you want to merge. Now click the **Merge Cells** button.

7. To remove a line from the table, click the **Eraser** button and then click the line you want to vamoose.

8. Repeat steps 4 through 7 to complete the table.

Note, too, that the Tables and Borders toolbar is populated with various buttons for formatting the table borders, filling cells with color, and more.

Constructing Frames

As you might know from having read Chapter 12, "Fooling Around with Frames," creating framed pages is a tough row to hoe. Fortunately, Word 2000 has some nice new frame-related features that can take some of the fussing out of your framework.

You begin by creating a new Web page and then selecting the **Format, Frames, New Frames Page** command. This creates a new document and displays the Frames toolbar. The **Format, Frames** menu also sprouts a few new commands. Here's a summary of what these buttons and commands are all about:

➤ **Table of Contents in Frame** Creates a new frame that includes links to headings in the current page.

➤ **New Frame Left**   Creates a new frame to the left of the current frame.

➤ **New Frame Right**   Creates a new frame to the right of the current frame.

➤ **New Frame Above**   Creates a new frame above the current frame.

➤ **New Frame Below**   Creates a new frame below the current frame.

➤ **Delete Frame**   Expunges the current frame.

➤ **Frame Properties**   Displays the Frame Properties dialog box, shown in Figure 20.6. You use this dialog box to specify the page to appear in the frame, the name of the frame, the dimensions of the frame, the frame borders, and more.

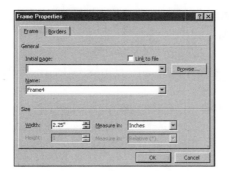

Figure 20.6

Use the Frame Properties dialog box to set up your frames the way you like them.

Spreadsheeting the Word: Creating Web Pages in Excel

Word 2000 seems like a natural application for building Web pages because its built-in commands are easily translated to Web page construction: text formatting, styles, tables, and so on. Excel, on the other hand, seems a tougher fit, what with its cells, formulas, pivot tables, and other spreadsheet arcana. Sure, its row-and-column format seems like it would translate nicely into building tables, but that's about it, right?

Excel Interactions

To interact with an Excel worksheet, the user must be surfing with Internet Explorer 4.01 or later.

Nope, not anymore. Excel 2000's beefed-up HTML muscles mean that it can go way beyond saving worksheet ranges as mere tables. It can actually save a worksheet as an *interactive* page in which a surfer can manipulate the data: enter and edit text, format cells, create formulas, move and copy cells, control pivot tables, and much more. In all, Excel 2000 gives you three different ways to save data as a Web page. Here are the ways, listed from least interactive to most interactive:

➤ Save a range of cells as a static (that is, non-interactive) page.

➤ Save an entire workbook. In this case, the data is static, but you can view the different worksheets.

➤ Save a range as an interactive Web page.

Saving a Range As a Static Web Page

A static page means that the user can't manipulate the data in any way (except to copy the data). This is fine if you have data that you only want to display to the user. Here's how you create such a page in Excel 2000:

1. Select the data that you want to publish:

   ➤ If you want to publish a specific range of cells or a chart, select the range or chart.

   ➤ If you want to publish an entire worksheet, make sure the cursor is somewhere inside that sheet.

2. Select **File**, **Save as Web Page** to ask the Save As dialog box to come out and play.

3. Activate the **Selection** option, as shown in Figure 20.7.

Figure 20.7

*Activate the **Selection** option.*

4. Fill in the other Save As data (choose a location, enter a **File name**, click **Change Title** to set the title) in the usual way.

5. Click **Save**.

Figure 20.8 shows an example of the kind of static page you end up with.

Saving a Workbook As a Series of Web Pages

Here are the steps to follow the save an entire workbook to the Web:

1. Select **File**, **Save as Web Page** to reunite with the Save As dialog box.

2. Make sure the **Entire Workbook** option is activated.

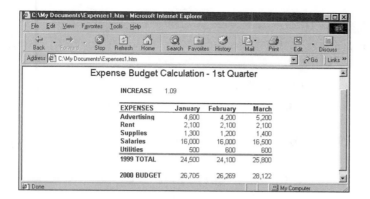

Figure 20.8

An example of an Excel range saved as a static page.

3. Fill in the other Save As data (choose a location, enter a **File name**, click **Change Title** to set the title) in the usual way.

4. Click **Save**.

Excel does three things at this point:

➤ It creates a new folder named *Filename*_files, where *Filename* is the filename you entered in the Save As dialog box.

➤ For each worksheet, it creates a file named sheet*nnn*.htm, where *nnn* is a number that represents each sheet's order within the workbook (the first sheet is sheet001.htm, the second sheet is sheet002.htm, and so on). All these files are stored in the new folder.

➤ It creates a page using the filename that you specify. This page acts as a kind of container for the worksheet pages.

Figure 20.9 shows an example of a workbook saved as a Web page.

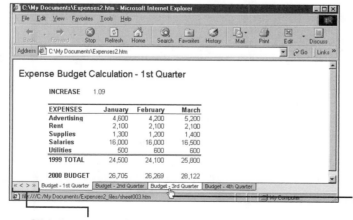

Figure 20.9

An example of an Excel workbook saved as Web pages.

Click a tab to see a different sheet page.

Click these controls to cycle through the sheet pages.

Saving a Range As an Interactive Web Page

Now we come to the fun part of the Excel show: creating truly interactive worksheet Web pages. Here's how it works:

1. Select the data that you want to publish:
    - ➤ If you want to publish a specific range of cells or a chart, select the range or chart.
    - ➤ If you want to publish an entire worksheet, make sure the cursor is somewhere inside that sheet.

2. Select **File**, **Save as Web Page** to drag the Save As dialog box in by the scruff of the neck.

3. Activate the **Selection** option.

4. If you don't want to specify any publishing options, activate the **Add interactivity** check box and skip to step 6. Otherwise, click the **Publish** button.

5. The Publish as Web Page dialog box that materializes (see Figure 20.10) offers the following options:
    - ➤ **Choose**   Select what part of the workbook you want to publish.
    - ➤ **Add interactivity with**   Activate this option to create an interactive page. You also need to use the list to select the type of interaction the page requires. This is usually **Spreadsheet functionality**, but you can also select **PivotTable functionality** (if you want to be able to manipulate a pivot table) or **Chart functionality** (if you selected a chart).
    - ➤ **Open published Web page in browser**   Activate this check box to see the resulting page in Internet Explorer. (This is a good idea, and it saves you loading the page by hand later on.)

Figure 20.10

Use the Publish as Web Page dialog box to specify how you want the interactive page published.

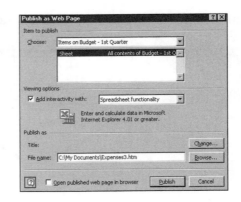

6. Fill in the other data (choose a location, enter a filename, change the title) in the usual way.

7. Click **Save** (or **Publish** if you're in the Publish as Web Page dialog box).

Figure 20.11 shows the resulting interactive page. This is an honest-to-goodness Excel range, so you can manipulate the data to your heart's content.

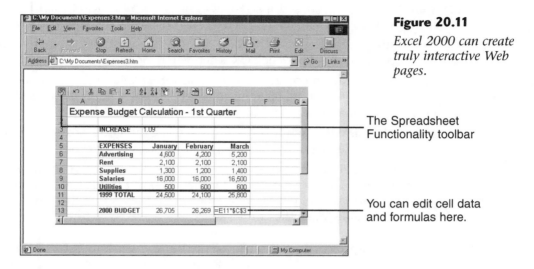

Figure 20.11

Excel 2000 can create truly interactive Web pages.

The Spreadsheet Functionality toolbar

You can edit cell data and formulas here.

PowerPoint to the People: Putting Slide Shows on the Web

If you've created a nice PowerPoint slide show that you want to share with people in some other location, you could use the Pack and Go Wizard to bundle everything up into a neat, portable package. That works fine, but it's a bit of a hassle. If the other location has Internet access, however, then it's *way* easier to just put the slide show on the Web and view it using Internet Explorer 4.0 or later. Here's what you do:

1. Select **File**, **Save as Web Page** to rendezvous with the Save As dialog box.
2. Click **Publish**. PowerPoint talks the Publish as Web Page dialog box into putting in an appearance, as shown in Figure 20.12.

Figure 20.12

Use the Publish as Web Page dialog box to set up the specifics of converting your slide show to a page.

3. Either choose **Complete presentation** or activate **Slide number** and then use the two spin boxes to specify the slides you want included.

4. If you want your speaker notes displayed alongside each slide, leave the **Display speaker notes** check box activated.

5. Click **Web Options** and deal with the following check boxes in the **General** tab of the Web Options dialog box (click **OK** when you're done):

   ➤ **Add slide navigation controls**   These controls enable the surfer to move from slide to slide. You might want to deactivate this option if your slide show has automatic timings.

   ➤ **Show slide animation while browsing**   Activate this check box if you want the surfer to see all the nifty animations that you've added to your show.

   ➤ **Resize graphics to fit browser window**   When this option is activated, the slide show's graphics are reduced if they won't fit inside the browser window. This is a good idea because otherwise it means that the surfer might not be able to see the entire slide.

6. Use the **Browser support** options to choose the browser versions you want to cover. Note that if you go with the 3.*x* browsers, you won't get the slide navigation controls or animations, and the graphics quality will be quite poor.

7. Fill in the other options (choose a location, enter a **File name**, click **Change** to set the title) in the usual way.

8. Activate the **Open published Web page in browser** check box to see the resulting page in Internet Explorer.

9. Click **Publish**.

Figure 20.13 shows Internet Explorer running a Web page slide show.

Publishing Access 2000 Forms As Data Access Pages

If you thought the interactive pages that Excel 2000 churns out were the cat's pajamas, then you'll be equally impressed with the new *data access pages* that Access 2000 can create. A data access page is a Web-based Access form that enables surfers to move from record to record, change existing data, and even add and delete records!

Access offers several methods for creating data access pages, but the Page Wizard is probably the easiest way to go. Here's how to use it:

1. From the database window, select **Insert**, **Page**. Access spits out the New Data Access page dialog box.

2. Click **Page Wizard**, use the list to choose the table or query that has your data, and then click **OK**. The Page Wizard appears in a cloud of smoke.

The outline

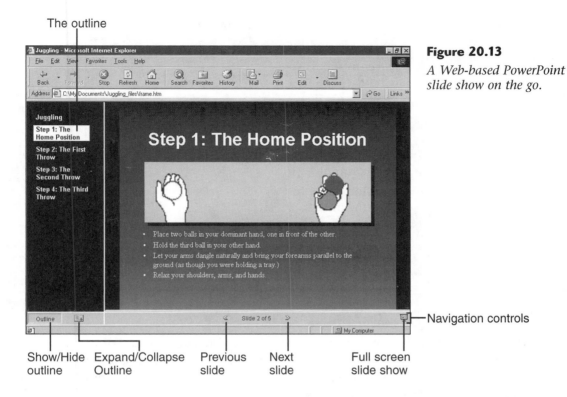

Figure 20.13
A Web-based PowerPoint slide show on the go.

Navigation controls

Show/Hide outline Expand/Collapse Outline Previous slide Next slide Full screen slide show

3. For each field that you want on the page, highlight it in the **Available Fields** list and click the > button. (Alternatively, you can select every field by clicking the >> button.) Click **Next** when you're done.

4. The wizard now wonders if you want to add grouping levels to the page. Users won't be able to edit the data if you add groupings, so just click **Next** to skip this.

5. The wizard asks you if you want to sort the data. If you do, select one or more sort fields, choosing either ascending or descending for each one, and then click **Next**.

6. In the final wizard dialog box, enter a title for the page, activate the **Open the page** option, and click **Finish**.

7. Select **File**, **Export** to get a load of the Export Data Access Page dialog box.

8. Choose a location and a name for the Web page, and then click **Save**.

9. To load the page into Internet Explorer, select **File**, **Web Page Preview**.

Figure 20.14 shows an example data access page. You can use the controls along the bottom of the page to move from record to record, add a new record, delete a record, sort and filter the data, and more.

Figure 20.14

Internet Explorer showing an Access 2000 data access page.

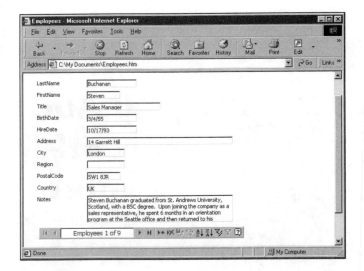

The Least You Need to Know

This chapter showed you how to take advantage of the large number of Web page goodies that come with the Office 2000 suite. You learned the basic techniques for saving files as Web pages, inserting links, and crafting a page using Word. You also learned how to publish Web pages from Excel, PowerPoint, and Access.

Chapter 21, "All Aboard the FrontPage Express," looks at yet another Microsoft Web page tool: the FrontPage Express HTML editor.

All Aboard the FrontPage Express

In This Chapter

➤ Easy commands for formatting Web page text and paragraphs

➤ How to add multimedia tidbits, such as images and sounds

➤ Working with links

➤ Constructing tables with your bare hands

➤ Web page creation in the express lane

Our look at WYSIWYG Web weaving continues in this chapter as I show you how to wield FrontPage Express, the HTML editing program that comes with Internet Explorer 4.0 and later, as well as Windows 98. FrontPage Express is the little brother of FrontPage, Microsoft's high-end Web publishing system. However, that doesn't mean FrontPage Express is a lightweight program, not by a long shot. FrontPage Express is loaded with menu commands and toolbar buttons that make working with standard page knickknacks—such as links, images, lines, and formatting—a walk in the Web park. There are also tools for adding more complex elements, such as tables and Java applets. As if that wasn't enough, there's even a collection of templates and wizards that help you transform your pages from zero to hero in no time flat. This chapter shows you how to wield these and other Web page wonders.

Check This Out

Downloading FrontPage Express

You can get the latest version of FrontPage Express from Microsoft's Windows Update Web site:

`http://windowsupdate.microsoft.com/`

Starting FrontPage Express

Depending on which version of Internet Explorer or Windows you're running, you use one of the following techniques to start FrontPage Express:

➤ **Start, Programs, Accessories, Internet Tools, FrontPage Express**

➤ **Start, Programs, Internet Explorer, FrontPage Express**

Figure 21.1 shows the FrontPage Express window that falls in.

Getting a Web Page Off the Ground

As you'll see, FrontPage Express has all the bits and pieces you need to create top-notch Web pages. To make forging your pages even easier, the program also boasts several wizards and templates that you can use to get your pages off to a fine start. Here's how you create a new page in FrontPage Express:

Standard toolbar   Format toolbar

Figure 21.1

The FrontPage Express window.

New button

Forms toolbar

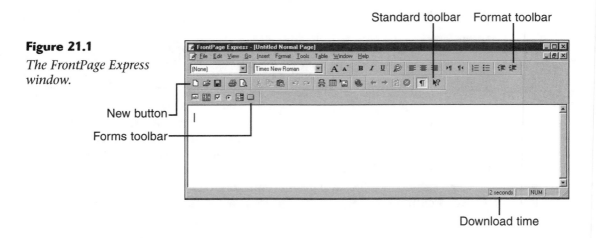

Download time

1. Select the **File, New** command, or press **Ctrl+N**. FrontPage Express tosses the New Page dialog box onscreen (as shown in Figure 21.2).

306

Download Time

As pointed out in the figure, the FrontPage Express status bar displays the download time for the current file. This is the approximate number of seconds it will take to load the page for someone surfing with a 28.8Kbps connection.

Figure 21.2

FrontPage Express has a few templates and wizards.

2. Select one of the following templates and wizards:

   Normal Page   This option just creates an empty Web page.

   Confirmation Form   This option creates a page suitable for displaying after the user has submitted a form.

   Form Page Wizard   This wizard helps you to build a form for gathering data.

   New Web View Folder   This template produces a Web page that you could use to specify as the Web page for a folder displayed in Web View.

   Personal Home Page Wizard   This wizard helps you to put together a simple home page.

   Survey Form   This template also creates a form, but it takes the data submitted in the form and stores it in a file.

3. Click **OK**.

4. If you selected a wizard, fill in all the dialog boxes.

5. Many of the pages created using these templates and wizards contain "placeholders," which are fields in which you

Normal Page Shortcut

A quick way to get a new file based on the Normal Page template is to click the **New** button in the Standard toolbar.

type your own data. For example, in Figure 21.3 (a Web page created using the Personal Home Page Wizard), you need to edit the data with your own job title, responsibilities, and so on. Just use the normal text editing techniques to delete the existing information and type in your own.

Figure 21.3

You need to enter your own data into the place-holders created by the templates and wizards.

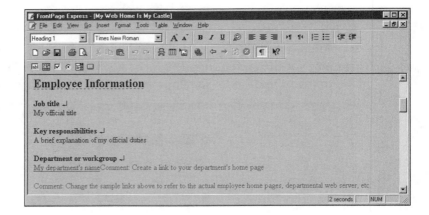

A Few Formatting Features

The pages created by the wizards and templates are an easy way to get a head start on your Web page chores. However, you might find that you have to make extensive modifications to these pages to end up with the design you prefer. Alternatively, you might elect to start with a blank page and create everything from scratch. Either way, you have to know how to wield the myriad Web page layout and formatting tools that ship with FrontPage Express.

Got a Hankering for HTML?

If you find you miss seeing the HTML tags, or if you just want to tweak a tag or two, you can take a gander at the HTML codes that FrontPage Express spits out. To do so, select the **View, HTML** command. In the View or Edit HTML window that appears, feel free to edit the tags as necessary. Note, too, that FrontPage Express uses color codes to represents different HTML chunks, such as tag names and attribute names. When you're done, click **OK** to return to the FrontPage Express window.

Here's a quick look at a few basic techniques:

Adjusting the page title   To adjust the title of the Web page, select the **File**, **Page Properties** command. In the dialog box that appears, use the **Title** text box to enter a new title for the page, and then click **OK**.

Formatting fonts   The basic formatting options—bold, italic, underline, font, font size, font color, and so on—can be adjusted by selecting the **Format**, **Font** command. Use the Font dialog box (shown in Figure 21.4) to make your selections, and then click **OK**. (Note, however, that any typefaces you use are only visible on the user's browser if they have the appropriate font installed on their computer.) As you can see in Figure 21.4, many font options are available via the Format toolbar.

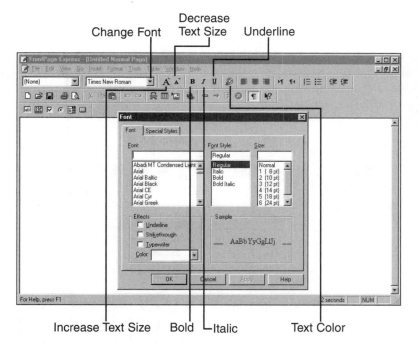

Change Font   Decrease Text Size   Underline

Increase Text Size   Bold   Italic   Text Color

Figure 21.4

You can use either the Font dialog box or the Format toolbar to set some character formatting options.

Setting the page background   To specify the page background, select the **Format**, **Background** command to display the Background tab of the Page Properties dialog box (shown in Figure 21.5). To set a background image, activate the **Background Image** check box and then enter the image filename (or click **Browse**). Alternatively, use the **Background** list to choose a background color.

Setting the default colors for text and links   While you're in the Background tab, you can also use the **Text** list to set the default color for the page text. You can use the other color lists to set the default colors for each **Hyperlink**, **Visited Hyperlink**, and **Active Hyperlink**. (The latter is a link that has been clicked and the user is waiting for the page to load.)

Figure 21.5

Use the dialog box to set the page background. You also use it to set the default colors for text and links.

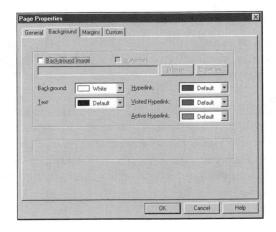

Working with headings FrontPage Express headings styles run from Heading 1 to Heading 6, which correspond to HTML heading tags <H1> through <H6>. To apply a heading style to a paragraph, either use the Change Style list in the Format toolbar, or select **Format**, **Paragraph** and choose the style you want in the Paragraph properties dialog box that appears (see Figure 21.6).

Figure 21.6

You can select a heading style either by using this dialog box or by using the Change Style list.

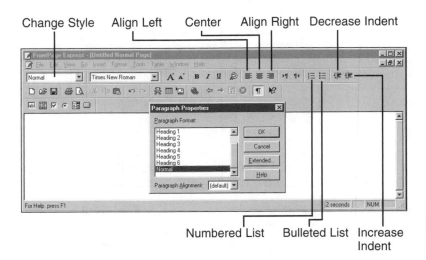

Aligning paragraphs FrontPage Express gives you three different paragraph alignment options: Left, Center, and Right. To set the alignment, either use the **Paragraph Alignment** list in the Paragraph Properties dialog box (see the previous figure), or click the appropriate alignment button in the Format toolbar. (This is equivalent to adding the ALIGN attribute to the <P> tag.)

Formatting bulleted and numbered lists To start one of these lists, select the **Format**, **Bullets and Numbering** command, and then use the List Properties dialog box to choose the style you want. Alternatively, you can set a basic list style by clicking either the **Bulleted List** or the **Numbered List** toolbar button. Either way, you then type each item and press **Enter** to move to the next item. To end the list, press **Enter** twice.

Indenting paragraphs   To indent a paragraph from the left margin, click the **Increase Indent** toolbar button. (FrontPage Express indents paragraphs by nesting <BLOCKQUOTE> tags.) If the indent is too large, you can move the paragraph closer to the left margin by clicking the **Decrease Indent** button.

Tossing in a Few Links

If want to add links to your page, here are the steps to follow:

1. Type in the link text you want to use and then highlight it.
2. Select the **Insert**, **Hyperlink** command (or press **Ctrl+K**). FrontPage Express displays the Create Hyperlink dialog box, shown in Figure 21.7.

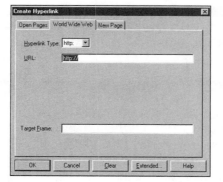

Figure 21.7

Use the Create Hyperlink dialog box to set up your hyperlink.

3. Use the **Hyperlink Type** list to choose the type of link you want. In most cases, you'll use the default **http:** selection, but several others are also available. For example, you can select **mailto:** if you want to create an email link.
4. Enter the link address in the **URL** text box.
5. If you're using frames, enter the name of the target frame in the **Target Frame** text box.
6. Click **OK** to insert the link.

Adding Multimedia to Your Page

If you feel like enhancing your page with a nice graphic or two, a background sound, or even a video, FrontPage Express is up to the challenge.

To insert an image, position the insertion point where you want the image to appear, and then select the **Insert**, **Image** command. Use the Image dialog box to pick out the GIF or JPEG file you want to use and then click **OK**.

Store HTML and Other Files in the Same Folder

Later on, you'll send all your files—the HTML file, the image files, the sound files, and so on—to your Web server. When you do, it's likely that you'll store all the files in one place: your home directory on the server.

So, whatever files you refer to in your page, your life will be infinitely simpler if you copy or move the file into the same folder that you're using to store your Web page. That way, when you specify the file in the Image dialog box (or wherever), you need only enter the name of the file and not the drive and folder. Otherwise, you'd have to strip out the extra drive and folder info before sending your files to the server.

After the image is in place, you can make a few adjustments by clicking the image and then selecting the **Edit**, **Image Properties** command. The Image Properties dialog box that pops up contains a whack of controls, but only a few are very useful:

Setting alternative text   Many Web users either have browsers that can't handle graphics, or else they surf with graphics turned off to speed things up. For these graphically-challenged folks, you should provide a text alternative so that they know what your image represents. To do so, enter the text in the General tab's **Text** area.

Creating a link   If you want to turn the image into a link, use the General tab's **Location** text box to enter the URL you want to use.

Setting alignment and spacing   Use the Appearance tab's **Alignment** list to set the image alignment relative to the surrounding text. You can also use the **Horizontal Spacing** and **Vertical Spacing** controls to set the distance between the image and the nearby text, and so give the image a bit of breathing room.

Specifying a size   Web page text loads much quicker if the browser knows how much room each image on the page takes up. Therefore, you should always activate the Appearance tab's **Specify Size** check box.

Next on the multimedia hit parade is specifying a background sound. This is a sound file that plays in the background automatically when the surfer loads your page. (Note that FrontPage Express inserts the <BGSOUND> tag, which is supported only by Internet Explorer.)

To insert a background sound, select the **Insert, Background Sound** command, enter the name of the sound file in the Background Sound dialog box that appears, and then click **OK**.

As with images, there are a few properties you can set for background sounds. To plop these properties onto the screen, select **File, Page Properties**. In the Page Properties dialog box that shows up, the General tab has a **Background Sound** group. In this group, use the **Loop** spin box to set the number of times the sound should play. Alternatively, activate the **Forever** check box to have the sound play indefinitely. (Boy, that had better be a *nice* sound!)

I don't recommend adding video files to a Web page because they're normally huge files and take far too long to download. However, if you know your visitors have fast connections (if they're on your corporate intranet, for example), a slick video can add a nice touch.

Again, the inserting part is criminally easy. First, position the insertion point where you want the video to play. Then select **Insert, Video**, enter the filename in the dialog box that flies in for the occasion, and click **OK**.

Are there video properties you can set? Of course! Click the video file to select it, and then run the **Edit, Image Properties** command. FrontPage Express loads up the Image Properties dialog box and selects the Video tab for you. Here's a look at the cast of options featured in this tab:

> **Video Source**   This text box holds the filename and location for your video.
>
> **Show Controls in Browser**   If you activate this check box, FrontPage Express sets things up so that the video displays simple controls that enable the surfer to start and stop the video.
>
> **Repeat**   These controls determine how many times the video plays. Use the **Loop** spin box to set the number of showings, and use the **Loop Delay** spin box to set the amount of time between each showing. If you'd prefer that your video play *ad nauseum*, activate the **Forever** check box.
>
> **Start**   When the **On File Open** check box is turned on, Internet Explorer starts playing the video as soon as anyone surfs to your page. If you activate the **On Mouse Over** check box, the video starts up when users puts their mouse pointers over the video.

Building Web Page Tables

The easiest way to get a table started is to click the **Insert Table** button in the Standard toolbar. FrontPage Express displays a grid. You then drag your mouse into

313

this grid to select the number of rows and columns you want, as shown in Figure 21.8. When you release the mouse, FrontPage Express cranks out the new table.

Figure 21.8

*Tables are a snap to build if you use the handy **Insert Table** button.*

Click the Insert Table button...

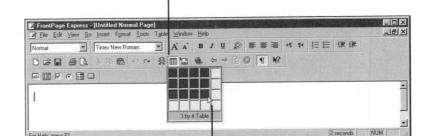

...then drag the mouse pointer into the grid.

You can get a bit more control over the finished table product if you following these steps, instead:

1. Move the insertion point to where you want the new table to appear.
2. Select the **Table, Insert Table** command. FrontPage Express displays the Insert Table dialog box, shown in Figure 21.9.

Figure 21.9

The Insert Table dialog box lets you specify a few extra table tidbits.

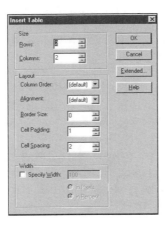

3. In the **Size** group, use the **Rows** and **Columns** spin boxes to set the number of rows and columns you want in the table. (If you're not sure about this, don't sweat it too much because you can always add and delete rows and columns later on.)
4. The **Layout** group offers up the following goodies:

   Column Order   This option determines the order in which the surfer navigates the cells by pressing Tab. The usual order is LTR (left-to-right), but you can also choose RTL (right-to-left). Of course, *why* you'd want to do this is the real question!

Alignment   This list is used to specify the table's horizontal alignment within the page.

Border Size   This spin box determines the size of the border that surrounds the table.

Cell Padding   This spin box sets the amount of white space that surrounds the data within each cell.

Cell Spacing   This spin box sets the amount of space between each table cell.

5. To set the width of the table, activate the **Specify Width** check box, and then use the text box to enter the width you want. (Note that you can enter a value either **in Pixels** or **in Percent**.)

6. Click **OK** to insert the table.

After your table is in place, the FrontPage Express **Table** menu boasts an impressive array of commands for table touch-ups. Here's a quick summary (make sure the insertion point is inside the table):

Insert Rows or Columns   Use this command to add more rows and/or columns to the table.

Insert Cell   This command adds a new cell to the table.

Insert Caption   When you select this command, FrontPage Express moves the insertion point just above the table so you can type in a caption that describes or names the table.

Merge Cells   If you selected two or more cells in advance, you can use this command to merge those cells into a single cell.

Split Cells   Use this command to split a single cell into two or more rows or columns.

Select Cell   This command selects the current cell.

Select Row   This command selects the current row.

Select Column   This command selects the current column.

Select Table   This command selects the entire table.

Caption Properties   Use this command to display the caption either at the top of the table or at the bottom. (Note that you need to put the insertion point into the caption before you can select this command).

Cell Properties   Selecting this command displays the Cell Properties dialog box shown in Figure 21.10. Use the controls in this dialog box to set the cell alignment and width, specify a background image or color, set the border colors, and more.

Table Properties   When you select this command, the Table Properties dialog box appears. This dialog contains many of the same options as you saw in the Cell Properties dialog box. (The difference is that the Table Properties options apply to the entire table.)

Figure 21.10

The Cell Properties dialog box is chock full of controls for customizing individual table cells.

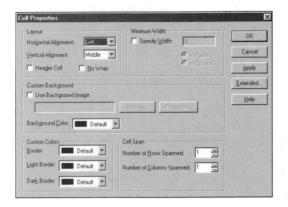

Creating a Scrolling Text Marquee

As I told you back in Chapter 10, "Making Your Web Pages Dance and Sing," a marquee is a special text box in which the text scrolls (usually) from right to left. (I also told you that they only work in Internet Explorer.) FrontPage Express makes it a snap to set up one of these marquee things. To try it, position the insertion point and then select the **Insert**, **Marquee** command. FrontPage Express coaxes the Marquee Properties dialog box (shown in Figure 21.11) onto the screen. Here's a rundown of the various options you get to play with:

Text   Use this text box to enter the text you want to display.

Direction   These options set whether the text moves right-to-**Left** or left-to-**Right**.

Movement Speed   Use these controls to set the speed of the scrolling text. The **Delay** spin box determines the number of milliseconds before the text starts scrolling. The **Amount** spin box determines the number of pixels that the text moves each time. (The larger the amount, the faster the text scrolls.)

Behavior   These options determine how the text moves in the box. Select **Scroll** to make the text move from one end of the box to the other and then repeat; select **Slide** to have the text move once from one end of the box to the other; select **Alternate** to have the text move back and forth within the box.

Align with Text   These options set how the marquee is aligned relative to the surrounding text.

Size   Activate the **Specify Width** and **Specify Height** check boxes to set custom values for the marquee's width and height. (In both cases, you can enter a value either **in Pixels** or **in Percent**.)

316

Repeat These controls determine the number of times the text scrolls. Activate **Continuously** for a never-ending scroll, or deactivate this check box and then use the spin box to set the number of times the text scrolls by.

Background Color Use this list to set the background color of the scroll box.

When you're done, click **OK** to add the marquee.

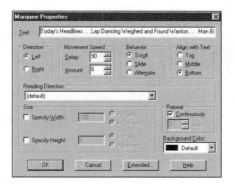

Figure 21.11

Use this dialog box to set up a scrolling marquee on your page.

Inserting Lines, Symbols, Comments, and Other Odds and Sods

To round out our look at the FrontPage Express Web page creation techniques, this section shows you how to insert a few more bits and pieces, including horizontal rules, special symbols, and more. All of these items are available using the following **Insert** menu commands:

Break This command inserts a *line break* (the <BR> tag).

Horizontal Line This command inserts a horizontal line (the <HR> tag) across the page.

Symbol This commands displays the Symbol dialog box, which contains a list of special characters you can insert into the page. Highlight the character you want, and then click **Insert**.

Comment Use this to add *comments* to your Web page. A comment is text that appears within the file, but it isn't displayed by the browser. This is handy for things like writing explanatory notes about the page contents.

File You can use this command to insert the contents of another file into your Web page. You'll use this most often to insert other HTML files, but you can also insert text files, WordPad files, and more.

Other Components This advanced command displays a submenu of components you can insert, including ActiveX controls and Java applets.

Form Field   This command displays a list of form controls that you can insert. In most cases, you're better off using one of the form-related wizards to set up a Web page form.

The Least You Need to Know

This chapter gave you a tour of FrontPage Express, Microsoft's excellent WYSIWYG Web page editor.

To close our look at alternative ways to put together Web pages, Chapter 22, "Assorted Other Ways to Create HTML Documents," looks at a few more methods you can use.

Assorted Other Ways to Create HTML Documents

The last few chapters concentrated on individual HTML programs: Netscape Composer, the Office 2000 tools, and FrontPage Express. You can think of these chapters as single-course meals: nourishing enough, but lacking in variety. This chapter, however, takes more of a smorgasbord approach. I ply you with various Web page production snacks, including a savory selection of HTML editors (the best of the rest), some tasty techniques for slicing HTML codes from existing pages, some mouthwatering Web-based page-creation engines, and some scrumptious software for converting existing files into HTML format. Hope you brought your appetite!

Other HTML Editors

When people ask me which HTML editor I use for my own pages, I have to answer, somewhat sheepishly, "I don't." That's right: I shun the fancy-schmancy editors and hand-code all my pages using a humble text editor. Why the Neanderthalic approach? Well, I've yet to find an editor that makes my pages look exactly the way I want them to look. I find myself constantly viewing and tweaking the HTML tags to get what I'm looking for. In the end, it's just faster for me to work with the tags directly.

Text Editors Extraordinaire

Just for the record, the text editor I use is called UltraEdit. I like it because it understands HTML (for example, it uses color coding to distinguish tags from regular text) and it has lots of powerful features. Even better, there's a copy of UltraEdit on this book's CD. (And, no, I don't own stock in the company or get a kickback for this.) However, there are many other text editors that put Notepad to shame. Here are their addresses (note that TextPad is also on the CD):

CuteHTML	`http://www.cutehtml.com/`
NoteTab Pro	`http://www.notetab.com/`
TextPad	`http://www.textpad.com/`
UltraEdit	`http://www.ultraedit.com/`

So although in early editions of this book I spent some time in this chapter reviewing HTML editors, I've decided against it for the last couple of editions because I'm just not up on the latest in HTML editing. Fortunately, there are plenty of folks on the Web who do use all the HTML editors and offer up in-depth reviews for your perusing pleasure:

Carl Davis's HTML Editor Reviews

`http://www.webcommando.com/editrev/index.html`

This site offers in-depth reviews on all kinds of HTML editors. He runs through all the interesting and useful features for each editor, and isn't shy about telling what's bad about them, too.

PC Magazine Reviews of HTML Editors

`http://www.zdnet.com/pcmag/stories/reviews/0,6755,2256995,00.html`

This site provides unbiased and expert reviews of a few popular HTML editors by PC Magazine's resident HTML gurus.

Stroud's Consummate Winsock Applications List (32-Bit)

`http://cws.internet.com/32advhtml.html`

This is a great site for reviews of Windows 95, Windows 98, and Windows NT editors (see Figure 22.1).

Surfing This Chapter on Easy Street

This chapter is chock-full of links to Web pages and FTP sites. Rather than typing in these links yourself, you can take a load off your fingers by loading the file named assorted.htm from this book's CD. This file contains links to all the sites mentioned in this chapter.

Figure 22.1

The Consummate Winsock Applications list is the best place to go for reviews and links to Windows HTML editors.

Stroud's Consummate Winsock Applications List (16-Bit)

http://cws.internet.com/16advhtml.html

For Stroud's reviews of editors that happily runs on Windows 3.1 systems, see this page.

Winmag.com's WinList

http://winlist.winmag.com/

This site lists the Web authoring tools that are recommended by the editors at Winmag.com (formerly Windows Magazine), and provides excellent reviews of each program.

ZDNet Web Authoring Product Guide

http://www.zdnet.com/products/filter/guide/0,7267,6006713,00.html

This site includes well-written reviews of editors and other Webmeister programs by the experts at ZDNet.

HTML Editors on the CD

The CD's Webmaster's Toolkit also includes a few HTML editors to save you a download or two. You get NetObjects Fusion, HomeSite, and HTML Assistant Pro.

Grabbing HTML from an Existing Page

Have you ever come across a particularly striking Web page and wondered just how the heck the author pulled it off? Or have you been struggling to duplicate the layout of a favorite page, only to be thwarted by the intricacies of some obscure HTML tags? Well, I have good news for you: most Web browsers have a feature that enables you peek under the hood, so to speak, and eyeball the page's underlying HTML tags. Not only that, but it's also possible in most cases to make a copy of either the entire page or of a chunk of HTML that suits your needs. You can then incorporate this purloined code into your own pages.

Is this ethical? That depends. Obviously, if you just copy another author's page verbatim and reprint it on your own site, it's not only unethical, it's illegal. The key here is the page text and graphics, which are protected by copyright law (assuming they were created by the author of the Web page). The HTML tags, however, have no such protection, so there's nothing wrong with using them wholesale. After all, life's too short to be constantly reinventing HTML wheels. As long as you change the text between the tags, you're okay.

Here's how you grab a page's underlying HTML using Internet Explorer and Netscape:

➤ **Internet Explorer**   To copy the document as a whole, pull down the **File** menu, select the **Save As** command, and then use the Save As dialog box to save the file to disk. If you only need part of the document, pull down the **View** menu and select the **Source** command. Internet Explorer loads the text and tags into Notepad (see Figure 22.2), from which you can copy whatever HTML hunks you need.

➤ **Netscape**   To copy the entire page, pull down the **File** menu, select the **Save As** command, and then use the Save As dialog box to save the file to your hard disk. To grab just a piece of the page, first select the **View** menu's **Page Source** command (in some versions of Netscape, this command is called Document Source or just Source). Then copy the tags you need from the window that appears (highlight them and press **Ctrl+C**).

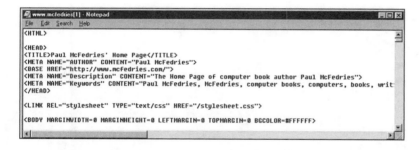

Figure 22.2

In Internet Explorer, selecting the View menu's Source command loads the document's HTML into Notepad.

If you're dealing with a framed site, things are a little different. If you use the above techniques, all you see is the code for the frameset page (the one that has the <FRAMESET> and <FRAME> tags). If what you're really after is the code for a page that's displayed in a frame, you have to use a different technique:

➤ **Internet Explorer:** Right-click the page inside the frame, and then click **View Source** in the menu that pops up.

➤ **Netscape:** Right-click the page inside the frame, and then click **View Frame Source** in the menu.

Web Pages That Create Web Pages

Word 2000's Web Page Wizard that I told you about in Chapter 20, "Suite Web O' Mine: The Office 2000 HTML Tools," enables you to create a simple home page just by filling in a few dialog boxes. The Web equivalent of dialog boxes are, of course, forms (which I talked about back in Chapter 11, "Need Feedback? Create a Form!"). So it makes sense that some intrepid soul would take the wizard concept, apply it to the Web itself, and come up with Web pages that help you create Web pages.

And, by golly, someone has actually done it! Actually, quite a few Websters have done it, so you have a choice of Web-based page-creation engines. Here's a rundown of some of the better ones.

Hayi Homepage Generator

```
http://www.lafayette.edu/acs/hayi/html-form1.html
```

This is a lengthy form that lets you specify, among other things, headings, text, colors, inline images, and hypertext links (see Figure 22.3). After you fill in the blanks, click the **Send** button at the bottom of the page to see how things look. You can then copy the page to your computer (as described in the previous section) for use on your Web site.

Figure 22.3

Part of the Hayi Homepage Generator.

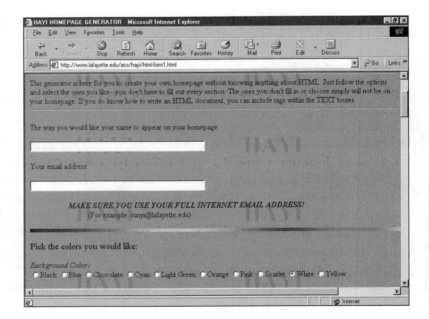

Make Your Own Home Page

```
http://www.goliath.org/makepage/
```

This is a form that lets you include an opening image, text, your own HTML, and links. For the latter, the page has dozens of suggested links to choose from. You can also select whether you want the results emailed to you or displayed onscreen (which you can then copy to your computer, as described in the previous section). After you complete the form, click the **Make me a home page** button to finish the job.

Netscape Page Wizard

`http://home.netscape.com/home/gold4.0_wizard.html`

Back in Chapter 19, "Netscape Composer and the Well-Tempered Web," I showed you how to use the Netscape Page Wizard to create Web pages online. However, you don't need to have Composer to take advantage of this feature.

Converting Existing Documents to HTML

Throughout this book I've concentrated on creating HTML documents from scratch. But what do you do if you have an existing non-HTML document—such as a spreadsheet, database, or word-processing file—and you want to publish it on the Web? In some cases, you might be able to tack on the appropriate HTML bric-a-brac by hand, but that can be time-consuming. A better approach is to find a program that automatically converts the document into its Web-ready, HTML equivalent. This section runs through a few conversion programs for popular file formats.

Office 2000 Conversions

In Chapter 20, I showed you how to take documents from Word, Excel, PowerPoint, and Access and save them as Web pages.

For starters, you should know that some HTML editors have conversion features built right in. For example, Web Edit Pro can convert some spreadsheet and database formats to HTML. Also, HTMLed Pro can convert RTF documents into HTML. (RTF is a document format developed by Microsoft. Many word processors—including Word and WordPerfect—can read and write RTF documents.) Otherwise, you might want to check out any of the following conversion programs.

The Ant

`http://telacommunications.com/ant/`

The Ant converts Word for Windows and Word for Mac documents to HTML (and vice-versa).

BeyondPress

`http://www.extensis.com/beyondpress/`

BeyondPress converts QuarkXPress files to HTML.

Database to HTML

```
http://www.guolo.com/english/dbf2html.htm
```

This program converts .dbf files to HTML.

Excel to HTML Converter

```
http://www.web100.com/sib/excel-to-html.html
```

This program converts Excel worksheet data into an HTML table. Works with Excel 5.0 for Windows and the Mac, as well as Excel 7 for Windows 95.

HTML Transit

```
http://www.infoaccess.com/
```

This is a powerful program that converts numerous documents types—including Word, Write, RTF, AmiPro, FrameMaker, and WordPerfect—into HTML.

InterLeaf

```
http://www.ileaf.com/
```

InterLeaf converts word-processing files (including Word, WordPerfect, and FrameMaker) to HTML.

Converters Galore

This collection of converters is by no means exhaustive. If you don't see the converter you need, or if you don't like any of my suggestions, here are a couple of sites that boast more extensive converter listings:

```
http://www.hypernews.org/HyperNews/get/www/html/converters.html
```

```
http://www.yahoo.com/Computers_and_Internet/Software/Internet/
World_Wide_Web/HTML_Converters/
```

The Least You Need to Know

This chapter closed out our look at painless page production by examining miscellaneous methods for creating Web documents. I showed you how to scoop out HTML from existing Web pages, examined some sites that let you create Web pages right on the Web, and listed some programs that enable you to convert documents in other formats to HTML.

From here, Part 6, "Rounding Out Your HTML Education" offers a few final thoughts on getting the most out of your Web page know-how. You learn about good HTML style, places on the Web to find the things you need, and how to make money from Web pages.

Part 6
Rounding Out Your HTML Education

Okay, that's it; the show's over. Our HTML box is now empty and all the shiny Web page baubles, bangles, and bric-a-brac have been brought out for your consideration. It's true: your basic HTML education is over, finito, sayonara, done like dinner. You know it all. Been there, done that.

Well, so now what? Ah, now it's time for a bit of HTML finishing school. The next two chapters help bring everything together by giving you pointers on good HTML and Web design style, and by offering you tons of links to Web sites that have resources or know-how that you'll find useful for the rest of your Webmaster career. The final chapter of the book gets downright mercenary by showing you how to convert your Web page prowess into cold, hard cash.

Chapter 23

The Elements of Web Page Style

In This Chapter

➤ Prose prescriptions for Web page writing

➤ Ideas for organizing your pages

➤ Tips on using graphics

➤ Things to keep in mind when dealing with links

➤ The dos and don'ts of world–class Webcraft

The least you can do is look respectable—Mom

With all that you've learned so far, you might be able to dress up your Web pages, but can you take them anywhere? That is, you might have a Web page for people to read, but is it a readable Web page? Will Web wanderers take one look at your page, say "Yuck!", and click the nearest link to get out of there, or will they stay awhile and check out what you have to say? Is your site a one-night surf, or will people add your page to their list of bookmarks?

My goal in this chapter is to show you there's a fine line between filler and killer, between "Trash it!" and "Smash hit!," and to show you how to end up on the positive side of that equation. To that end, I give you a few style suggestions that help you put your best Web page foot forward.

Content Is King: Notes About Writing

Most of the hubbub and hoopla surrounding the Web these days focuses on gorgeous graphics, fancy fonts, and other stylistic considerations. And, as you've read in several places in the book we're just now starting to see new innovations that make Web pages truly interactive.

But to the people who lust for flashy images and other eye candy, and to the pie-in-the-sky types who yearn for the Web's hands-on future, I have one thing to say: It's the content, stupid! For now and the foreseeable future, at least, this is the central fact of Web page publishing, and it often gets obscured behind all the hype.

And, unless you're an artist or a musician or some other right-brain type, content means text. The vast majority of Web pages are written documents that rely on words and phrases for impact. It makes sense, then, to put most of your page-production efforts into your writing. Sure, you spend lots of time fine-tuning your HTML codes to get things laid out just so, or tweaking your images, or scouring the Web for "hot links" to put on your page, but you should direct the majority of your publishing time towards polishing your prose.

That isn't to say, however, that you need to devote your pages to earth-shattering topics composed with a professional writer's savoir-faire. Many of the Web's self-styled "style gurus" complain that most pages are too trivial and amateurish. Humbug! These ivory tower, hipper-than-thou types are completely missing the point of publishing on the Web. They seem to think the Web is just a slightly different form of book and magazine publishing, where only a select few deserve to be in print. *Nothing could be further from the truth!* With the Web, anybody (that is, anybody with the patience to muddle through this HTML stuff) can get published and say what they want to the world.

In other words, the Web has opened up a whole new world of publishing opportunities, and we're in "anything goes" territory. So when I say, "Content is King," I mean you need to think carefully about what you want to say and make your page a unique experience. If you're putting up a page for a company, the page should reflect the company's philosophies, target audience, and central message. If you're putting up a personal home page, put the emphasis on the personal:

Write about topics that interest you.   Heck, if *you* are not interested in what you're writing about, I guarantee your readers won't be interested, either.

Write with passion.   If the topic you're scribbling about turns your crank, let everyone know. Shout from the rooftops that you love this stuff—you think it's the greatest thing since they started putting "Mute" buttons on TV remotes.

Write in your own voice.   The best home pages act as mirrors that show visitors at least an inkling of the authors' inner workings. And the sure-fire way to make your page a reflection of yourself is to write the way you talk. If you say "gotta" in conversation, go ahead and write "gotta" in your page. If you use contractions such as "I'll" and "you're" when talking to your friends, don't write "I will" and "you are" to your readers. Everybody—amateurs and professional scribes alike—has a unique writing voice; find yours and use it unabashedly.

Spelling, Grammar, and Other Text Strangers

Having said all that, however, I'm not proposing Web anarchy. It's not enough to just slap up some text willy-nilly, or foist your stream-of-consciousness brain dumps on unsuspecting (and probably uninterested) Web surfers. You need to shoot for certain *minimum* levels of quality if you hope to hold people's attention (and get them to come back for more).

For starters, you need to take to heart the old axiom, "The essence of writing is rewriting." Few of us ever say exactly what we want, the way we want, in a first draft. Before putting a page on the Web, reread it a few times (at least once out loud, if you don't feel too silly doing it) to see if things flow the way you want. Put yourself in your reader's shoes. Will all this rambling make sense to him or her? Is this an enjoyable read, or is it drudgery?

Above all, check and recheck your spelling (better yet, run the text through a spell checker, if you have one). A botched word or two won't ruin a page but, if nothing else, the gaffes will distract your readers. And, in the worst case, if your page is riddled with spelling blunders, your site will remain an eternally unpopular Web wallflower.

Spell Check Solutions

Correct spelling is important, so rather than trust your own sense of what's right, you ought to run your text through a handy spell checker. Most high-end word processing programs (such as Word) have one, and lots of HTML editors (such as Netscape Composer) are spell-check equipped. If there's no spell checker in sight, consider downloading a great little program called Spell Checker for Edit Boxes. It's free and it can be found here:

```
http://clever.net/quinion/mqa/spell.htm
```

Grammar ranks right up there with root canals and tax audits on most people's "Top Ten Most Unpleasant Things" list. And it's no wonder: all those dangling participles, passive voices, and split infinitives. One look at that stuff and the usual reaction is "Yeah, well, split *this*!" Happily, you don't need to be a gung-ho grammarian to put up a successful Web page. As long as your sentences make sense and your thoughts proceed in a semi-logical order, you'll be fine. Besides, most people's speech is reasonably grammatical, so if you model your writing after your speech patterns, you'll come pretty close.

I should note, however, that this write-the-way-you-talk school of composition does have a few drawbacks. For one thing, most people get annoyed having to slog through too many words written in a "street" style; for example, writing "cuz" instead of "because," "U" instead of "you," or "dudz" instead of "dudes." Once in a while is okay, but a page full of that stuff will rile even the gentlest soul. Also, don't overuse "train of thought" devices such as "um," "uh," or the three-dot ellipsis thing....

Remember, It's the "World" Wide Web

Although you should always squash all spelling bugs before a page goes public, try to maintain a charitable attitude about other people's howlers. Although the lion's share of pages are written in English, not all the authors have English as their native tongue, so some pages include spelling that's, uh, creative. If an email link is provided on the page, send a gentle note pointing out the slips of the keyboard and offer up the appropriate corrections.

More Tips for Righteous Writing

Thanks to the Web's open, inclusive nature and its grass-roots appeal, there are, overall, few prescriptions you need to follow when writing your page. Besides the ideas we've talked about so far, here are a few other stylistic admonishments to bear in mind:

> **Keep exclamation marks to a minimum!**   Although I told you earlier to write with passion, keep an eye out for extraneous exclamation marks! Yeah, you might be excited but, believe me, exclamation marks get old in a hurry! See?! They make you sound so darned perky! Stop!

DON'T SHOUT! Many Web spinners add emphasis to their epistles by using UPPERCASE LETTERS. This isn't bad in itself, but please use uppercase sparingly. An entire page written in capital letters feels like you're shouting, WHICH IS OKAY FOR A USED-CAR SALESMAN ON LATE-NIGHT TV, but it is inappropriate in the more sedate world of Web-page prose. Unless you think most of your readers will be using a non-graphical browser, use *italics* to emphasize important words or phrases.

Avoid excessive font formatting. Speaking of italics, it's a good idea to go easy on those HTML tags that let you play around with the formatting of your text (as described in Chapter 3, "From Buck-Naked to Beautiful: Dressing Up Your Page"). **Bold**, *italics*, and `typewriter text` have their uses, but overusing them diminishes their impact and can make a page tough to read.

Be good, be brief, be gone. These are the "three B's" of any successful presentation. Being good means writing in clear, understandable prose that isn't marred by sloppy spelling or flagrant grammar violations. Also, if you use facts or statistics, cite the appropriate references to placate the doubting Thomases who want to check things for themselves. Being brief means getting right to the point without indulging in a rambling preamble. Always assume your reader is impatiently surfing through a stack of sites and has no time or patience for verbosity. State your business and then practice the third "B": Be gone!

The Overall Organization of Your Web Pages

Let's now turn our attention to some ideas for getting (and keeping) your Web page affairs in order. You need to bear in mind, at all times, that the World Wide Web is all about navigation. Heck, half the fun comes from just surfing page-to-page via hypertext links. Because you've probably been having so much fun with this HTML stuff that you've created multiple pages for yourself, you can give the same navigational thrill to your readers. All you need to do is organize your pages appropriately and give visitors some way of getting from one page to the next.

What do I mean by organizing your pages "appropriately?" Well, there are two things to look at:

➤ How you split up the topics you talk about

➤ How many total documents you have

The One-Track Web Page: Keep Pages to a Single Topic

If there's one cardinal rule in Web-site organization, it's this: one topic, one page. Cramming a number of disparate topics into a single page is not the way to go. For one thing, it's wasteful because a reader might be interested in only one of the topics, but he still has to load the entire page. It can also be confusing to read. If you have, say, some insights into metallurgy and some fascinating ideas about Chia Pets, tossing them together in a single page is just silly. (Unless you have a *very* strange hobby!) Make each of your pages stand on its own by dedicating a separate page for each topic. In the long run, your readers will be eternally thankful.

There's an exception to this one-page, one-topic rule for the terminally verbose: if your topic is a particularly long one, you end up with a correspondingly long page. Why is that a problem? Well, lengthy Web pages have lots of disadvantages:

➤ Large files can take forever to load, especially for visitors accessing the Web from a slow connection. (This becomes even worse if the page is full of images.) If loading the page takes too long, most people aren't likely to wait around for the cobwebs to start forming; they're more likely to abandon your site and head somewhere else.

➤ If you have navigation links at the top and bottom of the page (which I talk about later on), they aren't visible most of the time if the page is long. (Unless, of course, you're using frames on your page. Not sure what "frames" are? You can find out more about them by surfing back to Chapter 12, "Fooling Around with Frames.")

➤ Nobody likes scrolling through endless screens of text. Pages with more than three or four screenfuls of text are hard to navigate and tend to be confusing to the reader.

Web Channel Surfers

Some studies show that many Web ramblers don't like to scroll at all! They want to see one screenful and then move on. This is extreme behavior, to be sure, and probably not all that common (for now, anyway). My guess is that many folks make a snap judgment about a page based on their initial impression. If they don't like what they see, they catch the nearest wave and keep surfin'.

To avoid these pitfalls, consider dividing large topics into smaller subtopics and assigning each one a separate page. Make sure you include links in each page that make it easy for the reader to follow the topic sequentially (more on this later).

For example, I have an email primer on my Web site. It's a long article, so I divided it up into seven separate pages and then added navigation links to help the reader move from section to section. Figure 23.1 shows one of those sections.

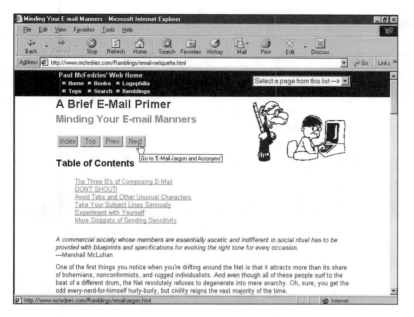

Figure 23.1

Break down long-winded topics into several pages with navigation links on each page.

Use Your Home Page to Tie Everything Together

Most people begin the tour of your pages at your home page. With this in mind, you should turn your home page into a sort of electronic launch pad that gives the surfer easy access to all your stuff. Generally, that means peppering your home page with links to all your topics. For example, check out the Yahoo! home page shown in Figure 23.2. Yahoo! is a giant subject catalogue of Web locations, so the home page consists mostly of links that take you to the various subject areas (Arts, Business and Economy, and so on).

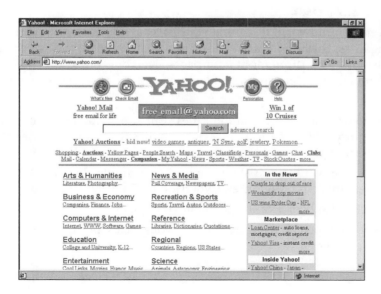

Figure 23.2

Yahoo!'s home page is mostly links to various subject areas.

Try to set up your home page so it makes sense to newcomers. Yahoo! is known as a subject catalogue of sites, so the subject-related links on its home page make immediate sense. Most people's home pages aren't quite so straightforward. Therefore, include a reasonable description of each link so visitors know what to expect.

For example, each page on my site contains a navigation header at the top of the page. On my home page, shown in Figure 23.3, I have a "What's What" section that explains how to use the navigation header.

Figure 23.3

For smoother surfing, include descriptions beside your home page links.

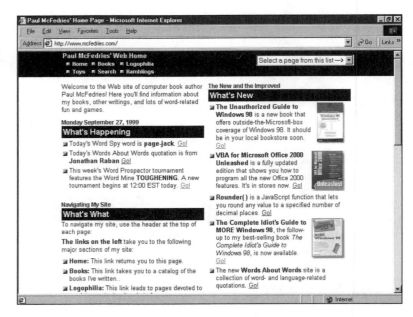

Use a Consistent Layout

Another thing to keep in mind when designing your pages is consistency. When folks are furiously clicking links, they don't often know immediately where they've ended up. If you use a consistent look throughout your pages, everyone will know that they're still on your home turf. Here are some ideas you can use to achieve a consistent look:

➤ If you have a logo or other image that identifies your site, plant a copy on each of your pages. Or, if you'd prefer to tailor your graphics to each page, at least put the image in the same place on each page.

➤ Preface your page titles with a consistent phrase. For example, "Jim Bob's Home Page: Why I Love Zima," or "Alphonse's CyberHome: The BeDazzler Page."

➤ Use the same background color or image on all your pages.

➤ If you use links to help people navigate through your pages, put the links in the same place on each page.

➤ Use consistent sizes for your headings. For example, if your home page uses the <H1> tag for the main heading and <H3> tags for subsequent headings, use these tags the same way on all your pages.

Figures 23.4 and 23.5 show you what I mean. The first is a page from my Word Spy site, and the second is from my Tech Word Spy site. As you can see, the two pages use an almost identical layout. So if you know how to get around in one site, you have no problem figuring out the other.

Figure 23.4
My Word Spy site.

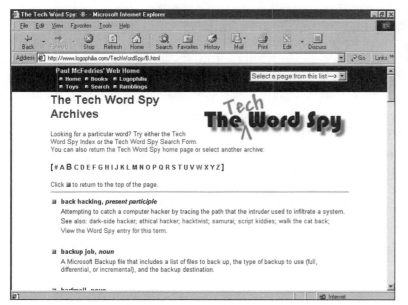

Figure 23.5
My Tech Word Spy site. Note the consistent layout between the two pages.

Organization and Layout Hints for Individual Pages

After you get the forest of your Web pages in reasonable shape, it's time to start thinking about the trees, or the individual pages. The next few sections give you a few pointers for putting together perfect pages.

Elements to Include in Each Page

For each of your Web pages, the bulk of the content that appears is determined by the overall subject of the page. If you're talking about Play-Doh, for example, most of your text and images are Play-Doh related. But there are a few elements that you should include in all your pages, no matter what the subject matter:

A title A Web site without page titles is like a cocktail party without "Hi! My Name Is..." tags.

A main heading Nobody wants to scour a large chunk of a page to determine what it's all about. Instead, include a descriptive, large heading (<H1> or <H2>) at the top of the page to give your readers the instant feedback they need. In some cases, a short, introductory paragraph below the heading is also a good idea.

A "signature" If you're going on the Web, there's no point in being shy. People appreciate knowing who created a page, so you should always "sign" your work. You don't need anything fancy: just your name and your email address will do. Many people also include their company name, address, phone number, and fax number.

Copyright info If the Web pages you create are for your company, the company owns the material that appears on the page. Similarly, the contents of personal home pages belong to the person who created them. In both cases, the contents of the pages are protected by copyright law, and they can't be used by anyone else without permission. To reinforce this, include a copyright notice at the bottom of the page.

The current status of the page If your page is a preliminary draft, contains unverified data, or is just generally not ready for prime time, let your readers know so they can take that into consideration.

A feedback mechanism Always give your visitors some way to contact you so they can lavish you with compliments or report problems. The usual way to do this is to include a "mailto" link somewhere on the page (as described in Chapter 5, "Making the Jump to Hyperspace: Adding Links").

A link back to your home page As I mentioned earlier, your home page should be the "launch pad" for your site, with links taking the reader to different areas. To make life easier for the surfers who visit, however, each page should include a link back to the home page.

Under Construction? Yeah, We Know!

Many Webmeisters include some kind of "Under Construction" icon on pages that aren't finished (a few examples of the species are on this book's CD). This is fine, but don't overdo it. The nature of the Web is that most pages are in a state of flux and are constantly being tweaked. (This is, in fact, a sign of a good Web site.) Scattering cute construction icons everywhere reduces their impact and annoys many readers.

Most of these suggestions can appear in a separate section at the bottom of each page (this is often called a *footer*). To help differentiate this section from the rest of the page, use an <HR> (horizontal rule) tag and an <ADDRESS> tag. Depending on the browser, the <ADDRESS> tag formats text in italics. Here's an example footer (look for footer.htm on the CD) you can customize:

```
<HR>
<ADDRESS>
This page is Copyright &copy; 200?, your-name-here<BR>
company-name-here<BR>
company-address-here<BR>
Phone: (###) ###-####<BR>
Fax: (###) ###-####<BR>
Email: <A HREF="mailto:your-email-address-here">your-email-address-
here</A>.
</ADDRESS>
<P>
Last revision: date/goes/here
<P>
Return to my <A HREF="home-page-URL-goes-here.htm">home page</A>.
```

Make Your Readers' Lives Easier

When designing your Web pages, always assume your readers are in the middle of a busy surfing session, and therefore won't be in the mood to waste time. It's not that people have short attention spans. (Although I'd bet dollars to doughnuts that the percentage of Web surfers with some form of ADD—Attention Deficit Disorder—is higher than that of the general population.) It's just the old mantra of the perpetually busy: "Things to go, places to do."

So, how do you accommodate folks who are in "barely-enough-time-to-*see*-the-roses-much-less-stop-and-smell-the-darn-things" mode? Here are a few ideas:

➤ Organize your pages so people can find things quickly. This means breaking up your text into reasonably sized chunks and making judicious use of headers to identify each section.

➤ Put all your eye-catching good stuff at the top of the page where people won't be able to miss it.

➤ If you have a long document, place anchors at the beginning of each section and then include a "table of contents" at the top of the document that includes links to each section. (I explain this in more detail in Chapter 5, "Making the Jump to Hyperspace: Adding Links.")

➤ Add new stuff regularly to avoid the "cobweb page" label. (A cobweb page is a page that hasn't been revised in some time.) You should also mark your new material with some sort of "new" graphic so regular visitors can easily find the recent additions.

Guidance for Using Graphics

As you saw back in Chapter 6, "A Picture Is Worth a Thousand Clicks: Working with Images," graphics are a great way to get people's attention. With images, however, there's a fine line between irresistible and irritating. To help you avoid the latter, this section presents a few ideas for using graphics responsibly.

For starters, don't become a "bandwidth hog" by including too many large images in your page. Remember that when someone accesses your Web page, all the page info—the text and graphics—is sent to that person's computer. The text isn't usually a problem (unless you're sending an entire novel, which I don't recommend), but graphics files are much slower. It's not unusual for a large image to take a minute or more to materialize if the surfer has a slow Internet connection. Clearly, your page better be *really* good if someone waits that long. Here are some ideas you can use to show mercy on visitors with slow connections:

➤ If your graphics are merely accessories, keep them small.

➤ Always use the <IMG> tag's WIDTH and HEIGHT attributes (see Chapter 6).

➤ It's acceptable to use graphics to get spiffy fonts because you can't be sure that surfers have the same font installed on their computers. However, don't rely on this too heavily, or your page could end up as nothing but a giant image!

Understanding the Bandwidth Thing

Bandwidth is a measure of how much stuff can be crammed through a transmission medium such as a phone line or network cable. Or, to put it another way, bandwidth measures how much information can be sent between any two Internet sites. Because bandwidth is a finite commodity, many Net veterans are constantly cautioning profligate users against wasting bandwidth.

Bandwidth is measured in bits-per-second (bps). Here, a bit is the fundamental unit of computer information where, for example, it takes eight bits to describe a single character. So a transmission medium with a bandwidth of 8bps would send data at the pathetically slow rate of one character per second. Bandwidth is more normally measured in kilobits per second (Kbps—thousands of bits per second). So, for example, a 28.8Kbps modem handles 28,800 bits per second. In the high end, bandwidth is measured in megabits per second (Mbps—millions of bits per second).

Always bear in mind that a certain percentage of your readership is viewing your pages either from a text-only browser or from a graphical browser in which they've turned off image loading. (Depending on the content of your page, the number of graphics-challenged surfers could be anywhere from 10 to 30% of your visitors.) If you're using an image as a link, be sure to provide a text alternative (by using the <IMG> tag's ALT attribute, as described in Chapter 6). For non-link graphics, you can use ALT to describe the picture or even to display a blank. If you must use lots of images, offer people a choice of a text-only version of the page.

Finally, be careful if you decide to use a background image on your page. The Internet has lots of sites that offer various textures for background images. (I tell you about some of these sites in the next chapter.) Many of these textures are "cool," to be sure, but they're too "busy" to display text properly. For example, check out the page shown in Figure 23.6. Now *that* is the mother of all ugly backgrounds! (Lucky for you, the figure doesn't show the background in color; the actual texture incorporates various shades of sickly green.) For maximum readability, your best bet is to combine solid, light backgrounds with dark text.

Some background textures just aren't worth it!

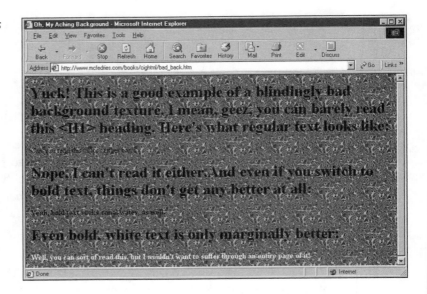

Link Lessons: Keeping Your Links in the Pink

To finish our look at Web page style, here are a few ideas to keep in mind when using links in your pages:

➤ In your link text, don't ask the reader to "click" something, because some of them won't have mice or other "clickable" devices. The verbs of choice are "select" and "choose."

➤ Make your link text descriptive. Link text really stands out on a page because most browsers display it underlined and in a different color. This means the reader's eye is drawn naturally toward the link text, so you need to make the text descriptive. That way, it's easy for the reader to know exactly what they're linking to. Always avoid the "here" syndrome, where your link text is just "here" or "click here." The snippet below shows you the right and wrong way to set up your link text. Figure 23.7 shows how each one looks in a browser.

```
<H3>Wrong:</H3>
The Beet Poets page contains various odes celebrating our favorite
edible
root, and you can get to it by clicking <A
HREF="beetpoet.htm">here</A>.
<H3>Right:</H3>
The <A HREF="beetpoet.htm">Beet Poets page</A> contains various odes
celebrating our favorite edible root.
```

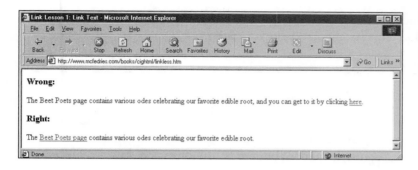

Figure 23.7
The reader's eye gravitates toward the link text, so make sure your text is descriptive.

➤ If you're presenting material sequentially in multiple pages, create "navigational links" to help the reader move forward and backward through the pages. For example, each page could have a **Previous** link that takes readers to the previous page, a **Next** link that takes them to the next page, and a **Top** link that returns them to the first page. (See Chapter 8, "Images Can Be Links, Too," for a bit more detail on this.)

The Difference Between "Previous" and "Back"

You might be wondering why the heck you'd want to bother with **Previous** and **Next** buttons when most browsers have similar buttons built in (usually called **Back** and **Forward**). Well, they're not really the same things. For example, suppose you surf to a site and end up on a page that's in the middle of a series of pages. If you select the browser's **Back** button, you find yourself tossed back to the site you just bailed out of. If you select the page's **Previous** button, however, you head to the previous page in the series.

➤ For maximum readability, don't include spaces or punctuation marks either immediately after the <A> tag or immediately before the </A> tag.

➤ If you're planning a link to a particular page, but you haven't created that page yet, leave the link text as plain text (for example, don't surround it with the <A> and </A> tags). Links that point to a nonexistent page (they're often called *vaporlinks*) generate an error, which can be frustrating for surfers.

➤ Try to keep all your links (both the internal and external variety) up-to-date. This means trying out each link periodically to make sure it goes where it's supposed to go.

➤ If you move your page to a new site, leave behind a page that includes a link to the new location (this is called a *Century 21 page*).

The Least You Need to Know

This chapter went beyond the specifics of HTML tags and told you about a few general concepts that should serve you in good stead when constructing your pages. Web page style guides abound on the Net, and

I'll tell you about a few of them, as well as a fistful of other Web page resources, in Chapter 24, "The Elements of Web Page Style."

Some HTML Resources on the Web

In This Chapter

➤ Where to go to get great graphics, sounds, and videos

➤ HTML style guide sites

➤ Web page access counters, without programming!

➤ HTML-related mailing lists and newsgroups

➤ A cornucopian compendium of cool HTML resources

The Internet is many things: It's a file repository, a communications medium, a shopping mall, a floor wax, a dessert topping, and a forum for all manner of kooks, crackpots, nut cases, and nincompoops. But the Internet—and the World Wide Web in particular—is mostly an information resource. Everywhere you go, some kind soul has contributed a tidbit or two about a particular subject. Of course, *you* might not be interested in, say, the mating habits of the Andorran Cow, but it's a good bet that some surfer somewhere is.

A Better Way to Surf This Chapter

To make surfing all these sites even easier, I've included a hypertext document on this book's CD that includes links to every site mentioned in this chapter. Look for the file named resource.htm.

What you *are* interested in, to be sure, is HTML. Now here's the good news: There are dozens, nay hundreds—okay billions—of HTML resources scattered throughout the Internet. The bad news, though, is the usual Internet gripe: How do you find what you need quickly and easily? This is where your purchase of this book—a savvy and prudent investment on your part—really pays off. Why? Because this chapter takes you through the best of the Net's HTML resources. I show you great Net locales for things like graphics and style guides, HTML-related newsgroups and mailing lists, and lots more.

Graphics Goodies

The CD that comes with this book is loaded with a few hundred bullets, buttons, bars, and icons for sprucing up your Web pages. They do for a start, but you might want to check out other images to give your page just the right touch. The next few sections show you a few of my favorite Web-based graphics stops. (Before we start, though, a caveat: Most of the graphics you find in these sites are free, as long as you don't use them commercially. Things change, of course, so you should always read the fine print before grabbing a graphic to use on your page.)

The Three B's: Buttons, Bars, and Bullets

Here are some sites to check out for the little accessories that add character to a page.

Celine's Original .GIFs

```
http://www.specialweb.com/original/
```

This site includes a nice collection of images created by Celine herself. If you use one of her images, she'll even put a link to your page on her graphics page.

Ender Design: Realm Graphics

```
http://www.ender-design.com/rg/
```

This is one of the best places to go for a wide variety of quality icons, balls, bullets, and more. And, if you're feeling gung-ho, you might want to use one of the few graphics-related documents (GIF versus JPEG, selecting a background, and more).

Image-O-Rama

`http://members.aol.com/dcreelma/imagesite/image.htm`

This site includes a large collection of graphics, especially the three B's. There's also an "Other Stuff" page that has a few cool icons, as well as a good collection of animated GIFs.

IconBAZAAR

`http://www.iconbazaar.com/`

This site includes the usual portfolio of Web page wonders, plus a few interesting variations on the standard themes (see Figure 24.1).

Figure 24.1

IconBAZAAR: Icons out the wazoo!

Jelane's Free Web Graphics

`http://www.erinet.com/jelane/families/`

This site has a great collection of graphical gadgets created by Jelane Johnson. Particularly interesting are the "families" of graphics that offer buttons and arrows and other images that use a common design.

McFedries.com Image Archives

`http://www.mcfedries.com/graphics/archives.html`

This is a collection of images that were distributed in earlier versions of the book.

netCREATORS Icon Page

`http://animatedgifs.simplenet.com/`

netCREATORS Icon page has oodles of images organized in dozens of categories.

Pixel Warehouse

`http://matrixvault.com/PW/`

This site includes lots of public domain images, and a well-crafted set of custom graphics that offer unique takes on the standard categories.

WebbGrafx

`http://www.february14th.com/grafx/`

The three B's are well represented at this site.

Yahoo!'s Icon Index

`http://www.yahoo.com/Arts/Design_Arts/Graphic_Design/Web_Page_Design_and_`
`Layout/Graphics/Icons/`

This site includes a seemingly endless list of sites that have collections of icons, bullets, and other images for Web pages.

Yet Another B: Background Textures

I don't like background images myself, but lots of Web welders swear by them. If you want to give them a try, you might find a few files at some of the sites mentioned in the last section. You can also find lots of *textures* (as background images are often called) in the following locations.

3D Webscapes

`http://3dzine.simplenet.com/3dwebscp/3dwebscapes.html`

This site offers "3D" background images. The site itself is horribly designed (it's almost a tutorial on how *not* to put together a Web site), but some of the images are interesting.

Absolute Background Textures Archive

`http://www.grsites.com/textures/`

This site claims to be "The Largest Collection of Free Background Textures on the Internet." I don't know if that's true, but with over 3,000 backgrounds on display, I can't imagine a bigger collection.

The Background Boutique

http://www.theboutique.org/

This site boasts a very nice collection of custom graphics in both regular and bordered styles.

Dr. Zeus' Textures

http://www.best.com/~drzeus/Art/Textures/Textures.html

At this site you can find some truly unique and way-out images. Most of them are totally useless for displaying text, but they sure look wild!

Netscape's Background Sampler

http://www.netscape.com/assist/net_sites/bg/backgrounds.html

This site has a truckload of textures from the folks who started all this background nonsense in the first place.

Pattern Land

http://www.netcreations.com/patternland/index.html

"Where all your pattern fantasies come true!" I bet you didn't even know you had pattern fantasies.

The Pixel Foundry

http://www.pixelfoundry.com/bgs.html

You can find hundreds of backgrounds at The Pixel Factory, including a "Gentle Tiles" category that offers images that don't interfere with page text. Yes!

Silk Purse Backgrounds

http://www.silkpursegraphics.com/backgrnd.html

This site has an unusual collection of images. They're copyrighted by the author, but they can be used for non-profit purposes.

Texture Land

http://www.meat.com/textures/

This site has a very unusual collection of backgrounds.

The Wallpaper Machine

http://www.cacr.caltech.edu/cgi-bin/wallpaper.pl

This interesting site displays a different background each time you refresh the page. When you see one that you like, grab it for use on your own pages.

Yahoo!'s Background Index

http://www.yahoo.com/Arts/Design_Arts/Graphic_Design/Web_Page_Design_and_
Layout/Graphics/Backgrounds/

If none of the above pages suits your fancy, Yahoo! has a list of a few dozen sites that feature background images.

The A/V Web: Sound and Video Sites

Back in Chapter 10, "Making Your Web Pages Dance and Sing," I showed you how to turn your Web page into a multimedia machine with sounds and videos. If you don't have a ready supply of A/V material on hand, here's a list of some sites that'll get you started.

The Daily .WAV

http://www.dailywav.com/

This site posts a new WAV file each weekday. It also has an extensive archive of WAV and MIDI files.

SoundAmerica

http://www.soundamerica.com/

This site has thousands of sound clips from all walks of life, including cartoons, movies, TV, and more. It also has a nice collection of MIDI music.

MidiWeb

http://www.midiweb.com/

This site is an excellent source of information and tutorials on MIDI. This site also boasts a nice collection of MIDI files, MIDI utilities, and links to other MIDI-related Web sites.

Whoopie!

http://www.whoopie.com/

With a name like that, a site better be good—real good. And this one certainly is (see Figure 24.2). Here, you can find links to all kinds of sound, MIDI, and video files, as well as pointers to plug-ins and helper applications.

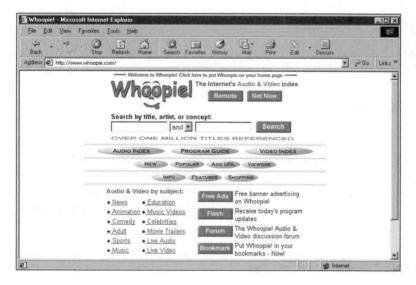

Figure 24.2

Whoopie!: A bad name for a great site.

Yahoo!'s Audio Index

http://www.yahoo.com/Computers_and_Internet/Multimedia/Audio/

Lots of links to audio sites, including sites that offer audio archives.

Yahoo!'s Video Index

http://www.yahoo.com/Computers_and_Internet/Multimedia/Video/

Links to all things video, including a decent set of entries for collections of video-related links.

A Guide to HTML Style Guides

Although we talked about HTML style in Chapter 23, "The Elements of Web Page Style," we didn't have room to cover everything. Fortunately, there's no shortage of Web wizards who are only too happy to give you their two-cents worth. Here's a list of some of the better ones.

Art and the Zen of Web Sites

http://www.digiweb.com/tkarp/webtips.html

This is a thoughtful article on how best to approach and design a Web site (although its extreme length violates one of the cardinal principles of good design!).

Composing Good HTML

http://www.cs.cmu.edu/~tilt/cgh/

This site includes a guide by Eric Tilton that's a bit on the advanced side. It has a good section on common errors that crop up in HTML documents.

High Five Award Page

http://www.highfive.com/

Although it's not strictly a Web style guide per se, this site presents the weekly "High Five" award to pages that exhibit "excellence in site design." Although the High Five site itself is rather badly designed (go figure!), checking out the winners gives you a good idea of what the top sites are doing to make themselves stand out from the Web crowd. (See also the WEB WONK page, later in this section.)

The Sevloid Guide to Web Design

http://www.sev.com.au/webzone/design.htm

Arranged in a tips and tricks format, this site offers over 100 pointers on good Web design.

Style Guide for Online Hypertext

`http://www.w3.org/hypertext/WWW/Provider/Style/Overview.html`

This is a friendly manual on good Web page design by no less an authority than Tim Berners-Lee, the fellow who invented the World Wide Web.

Top Ten Ways to Tell If You Have a Sucky Home Page

`http://jeffglover.com/sucky.html`

This is a tongue-in-cheek (sort of) look at the 10 worst things you can do in a Web page. (Number 11? Using dumb words like "sucky"!)

Web Pages That Suck

`http://webpagesthatsuck.com/`

The premise of this fun site is simple: learn good Web site design by checking out (and, usually, laughing at) Web sites that feature bad design.

WEB WONK

`http://www.dsiegel.com/tips/index.html`

A page from David Siegel, proprietor of the High Five Award Page (see my earlier reference). WEB WONK, shown in Figure 24.3, offers a few handy tips on making pages look their best.

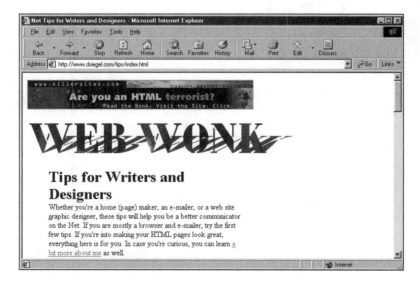

Figure 24.3
David Siegel's WEB WONK page.

WebHome Improvement

http://www.htmltips.com/

This site includes a nice compendium of design tips in categories such as Content, Presentation, and Usability.

Webmonkey Design Collection

http://www.hotwired.com/webmonkey/design/

This site includes a series of articles with loads of great tips and ideas about designing Web sites.

What Is Good Hypertext Writing?

http://www.cs.tu-berlin.de/~jutta/ht/writing-html.html

This site is an excellent guide (though a bit on the pedantic side) to Web page writing and editing.

Yale Style Manual

http://info.med.yale.edu/caim/manual/

This is a stuffy but exhaustive guide to all aspects of Web site design.

Counter Check: Tallying Your Hits

Okay, you've labored heroically to get your pages just right, a Web server is serving them up piping hot, and you've even advertised your site shamelessly around the Internet. All that's left to do now is wait for the hordes to start beating a path to your digital door.

But how do you know if your site is attracting hordes or merely collecting dust? How do you know if you've hit the big-time, or just hit the skids? In other words, how do you know the number of people who've accessed your pages? Well, there are two ways you can go:

> ➤ **Ask your hosting provider** Many companies can supply you with statistics that tell you the number of "hits" your site has taken.
> ➤ **Include a counter in your Web page** A counter is a little program that increments each time some surfer requests the page.

A Counter Caution

Counters are fun, and they're certainly a handy way to keep track of the amount of activity your page is generating. There are, however, three counter-related caveats you should know about:

➤ The counter program sits on another computer, so it takes time for the program to get and send its information. This means your page loads a little slower than usual.

➤ If the computer that stores the counter program goes "down for the count," the count won't appear on your page.

➤ Counters are notoriously fickle beasts that tend to reset themselves to 0 whenever they feel like it.

Creating a counter program is well beyond the scope of a humble book such as this (insert sigh of relief here). However, a few community-minded programmers have made counter programs available on the Web. Happily, you don't even have to copy or install these programs. All you have to do is insert a link to the program in your page, and the counter is updated automatically whenever someone checks out the page. This section provides you with a list of some counter programs to try.

The Counter.com

http://www.thecounter.com/

This is a free counter that doesn't require placing an ad on your site.

eXTReMe Tracker

http://www.extreme-dm.com/tracking/

This is a great service that offers a wide range of tracking options.

Net-Trak

http://net-trak.stats.net/

This full-featured service not only gives you a basic hit counter, but it also can track unique visitors, daily hits, average hits, hits by browser, and much more (see Figure 24.4).

Figure 24.4

The home page for Net-Trak.

sitegauge

http://www.sitegauge.com/

This is a sophisticated—and free—Web site monitoring tool with loads of features.

The WebCounter

http://www.digits.com/

This is a nicely implemented, no-frills counter. Note that busy sites (those getting more than 1,000 hits a day) have to pay a subscription fee to use this counter.

Yahoo!'s Access Counter Index

http://www.yahoo.com/Computers_and_Internet/Internet/World_Wide_Web/
Programming/Access_Counts/

As usual, Yahoo! has a long list of sites that supply counters.

HTML Mailing Lists

HTML is a huge topic these days, so there's no shortage of HTML-related chinwagging and confabulating on the Net. If you're stumped by something in HTML, or if you're looking for ideas, or if you just want to commune with fellow Web fiends, there are mailing lists and Usenet newsgroups to welcome you with open arms.

Here are a few mailing lists you might want to subscribe to.

ADV-HTML

This is a moderated mailing list for intermediate-to-advanced HTML hounds. To get subscription information, send a message to LISTSERV@UA1VM.UA.EDU. In the message body, enter **info ADV-HTML.**

CIGHTML

As I mentioned in the Introduction, this is a mailing list that I've set up exclusively for people smart enough to have purchased this book. You and your peers get to discuss HTML tips and pitfalls, ask questions, and get semi-sage advice from yours truly. To subscribe, send a message to the listmanager@mcfedries.com. In the Subject line of the message, type **join cightml.**

HTML-Haven

http://members.xoom.com/web_lady/
html/html-haven.html

This is a general discussion list for novices and experts, alike. To subscribe, send a note to html-haven-subscribe@onelist.com.

Using Usenet Discussions

Usenet also has tons of HTML and Web authoring discussions. Here's a rundown:

HTML Writers Guild Lists

The HTML Writers Guild (http://www.hwg.org/) maintains quite a few mailing lists. To see a list of them, head for the following page:

http://www.hwg.org/lists/archives.html

> **comp.infosystems.www.authoring.html**   This busy group is chock-full of HTML tips, tricks, and instruction.

> **comp.infosystems.www.authoring.images**   This group focuses on using images in Web pages.

> **comp.infosystems.www.authoring.misc**   This is a catch-all group that covers everything that doesn't fit into the other groups.

comp.infosystems.www.authoring.site-design This group concentrates on big picture issues of overall site layout and design.

comp.infosystems.www.authoring.stylesheets This group looks at the ins and outs of those new-fangled style sheet things you learned about back in Part 3, "High HTML Style: Working with Style Sheets."

comp.infosystems.www.authoring.tools This newsgroup looks at HTML editors and other Web page authoring tools.

A List of HTML Lists

To finish off our look at HTML resources on the Net, this section looks at a few all-purpose, everything-but-the-kitchen-sink sites. The following pages offer one-stop shopping for links that cover all aspects of Web page production.

Essential Links to HTML

http://www.el.com/elinks/html/

This is a nice collection of links to high-quality sites.

Haznet's Fallout Shelter

http://www.hudziak.com/haznet/

This "Webmaster Resource Clearinghouse" is chock full of links to great sites. Its unique feature is a "Geiger Meter" that rates each link.

HTML Writers Guild

http://www.hwg.org/

This is the semi-official headquarters for Webmeisters from around the world. Besides lots of links, you can also find tutorials, news, classes, and much more.

HyperText Markup Language

http://www.w3.org/MarkUp/

This is the W3C's home for the HTML specs that I mentioned earlier. It also includes a list of HTML links.

Macmillan's Web Design Resource Center

http://www.mcp.com/resources/webdesign/

A nice collection of links for Websters of all skill levels. Brought to you by the same people who brought you this book!

Nuthin' But Links

http://pages.prodigy.com/bombadil/

This includes a long list of HTML links, as well as other Internet- and computer-related links.

WebMonkey

http://www.hotwired.com/webmonkey/

HotWired has put together this useful site that's filled to the gills with resources, tutorials, and much more.

Yahoo!'s HTML Index

http://www.yahoo.com/Computers_and_Internet/Information_and_Documentation/
Data_Formats/HTML/

This is an absurdly impressive (bordering on overkill) list of HTML resources from the bottomless Yahoo! library.

The Least You Need to Know

This chapter showed you some of the "in" places to go on the Net for Web page resources, materials, and discussions. We looked at sites for graphics and back-grounds, sound and video files, HTML style guides, hit counters, mailing lists, Usenet newsgroups, and more.

The next chapter shows you how to use all your hard-won HTML knowledge to do something really radical: make money!

Chapter 25

Show Me the Money: Turning Your HTML Skills into Cash

Dear Paul,

Just want to let you know that I am actually getting paid to design and produce Web sites, and it's all your fault for writing your HTML book.

—Patsy West (http://www.websitewiz.com/)

That's a real note sent to me from a real reader of the book. And it's no fluke, either, because I've received dozens of similar messages from readers over the years. I'm not at all surprised, because Web page designing is one of *the* hottest fields right now. People who know how to cobble together Web pages are in great demand and are being snapped up by companies large and small. If you've read the whole book and if you have at least a bit of design skills, then you too can get a job as a Web page producer.

What if you like your day job, or are a student and don't have time to go into full-time Webmastering? An alternative is to turn your home page into a money machine. There are all kinds of affiliate programs available on the Web that will pay you cash. They won't make you rich, but they're a great way to earn some extra income and they don't require a ton of work.

This chapter takes you through the ins and outs, as well as the potential pitfalls, of Web design jobs and making money from your site.

Turning Pro: Becoming a Paid Web Designer

This section gives you some tips and pointers on becoming a paid page purveyor. My focus here is on setting up a freelance Web design business. You learn how to set up your business, how to find contracts, what to charge, and more.

Going Captive: Designing As a Full-Time Job

If your interest lies more in getting a full-time job as a corporate Web spinner, read this section anyway. For one thing, it helps immensely if you have a page "portfolio" that you can show to prospective employers. For another, many full-time page designers got their start by doing a great job on a freelance project for a company.

Getting Started: Your Business Plan

If you want to do this freelance Web design business thing right, then there's one step that you shouldn't skip: creating a business plan. This doesn't mean you have to forge a fifty-page tome with all kinds of charts and economic analyses. No, all you really want is to get a handle on the type of business that you're creating and running. To that end, you need to ask and answer ten basic questions:

➤ **What's my goal?**   It's tough to get anywhere if you don't have a final destination in mind. You need a concrete, realistic goal: To be able to quit the corporate rat race; to save up enough for the family vacation; to pay my way through school.

➤ **What's my target market?**   Although general Web design is still a reasonable area to shoot for, your chances of success improve immensely if you can target one or more smaller markets. Do you have a particular field of expertise? Are there particular kinds of Web sites you do better than others?

➤ **What's my name/domain?** Think long and hard about the name you want to use. Lots of rookie Web weavers seem to change their business name every six months or so, which is no way to build your "brand." As soon as you've thought of a great name, *immediately* go to Network Solutions (`http://www.networksolutions.com/`) and register the corresponding domain name. Having a "dot com" domain instantly makes your business look more solid and respectable. You think anyone's going to give money to someone with a 100-character long URL from GeoCities? I don't think so.

➤ **What are my expenses?** This is crucial, particularly because your income might take a while to build. Do you need to upgrade your computer or your Internet connection? Do you need other equipment, such as a scanner or a digital camera? What about software such as HTML editors or graphics programs? If you don't know JavaScript or CGI, will you have to hire someone to program for you? Break everything down into two categories: startup costs and ongoing expenses. For the latter, don't forget living expenses such as food and shelter.

➤ **What will I charge?** This is one of the most important questions, and it's also one of the toughest to answer. See "Getting Paid: Web Design Rates," later in this chapter.

➤ **How will I allocate my time?** Come up with realistic estimates for how long it takes you to forge various kinds of pages: simple text-only pages, heavily-designed graphics pages, and so on. You also need to budget time for client discussions, accounts receivable, and other business-related tasks.

➤ **What will my income be?** After you've settled on your rates and allocated your time, you can then come up with a realistic projection of your income.

➤ **Do I need professional help?** No, not a psychiatrist! I'm talking here about an accountant and a lawyer. An accountant can help you to set up books and can tell you whether some expenses are deductible (particularly if you work out of your home). You need a contract for each job, and a lawyer can help you create one that suits you and your business. (See "Legalese: Notes About Contracts," later in this chapter.)

➤ **How will I promote my business?** This isn't a better mousetrap you're building, so people won't automatically beat a path to your Web door. You need to advertise not only online, but also in the real world, too. (See "Getting the Word Out: Advertising and Promotion," later in this chapter.)

➤ **What about customer service?** No matter how you look at it, Web design is a service business. Therefore, you need to be prepared to offer a high level of customer service. Think about your policies regarding project updates, post-project follow-up, handling complaints, and so on.

Getting Paid: Web Design Rates

What you charge for your services is obviously a critical part of your business success (or lack thereof). If you charge too much, people won't hire you; if you charge too little, you'll leave money on the table (at best) or fail due to lack of profits (at worst). Unfortunately, the Web design business is still wet behind its electronic ears, so there are no set rates. In any case, what you charge depends on a number of factors:

➤ **Your level of experience** The more the monetarily merrier.

➤ **What skills you have** Someone with good writing, graphics, or programming skills can charge more than someone who just knows HTML inside and out.

➤ **The type of client** You can get away with charging more to a corporation than you could to a Mom and Pop shop or a non-profit organization.

➤ **What type of page you're creating** You should charge one (lower) price for simple text pages or for converting existing documents to HTML; you should charge another (higher) price for pages that require creative writing, custom graphics, or programming.

➤ **How much consulting is involved** You can boost your rate if a job requires long consultations with the client.

Check This Out

Contracting Out

It's a rare Web designer who has the Big Four skills: HTML, writing, graphics, and programming. If you lack one or more of these assets, you can always hire someone to work with you on a project-by-project basis.

With all that in mind, the next question to think about is how you want to charge the client: by the hour or by the project?

Per-hour pricing is the most common, particularly for new Web designers. Before delving into this, you should be familiar with one crucial concept: *billable hours*. These are hours that you actually work on a project. They don't include activities such as selling the client in the first place, eating lunch, or blowing away nasty aliens in a rousing game of Quake. With that in mind, coming up with that all-important hourly rate is tough. Here are two ways to go about it:

➤ **See what other designers are charging** Visit the Web sites of other page designers and check out their rates. See what kinds of sites they've produced. If you think you can do as good a job, then you might be able to charge the same amount.

➤ **The expenses-and-profits method** With this method, you calculate your average weekly expenses, add the amount of profit you'd like, and then divide by the weekly billable hours. For example, suppose your weekly expenses work out to $600. If you want to make a minimum 25% profit (a not unreasonable figure), then you need to add another $150, for a total weekly nut of $750. If you figure your week has 30 billable hours, then you'd set your rate at $25 per hour.

Watch the Clock!

Although you don't want to include non-productive time in your billable hours, be diligent about tracking even small blocks of time where you do real work. You'd be surprised to see how five minutes here and ten minutes there really adds up.

Some Pricing Resources

Yahoo! maintains a huge list of Web site designers. Here's where to find it:

```
http://dir.yahoo.com/Business_and_Economy/Companies/
Internet_Services/Web_Services/Designers/Complete_Listing/
```

Another great resource is a survey of HTML services pricing put together by Paul Uttermohlen:

```
http://columbusrealestate.com/paul/pricing.html
```

After you've gained enough experience, you might consider moving to a per-project fee. This means that you charge a single fee for all the work you do in a particular project. Most Web designers that I've talked to say that they usually make much more profit this way than they do using an hourly rate. However, going this route isn't for rookies in the field:

➤ You need to have top-notch skills. Per-project contracts are usually for a large number of pages, and you won't get those kinds of contracts unless your portfolio is of the highest quality.

➤ You need to be very experienced so that you can estimate with some exactitude just how long the project will take. You won't help your cause if you charge $1,000 for a project that you thought would take you 20 hours, and it ends up taking you 100 hours.

➤ These kinds of projects are really only sellable to large businesses.

Legalese: Notes About Contracts

Having a contract for each project is something that new Web designers rarely think about. However, it's absolutely crucial because it helps ensure that you get paid; it prevents your client from suing your pants off because of a misunderstanding; it specifies copyright issues; and it outlines everyone's rights and responsibilities.

By far the best advice I can give you in this area is this: *see a lawyer!* Although I give you a few good resources to check out in a sec, don't fool yourself into thinking you can do this on your own. By all means put together a contract that makes sense for your business, but make sure you run it by a lawyer who is versed in this type of thing. I guarantee you'll be glad you did.

With that out of the way, the following is a list of resources devoted to Web design contracts and legal issues.

Ivan Hoffman's Articles for Web Site Designers and Site Owners

http://www.ivanhoffman.com/web.html

Mr. Hoffman is *the* expert on legal issues involving creative adventures, including Web site design. This page is loaded with truly useful data on Web design contracts, copyrights, and much more.

Easy Site Surfing

For your surfing convenience, all the links in this chapter can be found in the file money.htm on the CD.

HTML Writers Guild sample contract

ftp://ftp.hwg.org/pub/archives/docs/
legal/consult.txt

This site shows a very basic contract that offers a good place to start.

Web Developer's Contract Swap File

http://provider.com/contracts.htm

This site is a great resource with tons of links to contract info.

Website Design Contract

```
http://www.wilsonweb.com/worksheet/
pkg-con.htm
```

This site has an elaborate contract by Ralph Wilson.

Website Development Agreements: Planning and Drafting

```
http://www.digidem.com/legal/wda/
```

This site offers an exhaustive (and often intimidatingly technical) look at the issues involved in creating Web design contracts.

Check This Out

Handling Design Changes

Make sure your clients understand (put it in writing, too!) that any design or content changes that aren't in the contract result in extra charges.

Getting the Word Out: Advertising and Promotion

With Web site design being such a growing concern, you better believe that there are thousands of like-minded souls out there competing for those client bucks. To help your business stand out from the herd, you need to blow your own horn by doing a little advertising and promotion.

By far the best marketing tool in existence is a little thing called word-of-mouth. Impressed clients naturally sing your praises to other people, and that recommendation might be all some soul needs to come knocking on your door. In other words, the most effective advertising is to do the highest quality work, meet your deadlines, operate responsibly and ethically, and offer great customer service.

There are also plenty of other things you can do to spread the gospel of you even further afield. Here are some ideas for online promotion:

➤ Include at the bottom of all your email messages a brief (nothing too elaborate) "ad" about your business. Even just the URL of your business home page is good. (Remember, too, that most email programs can be set up to automatically tack on a "signature" to the bottom of each outgoing message.)

➤ Join mailing lists and participate in newsgroups and discussion lists related to your area of expertise.

➤ Be sure to use <META> tags on your pages so search engines index your site (see Chapter 7, "Publishing Your Page on the Web"). When constructing your keywords, use words and phrases related to the market or markets in which you specialize. This helps differentiate your site.

➤ Even with <META> tags, don't assume all search engines will find you. Register your site with the major search engines directly.

DesignShops.com

Besides registering your business with DesignShops.com, you should also bookmark this first-rate site. It's crammed full of articles, links, and other resources targeted at Web design businesses.

➤ Make sure your contact information is present and easy to find on your Web pages.

➤ Register your business with DesignShops.com, shown in Figure 25.1:
   `http://designshops.com`

Figure 25.1

DesignShops.com is an excellent resource for Web designers.

➤ Write articles for other Web sites or online magazines. Along similar lines, you could create your own e-newsletter that offers site tips, business ideas, and whatever else you think might interest prospective customers.

➤ Look for Web sites that list local business in your area and register your business with them.

➤ Get all your friends and relatives to link to your site.

➤ Make sure your own site is always up-to-date and well-designed. Nothing turns off a prospective client more than an ill-maintained business home page.

➤ At the bottom of every client page, put a small, tasteful logo that links back to your site. (Make sure your client is okay with this.)

➤ Show samples of your work on your Web site.

You don't have to restrict all your promotion efforts to cyberspace. Here are some ideas for advertising your business in the real world:

➤ Get business cards or flyers made up and plaster them around town in grocery stores, community centers, and other appropriate public spaces.

➤ Check to see if local businesses have a Web presence. If not, send them a proposal.

➤ Create free pages for churches, charitable organizations, community groups, and schools.

➤ Chat up the nerds at the local computer or electronics store. Be sure to leave them a stack of business cards so that they can refer people your way.

➤ Advertise in community newspapers.

➤ Give talks or presentations to local computer user groups, community groups, clubs, or even the Chamber of Commerce.

Street Cred: Web Design Certification

As I said in the previous section, getting your new business noticed is vital if you want a steady stream of contracts. One good way to do that and to assure prospective clients that you really know what the heck you're doing is to get some kind of Web design certification. There are tons of certification programs available, but the following six are the best and most respected.

Association of Internet Professionals

http://www.association.org/

This is more of an umbrella group that exists to, in a sense, "certify the certifications."

Association of Web Professionals

http://www.a-w-p.org/cert.htm

This Association offers three programs—Certified Web Designer, Certified Web Manager, and Certified Web Technician.

NetGuru

http://www.ngt.com/

This organization offers a Certified Internet Webmaster program.

Penn State

http://webmaster.outreach.psu.edu/

This school offers a Webmaster Certificate Program.

Sysoft

http://netra.sysoft.com/web/

Sysoft offers Certified Webmaster and Certified Advanced Webmaster certifications.

World Organization of Webmasters

http://www.naw.org/education_index.html

This organization offers a Certified Professional Webmaster program.

A Mailing List for Page Pros

If you decide to start your own Web design shop, or even if you're seriously thinking about it, you'd do well to check out a mailing list called hwg-business. It's run by the HTML Writers Guild and it covers most aspects of running a Web design business. You can find out more about it here:

http://www.hwg.org/lists/hwg-business/index.html

Joint Ventures: Working with Affiliate Programs

An *affiliate program* (also sometimes called a referral program) is a partnership with a Web site that sells stuff. The basic idea is that you put on your page a link to a specific product from the selling site. If someone clicks your link and ends up purchasing the product, you get a piece of the action—typically, a percentage of the selling price.

For example, the granddaddy of all affiliate programs is the Associates Program run by Amazon.com (see Figure 25.2). In the books portion of the program, if someone purchases a book after linking to Amazon through your site, you get a "referral fee," which is usually a cool 15% of the purchase price. So, if someone buys a $30 book, your cut is $4.50. It redefines the phrase "easy money"!

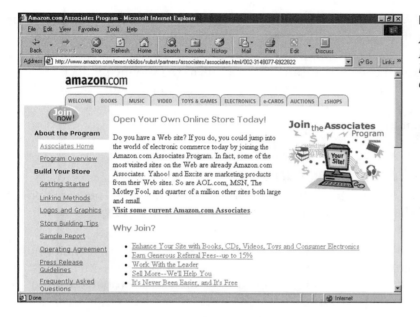

Figure 25.2

Amazon.com's Associates Program pays you boffo bucks for sending paying customers their way.

Even better, there are affiliate programs available for more than just books. There are programs for CDs, videos, computer software and hardware, food, liquor, furniture, and even cars. This means you can select a program that fits in with the type of site you have.

Non-Commission Programs

Although most affiliate programs are commission-based, some are based on other criteria. For example, some programs pay a flat fee for each *new* visitor who purchases something. Other programs offer *click-through* incentives that pay for each new visitor sent to the site.

Setting Up an Affiliate Program

Setting up an affiliate program typically requires these steps:

1. Go to the site offering the program and sign up for it.

2. Create a "store" on your site. This doesn't have to be anything elaborate, although most programs also offer program-related graphics and other helping hands.

3. For each product you want to feature, set up a link to the specific product on the program site. You usually include some kind of code in the link address that identifies your site as the referrer.

4. Sit back and wait for the checks to come rolling in.

Choosing an Affiliate Program

The hardest part about setting up an affiliate program is choosing one. There are hundreds available, and they all have different features. Here are a few things to watch for when choosing a program:

➤ **Commission rates**   These vary widely. Amazon's 15% is on the high end of the scale and most programs offer between 3 and 10%. Some programs offer a sliding scale where your commission goes up after the total sales attributed to your links goes over a certain amount.

➤ **Commission exceptions**   Some programs offer their highest commission rate only on certain items. Amazon, for example, offers only a 5% commission on its other products (such as CDs and videos). It's also typical to offer a reduced commission on products that are heavily discounted.

➤ **Direct versus general links**   Most programs pay a much higher commission if a sale was generated from a direct link to a product. (As opposed to linking to the program's home page, for example.)

➤ **The commission base**   Some programs base the commission on the selling price of the product, others base it on the profit earned by each sale.

➤ **Site restrictions**   Many programs reject sites that have "unsuitable" themes such as sex, violence, discrimination, or the promotion of illegal activities.

➤ **Check thresholds**   Many programs won't issue you a check until your commission reaches a certain threshold.

➤ **Exclusivity**   Some program agreements demand exclusivity, meaning that you can't also include a rival program on your site.

Whew! That's a lot to worry about. Fortunately, a few good people on the Web have made it their full-time job to monitor and review these affiliate programs. The following are the four sites that I think do the best job.

Associate Programs Directory

http://www.associateprograms.com/

This directory has hundreds of programs broken down into dozens of categories. Includes ratings from program users as well as a free newsletter.

Mark Welch's Commission Based Advertising Page

http://www.markwelch.com/bannerad/baf_commission.htm

This breathtakingly-comprehensive listing of affiliate programs shows commission rates and restrictions. It also displays "Be wary" and "Not Recommended" for those programs that are unreliable or don't seem quite on the up-and-up.

Refer-It

http://www.refer-it.com/main.cfm

Refer-It lists hundreds of programs, which is good, but the descriptions are often written by the companies offering the programs, which is bad. Still, it's a good place to learn about commission rates and the number of affiliates associated with each program.

Sitecash.com

http://www.sitecash.com/

This site offers a good overview of affiliate programs and has a limited number of program reviews.

Affiliate Program Pointers

To close this section, here are a few pointers for getting the most out of affiliate programs:

➤ **Choose a program that fits**   Affiliate programs work best when you have lots of prospective buyers visiting your site. Therefore, you should always select a program that fits in with your site's theme. If you have a gardening site, for example, joining a CD-based program doesn't make much sense.

➤ **Sell your links**   You want people to not only click the program links, but also buy the item on the other end of the wire. You can encourage people to do that by selling the product on your end: writing a review, listing the product's features, and so on.

➤ **Make your "store" attractive**   Don't just slap up a few links. Use the HTML skills you've learned from this book to build a nice "store" that makes people come back for more. And don't forget to take advantage of whatever design help the affiliates program offers.

The Least You Need to Know

This chapter closed the main part of the book by showing you two ways to convert your coding skills into cold, hard cash. The first part of the chapter showed you how to start up a Web design business, including creating a business plan, setting rates, advertising, and more. The second part of the chapter told you about affiliates programs: what they are, how to choose one, and how to get the most out of them.

WHAT?

Speak Like a Geek Glossary

404   Used to describe a person who is clueless. This comes from the following Web server error message:

`404 Not Found. The requested URL was not found on this server.`

access counter   A small program inserted in a Web page that tracks the page's *hit* count (how many times it's been accessed).

access provider   See *service provider*.

anchor   A word or phrase in a Web page that's used as a target for a link. When the user selects the link, the browser jumps to the anchor, which might exist in the same document or in a different document.

applet   A *Java* program. See also *craplet* and *dancing baloney*.

arachnerd   A person that spends way too much time either surfing the Web or fussing with their home page.

bandwidth   A measure of how much stuff can be stuffed through a transmission medium such as a phone line or network cable. There's only so much bandwidth to go around at any given time, so you see lots of Net paranoia about "wasting bandwidth." Bandwidth is measured in *bits per second*.

Barney page   A page whose sole purpose in life is to capitalize on a trendy topic. The name comes from the spate of pages bashing poor Barney the Dinosaur that were all the rage a while back. Recent Barney pages have been dedicated to O.J. and Princess Diana. Also known as a *Macarena page*.

bit   The fundamental unit of computer information (it's a blend of the words "binary" and "digit"). Computers do all their dirty work by manipulating a series of high and low electrical currents. A high current is represented by the digit 1 and a low current by the digit 0. These 1's and 0's—or bits—are used to represent absolutely everything that goes down inside your machine. Weird, huh?

bits per second (bps)   Another, more common, measure of *bandwidth*. Because it takes eight bits to describe a single character, a transmission medium with a bandwidth of, say, 8bps would send data at the pathetically slow rate of one character per second. Bandwidth is more normally measured in kilobits per second (Kbps—thousands of bits per second). So, for example, a 28.8Kbps modem can handle 28,800 bits per second. In the high end, bandwidth is measured in megabits per second (Mbps—millions of bits per second).

body   The section of the Web document in which you enter your text and tags. See also *head*.

bookmarks   In a Web browser (particularly Netscape), a list of your favorite Web pages, which you can set while you are surfing. To return to a page, just select it from the list. See also *favorites*.

bps   See *bits per second*.

browser   The software you use to display and interact with a Web page.

byte   Eight *bits*, or a single character.

Century-21 site   A Web site that has moved to a new location and now contains only a link to the new address.

CGI   See *Common Gateway Interface*.

CGI Joe   A programmer who specializes in the *Common Gateway Interface* (CGI) scripts that accept and handle input from most Web page *forms*.

character reference   Sounds like something you'd put on your résumé, but it's really an HTML code that lets you insert special characters in your Web pages (such as é). See also *entity name*.

clickstream   The "path" a person takes as they navigate through the World Wide Web.

client-side image map   An *image map* where the links are processed by the browser instead of the server. See also *server-side image map*.

cobweb page   A Web page that hasn't been updated in a long time.

Common Gateway Interface (CGI)   A programming technology that enables a Web server to accept data (usually from a form), process that data, and then send the browser some kind of result. See also *CGI Joe*.

cornea gumbo   A Web page that is an overdesigned, jumbled, soup of colors, fonts, and images.

craplet   A poorly designed, aesthetically unpleasing, or just generally useless Java *applet*. See also *dancing baloney*.

cyberscriber   A person who publishes something in an Internet forum (such as a Web page or a Usenet newsgroup).

cyberspace   The place you "go" when you reach out beyond your own computer (usually via modem) and interact with information or people on other computer systems. See also *meatspace*.

cybersquatting   The practice of obtaining and holding an Internet domain name that uses a company's registered trademark name.

cyberstyle   The writing style used in most online communications. This style is characterized by one or more of the following traits: frequent use of abbreviations, acronyms, and jargon; "street" slang (e.g., using "cuz" instead of "because"); typos, misspelled words, and a general inattention to grammar and sentence structure; a rambling, stream-of-consciousness style.

cybersurfer   A person who surfs *cyberspace*.

dancing baloney   Web page-based animated images, Java applets, and other bells and whistles that are not only useless, but also detract from the overall quality of the page. See also *craplet*.

dead tree edition   The paper version of an online magazine or journal.

deep link   A Web page link that points to a file within a site rather than to the site's home page.

dirt road   A frustratingly slow connection to a Web site. "Geez, that GIF still hasn't loaded yet? The Web server must be on a dirt road." See also *JPIG* and *spinner*.

domain name   The part of your email address to the right of the @ sign. The domain name identifies a particular site on the Internet.

egosurfing   Scanning the Internet's archives and search engines for mentions of your own name.

emotag   Mock HTML tags used in writing to indicate emotional states. "<FLAME>That guy on the mailing list is the rudest jerk I've ever had the misfortune of dealing with.</FLAME>"

emoticon   See *smiley*.

entity name   An HTML code that lets you insert special characters in your Web pages. See also *character reference*.

FAQ   The aficionado's short form for a Frequently Asked Question. The correct pronunciation is *fack*. See *Frequently Asked Questions list*.

favorites   In Internet Explorer, a list of Web pages that you've saved for subsequent surfs. To return to a page, just select it from the list. See also *bookmarks*.

flooded   A page rendered unreadable because of a poorly chosen background image. "I had to bail out of that page because the background was flooded with some butt-ugly tartan." See also *wrackground image*.

form   A Web document used for gathering information from the reader. Most forms have at least one text field where you can enter text data (such as your name or the keywords for a search). More sophisticated forms also include check boxes (for toggling a value on or off), radio buttons (for selecting one of several options), and command buttons (for performing an action such as submitting the form).

frames   Rectangular browser areas that contain separate chunks of text, graphics, and HTML. In other words, you can use frames to divide the browser window into two or more separate pages.

Frequently Asked Questions list   A list of questions that, over the history of a newsgroup or Web site, have come up most often. If you want to send a question to a newsgroup or to a Web site's administrator, it's proper *netiquette* to read the group's FAQ list to see if you can find the answer there first.

FTP (File Transfer Protocol)   This is the usual method for sending your HTML files to your Web server. Note that it's okay to use FTP as both a noun (a method for transferring files) and a verb ("Your images aren't showing up because you forgot to FTP the graphics files to your home directory").

geek   Someone who knows a lot about computers and very little about anything else.

GIF   Graphics Interchange Format. One of the two most commonly used graphics format on the Web. See also *JPEG*.

grammar slack   The tolerance exhibited by most Internet users for small spelling and grammar errors.

greenlink   To use the Web for monetary gain.

guru site   A Web site, put together by an expert on a particular subject, that contains a large amount of useful, accurate information on that subject.

hard launch   The release of a product or Web site for public consumption.

head   The top part of an HTML file. This is like an introduction to a Web page. Web browsers use the head to glean various types of information about the page (such as the title). See also *body*.

hit   A single access of a Web page. A hit is recorded for a particular Web page each time a browser displays the page.

hit count   The number of *hits* a particular page has had. Many pages have installed access counters to track (and display) the number of hits they've had.

hit-and-run page   A Web page that gets a huge number of *hits* and then disappears a week later. Most hit-and-run pages contain pornographic material and they get shut down when the Web site's system administrators figure out why their network has slowed to a crawl. See also *slag*.

home page   The main page of a Web site.

host   See *Web server*.

hosting provider   A company that provides you with storage space (usually at a fee) for your Web pages. The company runs a Web server that enables other people to view your pages.

hotlist   A collection of links to cool or interesting sites that you check out regularly.

HTML   HyperText Markup Language. The collection of tags used to specify how you want your Web page to appear.

HTML editor   A program that makes it easier to mark up a document by using menu commands and toolbar buttons to insert tags.

hypertext link   See *link*.

image map   A clickable image that takes you to a different link, depending on which part of the image you click. See also *client-side image map* and *server-side image map*.

inverse vandalism   Creating something for no other reason than the sheer fact that you *can* create it. Most Web pages are acts of inverse vandalism.

ISP (Internet service provider)   A company that offers access to the Internet.

Java   A programming language designed to create software (an *applet*) that runs inside a Web page. Can also be used to create standalone applications such as word processors and spreadsheets. See also *craplet* and *dancing baloney*.

Javlovian   Describes the automatic response that causes marketing types to come up with only cute, coffee-related names for *Java*-based products (for example, Cafe, Roaster, Java Beans, Latte, and so on ad nauseum).

JPEG   A common Web graphics format developed by the Joint Photographic Experts Group. See also *GIF*.

JPIG   A Web page that takes forever to load because it's either jammed to the hilt with graphics, or because it contains one or two really large images. See also *dirt road* and *spinner*.

Kbps   Kilobits per second (thousands of *bits per second*).

link   A word or phrase that, when selected, sends the reader to a different page or to an anchor.

link rot   The gradual obsolescence of the *links* on a Web page as the sites they point to become unavailable.

Macarena page   A Web page capitalizing on a current fad. They are usually full of fluff and have a short life expectancy. See also *Barney page*.

Mbps   Megabits per second (millions of *bits per second*).

meatspace   The flesh-and-blood real world; the opposite of *cyberspace*.

mouse potato   The computer equivalent of a couch potato.

multimediocrities   Lame Web pages that are jam-packed with second-rate pictures, sounds, and *applets*.

netiquette   An informal set of rules and guidelines designed to smooth Internet interactions. Netiquette breaches often result in the offender being flamed (sent a nasty email message).

nooksurfer   A person who frequents only a limited number of Internet sites.

notwork   A downed network.

one-link wonder   A Web page that contains only a single useful link.

page jack   To steal a Web page and submit it to search engines under a different address. Users who run a search and attempt to access the page are then routed to another—usually pornographic—site.

password trap   A Web site that uses a legitimate-looking interface to fool users into providing their passwords.

paster boy   A person who copies other peoples' HTML source code and pastes it into their own Web page in an effort to look like they know what they're doing.

pixel shim   A small, transparent, image (usually 1 pixel wide and 1 pixel tall) that Web page designers use to achieve exact placement of text and images.

plug-in   A program that attaches itself to a Web browser. The functionality of the program then becomes an integral part of the browser. An example is WebFX, a VRML plug-in for Netscape.

portal site   A Web site that combines a wide array of content and services in an effort to convince users to make the site their home page.

publish   To make a Web page available to the World Wide Web community at large.

read-only user   A person who uses the Internet exclusively for reading Web pages, email, and newsgroups instead of creating their own content.

roadblock   A Web page that serves no other purpose other than to let you know that there is nothing available at the URL, but that something will be coming soon.

search jack   To include in a Web page popular, but superfluous, search terms (such as "sex" or "Lewinsky") to appear in the results when people search for those terms.

server   A computer that sends out stuff. Check out *Web server* for an example.

server-side image map   An *image map* where the links are processed by the server. See also *client-side image map*.

service provider   A business that sells Internet connections to individuals and small companies. Also called an *access provider*.

shovelware   Content from an existing medium (such as a newspaper or book) that has been dumped wholesale into another medium (such as a Web page).

slag   To bring a network to its knees because of extremely high traffic. "That Babe of the Week page has totally slagged the network." See also *notwork*.

smiley   A combination of symbols designed to indicate the true intent or emotional state of the author. The classic smiley is the sideways happy face :-). Smileys are fine in moderation, but overusing them not only indicates that your writing isn't as clear as it could be, but it also brands you as a newbie. See also *emotag*.

spamdexing   To repeat a word dozens or even hundreds of times at the top of a Web page. The word is usually indicative of the subject matter of the site, and repeating it so many times is an attempt to fool Web search engines into thinking the site is a good representation of that subject. However, most search engines recognize this and refuse to index such a site.

spinner   An extremely slow link. The name comes from Mosaic's globe icon, which spins while the program tries to access a site. If the site is particularly slow, the only sign you have that anything is actually happening is the spinning globe. See also *dirt road* and *JPIG*.

stalker site   A Web site devoted to a celebrity, the content of which clearly indicates that the fan who created the site is obsessed with their subject.

surf   To leap giddily from one Web page to another by furiously clicking any link in sight; to travel through *cyberspace*.

tags   The HTML commands, in the form of letter combinations or words surrounded by angle brackets (<>). They tell a browser how to display a Web page.

target   See *anchor*.

title   A short description of a Web page that appears at the top of the screen.

ubiquilink   A link found on almost everyone's *hotlist*. "Yahoo! must be on every hotlist on the planet. It's a total ubiquilink."

Uniform Resource Locator   See *URL*.

URL   A Web addressing scheme that spells out the exact location of a Net resource. For example, Yahoo!'s URL is `http://www.yahoo.com/`. See Chapter 5, "Making the Jump to Hyperspace: Adding Links," for an almost-comprehensible explanation of how URLs work.

vanity plate   An annoyingly large Web page graphic that serves no useful purpose. See also *JPIG*.

vaporlink   A link that points to a nonexistent Web page.

VRML   Virtual Reality Modeling Language. Used to create Web sites that are 3D "worlds" you "enter" using a VRML-enhanced browser. You can then use your mouse to "move" around this world in any direction.

Web host   See *Web server*.

Web server   A computer that stores your Web pages and hands them out to anyone with a browser that comes calling. Also known as a Web host.

wrackground image   A background image that ruins a page by making the text unreadable. See also *flooded*.

YOYOW   You own your own words. This refers to the copyright you have on the text in your Web pages.

Frequently Asked Questions About HTML

This appendix presents a list of FAQs (frequently asked questions) about HTML. The questions are listed in the following categories: General HTML, Graphics, Publishing, Multimedia, Forms, Frames, and Page Design. A longer list of FAQs is available on my Web site:

```
http://www.mcfedries.com/books/cightml/list/faq.html
```

General HTML Questions

How can I spell check my Web page?

You have two choices for getting your spelling letter-perfect:

➤ Compose your pages in a program that has a spell check feature. You can find such a feature in word processors (such as Word), HTML editors (such as Netscape Composer), or in text editors (such as UltraEdit—http://www.ultraedit.com/).

➤ Use a spell check program such as Spell Checker for Edit Boxes (see http://clever.net/quinion/mqa/spell.htm).

The browser shows the tags I put into the page. What's wrong?

I showed you how to solve this problem in Chapter 2, "Laying the Foundation: The Basic Structure of a Web Page." See the section titled "Help! The Browser Shows My Tags!"

Internet Explorer handles my link/graphic/whatever no problem, but Netscape doesn't. What's wrong?

The usual culprit here is that you've included a space in either a filename or a directory name. Netscape doesn't like spaces, so you need to rename your file or directory to remove the space. If you want to separate words in a file or directory name, a good substitute is the underscore character _.

What's the difference between the .htm and .html file extensions?

There's no difference whatsoever. Both are legit HTML file extensions, and browsers treat them equally.

How can I open a link in a separate browser window?

The usual method is to set the <A> tag's TARGET attribute equal to_blank</SPAN>:

```
<A HREF="whatever.html TARGET="_blank">New Window</A>
```

However, if you set the <A> tag's TARGET attribute equal to an undefined name—that is, it's not the name of a frame or one of the pre-fab names—then the browser opens a new window and assigns the TARGET value as the name of the new window.

For example, consider the following:

```
<A HREF="whatever.html" TARGET="LinkWindow">Click this!</A>
```

This opens a new window and displays the "whatever.html" page within that window. The browser assigns the name "LinkWindow" to that window. This means that you can load anything into that window just by referring to the same window name, like so:

```
<A HREF="another.html" TARGET="LinkWindow">Click this, too!</A>
```

This link displays the "another.html" page in the same window that the previous link opened.

Is there a way to make table columns have a constant width?

Absolutely! Provided you're only putting text in each cell, then you have to do two things:

➤ Specify an exact width for each cell.

➤ Use our old friend spacer.gif, the transparent 1×1 pixel image (see Chapter 6, "A Picture Is Worth a Thousand Clicks: Working with Images").

For example, if you want you a column to always be 100 pixels wide, use this:

```
<TD WIDTH=100>
Cell text goes here
```

```
<BR><IMG SRC="spacer.gif" WIDTH=100 HEIGHT=1>
</TD>
```

What is XML?

XML (eXtensible Markup Language) is still pretty high-falutin' stuff, and it's not really on the radar screens just yet (and least not for the likes of us). The basic idea is that XML enables the designer to create her own tags in such a way that an XML-smart browser knows what to do with those tags. This won't be a big deal for folks who just have straightforward pages. If you deal with databases or specialized fields (such as medicine or mathematics), however, you can create tags that describe database components or elements from your field of expertise. For example, a Math XML is already being proposed, and it'll enable math types to render equations and other elements that HTML just can't do:

```
http://www.w3.org/Math/
```

The problem with XML is that it requires some heavy-duty programming to "teach" the browser what each hand-built tag is supposed to do. For that reason, XML will remain a geeks-only technology for some time to come.

Finding non-geek info on XML is hard right now, but the following PC Magazine article isn't too bad:

```
http://www.zdnet.com/pcmag/features/xml98/intro.html
```

Instead of displaying the symbol represented by a character code or entity, I want to display the actual character code or entity. Is that possible?

Yes. All character codes and entities begin with an ampersand . So the easiest way to display the code is to remove the ampersand and replace it with the character code for the ampersand (&). For example, the character code for the copyright symbol is ©. To display the code, you'd use the following:

```
&#38;#169;
```

Graphics Questions

Is it possible to change the color of the border that appears around images used as links?

The image link border color is the same as the regular link color. Therefore, you can change the border color by using the LINK, ALINK, and VLINK attributes in the <BODY> tag. For example, if you want a red border, you use this:

```
<BODY LINK="#FF0000" ALINK="#FF0000" VLINK="#FF0000">
```

How do I create thumbnail images?

A thumbnail is just a smaller version of an existing image. What you need to do is load the original image into a graphics program and then use the program's "Resize" command to scale down the image to an appropriate size (which depends on the original image). Then use the program's File, Save As command to save the smaller image under a different name. I usually just add "-thumbnail" to the name. For example, if the original is mypic.jpg, I name the smaller version mypic-thumbnail.jpg.

To use the thumbnail, put it in your page with an <IMG> tag, and then set up that image as a link to the normal size file. Here's an example:

```
<A HREF="mypic.jpg">
<IMG SRC="mypic-thumbnail.jpg">
</A>
```

How do I make an image map with weird shapes, not just the usual rectangle, circle, or polygon?

You need to create a *server-side* image map, which requires a special program. Here are some to check out:

➤ **Image Mapper** `http://www.coffeecup.com/mapper/`

➤ **LiveImage** `http://www.liveimage.com/`

➤ **Mapedit** `http://www.boutell.com/mapedit/`

See also the following Yahoo! index:

`http://www.yahoo.com/Computers_and_Internet/`
`Internet/World_Wide_Web/Imagemaps/`

Image Map Programs on the CD

This book's CD contains the necessary files for two of these image map programs: LiveImage and Mapedit.

Why doesn't my image appear when I view my page in the browser?

The fact that you're not seeing your image is probably due to one of the following reasons:

➤ If you're viewing your page on your home machine, the HTML file and the image files might be sitting in separate directories on your computer. Try moving your image files into the same directory that holds your HTML file.

➤ If you're viewing your page on the Web, make sure you sent the image files to your server.

➤ Make sure you have the correct match for uppercase and lowercase letters. If an image is on your server and it's named "image.gif", and your IMG tag refers to "IMAGE.GIF", your image won't show up. In this case, you'd have to edit your IMG tag so that it refers to "image.gif".

How do I get those little banners to pop up when the user puts their mouse over an image?

Add ALT text to your <IMG> tag:

```
<IMG
SRC="vacation12.gif"
ALT="This is a picture of me getting mugged in Marrakesh">
```

Most modern browsers display that text as a banner when the mouse pointer sits over an image for a second or two.

When I use an image as a link, how do I remove the border around the image?

Add BORDER=0 to your <IMG> tag, as in this example:

```
<A HREF="something.html">
<IMG SRC="jiffy.gif" BORDER=0>
</A>
```

I'm an AOL user, and my uploaded images are distorted. What's the problem?

AOL compresses uploaded images, which causes problems for some files. There's a full explanation on the AOL Webmaster Info site:

```
http://webmaster.info.aol.com/
```

When you get there, click **Graphics Compression**.

How can I prevent people from stealing my Web page images?

This is extremely difficult, if not impossible, to do. However, here are three things that can help:

➤ Put a strongly worded copyright message on all of your pages.

➤ Disable the right-click functionality that most image thieves use to grab graphics. I have a script on my site that shows you how to do this:

```
http://www.mcfedries.com/JavaScript/NoRightClick.html
```

➤ Add a "digital watermark" to your images. See the Digimarc Corporation:

```
http://www.digimarc.com/
```

How can I reduce the size of a GIF or JPEG file?

There are a number of techniques you can try:

➤ Use a graphics program to reduce the size of the image.

➤ If the image is a GIF, use a graphics program to reduce the number of colors the image uses.

➤ If the image is a JPEG, use a graphics program to either reduce the number of colors or increase the image compression.

➤ Use a Web-based image optimization service. There's a good one at the Web Site Garage:

> `http://www.websitegarage.netscape.com/`

How can I slice up a large image to put in a table or use as an image map?

The easiest way I know is to use the Picture Dicer program:

> `http://www.ziplink.net/~shoestring/dicer01.htm`

Publishing Questions

How can I get my own domain name?

There are two types of domain names available:

➤ **A regular domain name of the form (or perhaps yourdomain.org).** To get one of these domains, you either need to contact Network Solutions (`http://www.networksolutions.com/`) directly, or you need to sign up with a Web hosting provider that does this for you. Either way, it will cost you US$70 up front for two years, and then US$35 per year after that. If you go the direct route, you have to find a Web host who is willing to host your domain.

➤ **A *subdomain* of the form yourdomain.webhostdomain.com.** There are many Web hosts who will provide you with this type of domain, often for free.

Why do I see only a list of my files when I plug my address into the browser?

In your directory, you need to have a file that uses your server's *default name*. I explained how this works in Chapter 7, "Publishing Your Page on the Web."

How do I register my site with search engines?

There are two routes you can take:

➤ **Manual** This route involves surfing to each search engine and then adding your site by hand. Look for a link named Add a Page, Add URL, or something similar.

➤ **Automatic** This route involves using a service that submits your site to a number of search engines. Here are some of the more popular ones:

Submit It (`http://www.submit-it.com/`)

Add Me (`http://addme.com/`)

Register It (`http://register-it.netscape.com/`)

See also the Yahoo! Promotion Index

```
http://dir.yahoo.com/Business_and_Economy/Companies/Internet_Serv
ices/Web_Services/Marketing/Promotion/
```

How do I copyright my page?

There is no official process you have to go through to copyright your Web page text. According to copyright law (see `http://lcweb.loc.gov/copyright/`), as soon as your text is published in a fixed form (such as being uploaded onto your Web server), then your copyright is automatically in place. To be safe, always include a copyright notice at the bottom of all your pages. The usual format is the word "Copyright", followed by the © symbol (use either © or ©), followed by the year of publication, followed by your name:

```
Copyright © 2000 Paul McFedries
```

Multimedia Questions

I have a MIDI version of a popular song. Is it okay to use it on my site?

Using MIDI variations of commercial music is definitely a copyright violation. As responsible Webmeisters, we should use *licensed* MIDI music wherever possible. The following page explains more about this and offers some licensed files:

```
http://www.liveupdate.com/sounds.html
```

How can I get a MIDI file to play as a background sound in both Internet Explorer and Netscape?

It's okay to use both the <BGSOUND> and <EMBED> tags in the same document:

```
<BGSOUND SRC="earsore.mid" LOOP=INFINITE>
<EMBED SRC="earsore.mid" AUTOSTART=TRUE HIDDEN=TRUE LOOP=0>
```

Can I use a sound file with a mouseover instead of an image?

To play a sound in JavaScript, you set the <SPAN STYLE="font-family: monospace">location.href</SPAN> property equal to the sound file you want to play, like so:

```
location.href="applause.au"
```

So with a mouseover, you'd tack this on to the end (note the semi-colon in between):

```
onMouseover="books.src='books-on.gif'; location.href='applause.au'"
```

Crescendo Is on the CD

This book's CD is home to a copy of the Crescendo plug-in.

Can I convert a .wav file to a MIDI file?

No, there isn't any way to do this.

Why doesn't Netscape play sounds when I test my pages?

You might need to get the proper plug-in. Check out the Crescendo page:

```
http://www.liveupdate.com/
```

Forms Questions

What is this "cgi-bin" thing that I see all over the Web?

"cgi-bin" is the name of a directory where CGI scripts and programs are stored.

How do I use a form's Submit button to create a link to another page?

You could set up cute little mini-forms that consist of just a single BUTTON control. You add the JavaScript `onClick` attribute and use it to set the location property to the address of the Web page you want to load:

```
<FORM>
<INPUT
   TYPE=BUTTON
   VALUE="Paul's Place"
   onClick="location='http://www.mcfedries.com'">
</FORM>
```

Create a separate mini-form for each link. Note, too, that you need to use a table if you want to line up the buttons side-by-each.

Is it possible to use JavaScript to take form data and record it on another page?

No, JavaScript can't create a page or add text to an existing page. This can only be done using CGI.

How can I use an image instead of the usual SUBMIT button?

Use the <INPUT TYPE=IMAGE> control:

```
<INPUT TYPE=IMAGE SRC="someimage.gif">
```

Replace *someimage.gif* with the name of the image file that you want to use. Two things to note:

➤ This type of button acts just like a SUBMIT button. That is, when the user clicks the image, the form is submitted to the server.

➤ When the user clicks the image, the browser sends not only the form data, but also the coordinates, in pixels, of the spot on the image where the user clicked. These are sent as "x" (the horizontal coordinate) and "y" (the vertical coordinate).

How do I get the email address of a person who fills in my form?

Include a field in the form and ask the user to enter her email address in that field. Note that although there *are* ways to grab a person's email address automatically, this is considered to be unethical. I think of it as equivalent to rifling through someone's purse or wallet to get their home address.

I'm using your MailForm service, but it doesn't seem to work. Is it still available?

Yes, MailForm is still available. If you're not getting messages, check the following:

➤ The most common MailForm mistake is to misspell one of the hidden field names. For example, lots of people accidentally spell the "MFAddress" field as "MFAdress."

➤ Double-check that your email address is correct in the MFAddress field.

➤ Make sure you have all your quotation marks in place.

➤ The MFReturn field only works if the "thank you" page is online. You can't specify a thank you page that's on your own computer.

➤ Check out the MailForm page for the latest updates and improvements:

```
http://www.mcfedries.com/books/cightml/mailform.html
```

Frames Questions

How do I set up my a frames without borders?

You need to add both FRAMEBORDER=0 and BORDER=0 to your <FRAMESET> tag, like so:

```
<FRAMESET COLS="25%,*" FRAMEBORDER=0 BORDER=0>
```

I have a frame with lots of links. Is there an easier way to specify the TARGET than adding it to every single <A> tag?

Yes! You can define a default target by including the <BASE TARGET> tag in the page header:

```
<BASE TARGET="YourFrameName">
```

Here, *YourFrameName* is the name of the frame that you want to use for all your links. It can also be one of the pre-fab frame names, such as "_top" or "_blank." After you put this in place, you don't need to use TARGET in your links (unless, of course, you want to use a different target for a particular link).

How do I change more than one frame from a single link?

The only way to do this is to have your link point to another frameset page. For example, suppose your original frameset page looks like this:

```
<FRAMESET COLS="100,*">
<FRAME SRC="menu.html" NAME="Left">

    <FRAMESET ROWS="50%,*">
    <FRAME SRC="one.html" NAME="TopRight">
    <FRAME SRC="two.html" NAME="BottomRight">
    </FRAMESET>

</FRAMESET>
```

This page sets up a frame on the left (named, boringly, "Left") and two frames on the right ("TopRight" and "BottomRight"). To change the two right frames in one fell swoop, set up your link to point to an identical frameset page that uses different SRC values in the "TopRight" and "BottomRight" frames:

```
<FRAMESET COLS="100,*">
<FRAME SRC="menu.html" NAME="Left">

    <FRAMESET ROWS="50%,*">
    <FRAME SRC="three.html" NAME="TopRight">
    <FRAME SRC="four.html" NAME="BottomRight">
    </FRAMESET>

</FRAMESET>
```

I don't want my site displayed in someone else's frames. Is it possible to prevent that?

Yes. Assuming your frames page is named "myframes.html", insert the following JavaScript into your page between the </HEAD> and <BODY> tags:

```
<SCRIPT LANGUAGE="JavaScript">
<!--
if (top != self)
    top.location.href="myframes.html"
//-->
</SCRIPT>
```

How do search engines index framed pages?

Here are some pointers about frames and search engines:

➤ Most search engines index only the frameset page (the one with the <FRAME-SET> and <FRAME> tags). Therefore, be sure to include <META> tags in this page.

➤ Some search engines don't index <META> tags, so you might consider putting some kind of indexable content between <NOFRAMES> and </NOFRAMES>.

➤ If you want the search engine to index your "inside" pages, then it's also a good idea to include a link to those pages between <NOFRAMES> and </NOFRAMES>. This gives the search engine an entry point into the rest of your site.

➤ The problem with the latter suggestion is that surfers can easily end up in an inside page that lacks your framed navigation controls. However, you can use JavaScript to "reframe" the page. I have a script on my site that does just that:

```
http://www.mcfedries.com/JavaScript/reframer.html
```

Page Design Questions

Is it possible to determine the resolution of the user's screen?

Yes, using JavaScript's screen.height property. In the following example, the script checks this property and then replaces the current page with another page that's optimized (presumably) for the user's screen resolution:

```
<SCRIPT LANGUAGE="JavaScript">
<!--

// Check for 640x480
if (screen.height == '480')
    location.replace('480.html')

// Check for 800x600
else if (screen.height == '600')
    location.replace('600.html')

// Check for 1024x768
else if (screen.height == '768')
    location.replace('768.html')

// Check for 1280x1024
else if (screen.height == '1024')
    location.replace('1024.html')

// Everything else
else
    location.replace('else.html')
//-->
</SCRIPT>
```

How do I create a stationary background that doesn't scroll along with the page text?

Add the BGPROPERTIES=FIXED attribute to your <BODY> tag:

```
<BODY BGPROPERTIES=FIXED>
```

You can also do it with style sheets:

```
<BODY STYLE="background-image:
url(http://www.wherever.com/whatever.gif);
                background-attachment: fixed">
```

Note, however, that both methods work only with Internet Explorer.

How do I center page text both vertically and horizontally?

You can use <CENTER> to center text horizontally, but there is no HTML tag for centering vertically. However, you can do it if you create a table for your entire page, and then use the VALIGN=MIDDLE and ALIGN=CENTER attributes within the main TD tag. Here's the skeleton:

```
<BODY>

<!--Set up a table for the entire window-->
<TABLE WIDTH=100% HEIGHT=100%>
<TR>
<TD VALIGN=MIDDLE ALIGN=CENTER>

<!--The real page text and stuff goes here-->

This text appears smack dab in the middle of the screen.

<!--Close the big table-->
</TD>
</TR>
</TABLE>

</BODY>
```

How do I provide users with an easy way to return to the top of a page?

Right below your <BODY> tag, add the following anchor:

```
<A NAME="top">
```

You can then send the surfer to the top of the page by including a link such as this:

```
<A HREF="#top">Return to the top of the page</A>
```

The CD: The Webmaster's Toolkit

As I've mentioned before, this book's whole purpose is to be a one-stop shop for budding Websmiths. To that end, the text is geared towards getting you up to speed with this HTML rigmarole without a lot of fuss and flapdoodle. But fine words butter no parsnips, as they say, so you'll also find a complete "Webmaster's Toolkit" on the CD-ROM that's pasted into the back of the book. This toolkit is jammed to the hilt with handy references, files, and software that should provide everything you need to get your Web authorship off to a rousing start. This appendix describes what's on the CD and tells you how to install it.

Accessing the Disc's Contents

To get to the goodies on the CD, there are two routes you can take:

➤ Use your browser to open the file named index.htm in the main folder of the CD. This gives you a nice, clickable interface to everything that's on the disc.

➤ Open the CD in Windows Explorer and access the files directly.

Webmaster References

With over 100 HTML tags and over 100 style sheet properties in existence, there's a lot to keep track of. To help you out, I've created a few references that give you the full scoop on all the available tags, styles, and more. Here's a summary:

HTML tag reference   This reference supplies you with the nitty-gritty on all the HTML tags. For each tag, you get a description of the tag, notes on using the tag, a complete list of the tag's attributes, browser support (including links to the appropriate Microsoft and Netscape pages, as well as to the official W3C page), and an example that shows the tag in action.

Style sheet reference   This reference runs through a complete list of the available style sheet properties. For each property, you get a description of the property, notes on using it, a list of the property's possible values, browser support, and an example that shows how the property works.

The 216 "safe" Web colors   This page shows you all the 216 so-called "safe" Web colors to use on your pages. ("Safe" means that these colors display well on almost all screens.) One table shows you the colors and another table shows you the corresponding RGB values.

The X11 color set   This page runs through all the colors that have defined names (such as Red, Blue, and Chartreuse).

The HTML Examples from the Book

Many of this book's chapters (especially those in Part 1, "Creating Your First HTML Page") are sprinkled with examples showing HTML tags on the go. If you'd like to incorporate some of these examples into your own Web work, don't bother typing your poor fingers to the bone. Instead, all the example files are sitting on the CD-ROM, ready for you to use. These example files are in the \Examples directory on the CD. Note, too, that everything is organized by chapter. The files for Chapter 1 are in \Examples\Chap01, the files for Chapter 2 are in \Examples\Chap02, and so on.

Web Graphics Sampler

Back in Chapter 6, "A Picture Is Worth a Thousand Clicks: Working with Images," you saw how a graphic or two can add a nice touch to an otherwise drab Web page. Then, in Chapter 24, "Some HTML Resources on the Web," I mentioned a few spots on the Web where you can find images to suit any occasion. But before you go traipsing off to one of these sites, you might want to check out what's on the CD-ROM. There you'll find hundreds of files that give you everything from simple bullets and lines to useful icons and pictures. There's even a section with some high-quality animated GIFs.

Programs for Web Weavers

The Webmaster's Toolkit is also loaded with a whack of software programs that can help you create better pages. The rest of this appendix presents a summary of the programs you'll find.

HTML Editors

Here's a list of the HTML editors that are in the Webmaster's Toolkit:

Dreamweaver   This is an excellent, professional-quality HTML editor that's loaded with great features for churning out top-notch pages. It also boasts some impressive site management features, templates, and much more.

CD site: /3rdParty/HTMLEdit/Macromedia/Dreamweaver/Dreamweaver2.exe
Web site: http://www.macromedia.com/

GoLive   This is an advanced HTML editor that's packed with features to make your Webmastering life easier. It uses a "visual design" model for precise control, and also supports esoterica such as style sheets, Dynamic HTML, and XML.

CD site: /3rdParty/HTMLEdit/Adobe/GoLive/gl4try.exe
Web site: http://www.adobe.com/

HomeSite   This is one of the best HTML editors on the planet. It has a great interface and it has more features than you can shake a stick at: a built-in spell checker, the ability to edit multiple documents at once, color-coded HTML tags, the ability to search-and-replace text across multiple files, and much more.

CD site: /3rdParty/HTMLEdit/Allaire/Homesite/Homesite_401_eval.exe
Web site: http://www.allaire.com/

HotDog Professional   This is one of the veterans of the HTML editor wars, and has emerged from the front lines better than ever. If you just want a good editor that doesn't offer a lot of unnecessary accessories, give HotDog a taste.

CD site: /3rdParty/HTMLEdit/Sausage/HotDog/hotdog55install.exe
Web site: http://www.sausage.com/

HTML Assistant   This is a decent HTML editor that gives you a graphical way to build your Web pages. It includes a built-in spell checker as well as easy methods for creating forms and tables.

CD site: /3rdParty/HTMLEdit/Brooklynnorth/HTMLAssistant/Pro97Demo.exe
Web site: http://www.brooknorth.com/

NetObjects Fusion   This is an extremely powerful editor that not only excels at regular HTML, but can also make it a breeze to create truly interactive sites that use JavaScript, Java, style sheets, and even dynamic HTML. It also features some amazing site management tricks (such as automatically updating links if you move or rename a page).

CD site: /3rdParty/HTMLEdit/NetObjects/Fusion/Nof401_trial.exe
Web site: http://www.netobjects.com/

Graphics Software

Chapter 6, "A Picture Is Worth a Thousand Clicks: Working with Images," gave you the basics for adding images to your pages. Here are a few tools that help take some of the drudgery out of graphics work:

ACDSee   If you just need to take a quick gander at an image, ACDSee is the program to use because this utility excels and displaying image files. It's extremely fast, so it's perfect for sneak peeks. However, it can also do a bit of image manipulation, and it can convert graphics from one format to another.

CD site: /3rdParty/Graphics/ACDSystems/ACDSee32/ACDC32241.exe
Web site: http://www.acdsystems.com/

GIF Animator   This is a great program for creating animated GIFs. It's a snap to use (I gave you the basics in Chapter 10, "Making Your Web Pages Dance and Sing"), and it's crammed with cool features such as a banner-creation tool, transitions, and image optimization.

CD site: /3rdParty/Graphics/Ulead/Gifanimator/Uga3t.exe
Web site: http://www.webutilities.com/

GraphX   This is a simple graphics viewer that can also convert graphics into GIF and JPEG formats for use on the Web.

CD site: /3rdParty/Graphics/Group42/Graphxviewer/Gv16_151.exe
Web site: http://www.group42.com/

LiveImage   Were you confused by my discussion of client-side image maps in Chapter 8, "Images Can Be Links, Too"? If so, then I suggest you check out LiveImage, which gives you an easy, graphical way to create client-side image maps without worrying about coordinates and other finicky stuff.

CD site: /3rdParty/Graphics/Liveimage/Liveimage/Liveimag.exe
Web site: http://www.liveimage.com/

Mapedit   This program gives you an easy, graphical method for defining *server-side* image maps (as opposed to the client-side image maps that I yammered on about in Chapter 8).

CD site: /3rdParty/HTMLEdit/Boutell/Mapedit/Map32dst.exe
Web site: http://www.boutell.com/

Paint Shop Pro   This is one of the best graphics programs on the market today. It supports all kinds of formats, offers great tools for creating drawings, makes effects such as drop shadows a breeze, and does much more.

CD site: /3rdParty/Graphics/Jasc/PaintShopPro/psp60ev.exe
Web site: http://www.jasc.com/

WebImage   This is a more powerful version of GraphX. It comes with lots of extra features, including image optimization and the capability to create image maps and transparent GIFs (for the latter, see Chapter 6).

CD site: /3rdParty/Graphics/Group42/Webimage/Wi32_211.exe
Web site: http://www.group42.com/

FTP Programs

I discussed using FTP to get your Web handiwork onto your Web host's server back in Chapter 7, "Publishing Your Page on the Web." To help out, the CD boasts two of the best FTP programs around:

CuteFTP   CuteFTP has a bizarre name, but it's an easy-to-use FTP program that gives you a no muss, no fuss way to fling files around the Net.

CD site: /3rdParty/FTP/Globalscape/CuteFTP/Cute3032.exe
Web site: http://www.globalscape.com/

WS_FTP Pro   This program's easy interface and long list of features have made it one of the most popular FTP utilities on the Net.

CD site: 3rdParty/Ftp/IPSwitch/WS_ftppro/f_x86t32.exe
Web site: http://www..com/

Web Browsers

You need a Web browser to view your pages, and the more browsers you use, the more sure you can be that all your visitors are seeing what you want to see. Unfortunately, the latest browsers redefine the word *humungous*, so downloading them becomes a weekend-long job. Because you probably have better things to do, the CD comes packed with the following browsers:

Internet Explorer   This is version 5 of the most popular browser (by far) on the Web.

CD site: /3rdParty/BrowsersInternet/Microsoft/IE5/EN/IE5Setup.exe
Web site: http://www.microsoft.com/

Netscape Navigator   This is version 4.7 of the former browser champ that's still used by a sizable portion of Web users.

CD site: /3rdParty/Browsers-Internet/Netscape/Netscape 47/Sd_cc32e47en.exe
Web site: http://home.netscape.com/

401

Audio Software

Lots of Web designers like to add music to their sites to enhance their visitors' visits. The CD has some audio tools that can help:

CoolEdit If you plan on adding audio to your pages (as explained in Chapter 10, "Making Your Web Pages Dance and Sing,") you can use CoolEdit to edit Windows' native WAV files.

CD site: `/3rdParty/Audio/Syntrillium/Cooledit/Cep12dmo.exe`
Web site: `http://www.syntrillium.com/`

Crescendo This is a plug-in that enables you to hear MIDI files.

CD site: `/3rdParty/Audio/LiveUpdate/Crescendo/`
Web site: `http://www.liveupdate.com/`

Koan Plugin This music plug-in supports not only MIDI files, but also MP3 files, as well.

CD site: `/3rdParty/Audio/Sseyo/Koanplugin/Koanplugin.exe`
Web site: `http://www.sseyo.com/`

Koan Pro Use this program to create MP3 files to use on your Web site.

CD site: `/3rdParty/Audio/Sseyo/Koanpro/Koanprodemo.exe`
Web site: `http://www.sseyo.com/`

Other Stuff

To wrap things up, the CD also contains the following miscellaneous tools:

Adobe Acrobat Rather than converting complex documents into HTML, many Web weavers are instead converting these files into Adobe's PDF (Portable Document File) format, which preserves formatting and graphics with remarkable fidelity. To view these PDF files, use the Adobe Acrobat program.

CD site: `3rdParty/Other/Adobe/Acrobat/ar40eng.exe`
Web site: `http://www.adobe.com/`

CommNet This is a data communications application that seamlessly integrates Internet Telnet and modem dial-up and capabilities into a single, fast, full-featured, and easy-to-use application. CommNet supports both Zmodem and Telnet Zmodem file transfers and VT100/full-color PC ANSI and SCO ANSI emulations.

CD site: `/3rdParty/FTP/Radient/Commnet/Cnet3210.exe`
Web site: `http://www.radient.com/`

Drag & Zip   This program is an add-on that gives Windows Explorer the capability to compress and decompress files.

CD site: `/3rdParty/Other/Canyon/Drag&Zip/DZ95.exe`
Web site: `http://www.canyonsw.com/`

TextPad   This is a powerful replacement for Windows' Notepad text editor.

CD site: `/3rdParty/Textedit/Helios/Textpad/Txpeng40.exe`
Web site: `http://www.textpad.com/`

UltraEdit   This is a great text editor that understands HTML (for example, it uses color coding to distinguish tags from regular text), enables you to work on multiple files at once, supports macros, and has lots of other powerful features.

CD site: `/3rdParty/Textedit/IDMComp/Ultraedit/Uedit32I.exe`
Web site: `http://www.idmcomp.com/`

WinZip   For faster service, many of the Net's files and documents are stored in a "compressed" format that makes them smaller. After you download a compressed file to your computer, you need to "uncompress" the file in order to use it. WinZip is a handy little utility that makes it a breeze to uncompress any file. You can also use it to compress your own files if you'll be shipping them out.

CD site: `3rdParty/Other/Nicomak/Winzip/winzip70.exe`
Web site: `http://www.winzip.com/`

Legal Stuff

By opening this package, you are agreeing to be bound by the following agreement:

This software product is copyrighted, and all rights are reserved by the publisher and author. You are licensed to use this software on a single computer. You may copy and/or modify the software as needed to facilitate your use of it on a single computer. Making copies of the software for any other purpose is a violation of the United States copyright laws.

This software is sold *as is* without warranty of any kind, either expressed or implied, including but not limited to the implied warranties of merchantability and fitness for a particular purpose. Neither the publisher nor its dealers or distributors assumes any liability for any alleged or actual damages arising from the use of this program. (Some states do not allow for the exclusion of implied warranties, so the exclusion might not apply to you.)

Index

413

Licensing Agreement

Read This Before Opening the Software

By opening this package, you are agreeing to be bound by the following agreement:

You may not copy or redistribute the entire CD-ROM as a whole. Copying and redistribution of individual software programs on the CD-ROM is governed by terms set by the licensors or individual copyright holders.

The installer and code from the author(s) are copyrighted by the publisher and the author(s).

This software is sold as-is, without warranty of any kind, either expressed or implied, including but not limited to the implied warranties of merchantability and fitness for a particular purpose. Neither the publisher nor its dealers or distributors assumes any liability for any alleged or actual damages arising from the use of this program. (Some states do not allow for the exclusion of implied warranties, so the exclusion may not apply to you.)

NOTE: This CD-ROM uses long and mixed-case filenames requiring the use of a protected-mode CD-ROM Driver.